THE FAMILY CREATIVE WORK SHOP

THE FAMILY CREATIVE WORKSHOP

16

Sculpture, Seashells
Seed Sprouting, Serigraphy
Sewing Without a Pattern
Shadow Theater, Shaker Furniture
Shelters and Tents
Ship Models, Silhouettes

Plenary Publications International, Inc.
New York and Amsterdam

Published by Plenary Publications International Incorporated 300 East 40th Street, New York, New York 10016, for the Blue Mountain Crafts Council.

Library of Congress Catalog Card Number: 73-89331. Complete set International Standard Book Number: 0-88459-021-6. Volume 16 International Standard Book Number: 0-88459-015-1

Manufactured in the United States of America. Printed and bound by the W. A. Krueger Company, Brookfield, Wisconsin.

Printing preparation by Lanman Lithoplate Company.

Publishers:
Plenary Publications International, Incorporated 300 East 40th Street New York, New York 10016

Steven R. Schepp
EDITOR-IN-CHIEF

Jerry Curcio
PRODUCTION MANAGER

Peggy Streep
EDITORIAL ASSISTANT

Editorial preparation:
Tree Communications, Inc.
250 Park Avenue South
New York, New York 10003

Rodney Friedman
EDITORIAL DIRECTOR

Ronald Gross
DESIGN DIRECTOR

Paul Levin
DIRECTOR OF PHOTOGRAPHY

Donal Dinwiddie
CONSULTING EDITOR

Jill Munves
TEXT EDITOR

Sonja Douglas
ART DIRECTOR

Rochelle Lapidus
Marsha Gold
DESIGNERS

Lucille O'Brien
EDITORIAL PRODUCTION

Eva Gold
ADMINISTRATIVE MANAGER

Ruth Forst Michel
COPYREADER

Editors for this volume:
Hyla Clark
Andrea DiNoto
SHADOW THEATER

Hyla Clark
Marilyn Nierenberg
SEASHELLS

Andrea DiNoto
SHIP MODELS

Michael Donner
SCULPTURE
SHELTERS AND TENTS

Linda Hetzer
SEWING WITHOUT A PATTERN

Nancy Bruning Levine
SILHOUETTES

Jill Munves
SERIGRAPHY

Marilyn Nierenberg
SEED SPROUTING

Mary Grace Skurka
SHAKER FURNITURE

Originating editor of the series:
Allen Davenport Bragdon

Contributing editor:
Dennis Starin

Contributing illustrators:
Marina Givotovsky
Lynn Matus
Sally Shimizu

Contributing photographers:
Steven Mays
Marilyn Nierenberg

Production:
Thom Augusta
Christopher Jones
Patricia Lee
Leslie Strong

Photo and illustration credits:
SEASHELLS: Photographs, page 1944, reprinted from *Art from Shells* by Stuart and Leni Goodman, Crown Publishers Inc., New York, N. Y., Copyright 1972. Shells, pages 1940 through 1942 courtesy of Seashells Unlimited, Inc., New York, N. Y., and Burry's Shell Museum, Pompano Beach, Florida. SEED SPROUTING: Bio Snacky sprouting trays distributed by Miracle Exclusives, Inc., 16 West 40th Street, New York, N. Y. SHADOW THEATER: The White Snake Lady, page 1986, is an East City Peiking puppet from the collection of Penny Jones. SHELTERS AND TENTS: Photographs of tepees, page 2020, left, archive photo by Fred R. Meyer, courtesy of the Museum of the American Indian, Heye Foundation; right, from *Woodstock Handmade Houses*, courtesy of Ballantine Books, Inc., New York, N. Y. SHIP MODELS: Photographs page 2024 from the Collection of the United States Military Academy Museum; page 2026, Smithsonian Institution Photo No. 73-8031.

Acknowledgement:
SHELTERS AND TENTS: Technical consultant, Dr. Glenden Redman, Vice President, Rockland County Council of the Boy Scouts of America.

The Project-Evaluation Symbols appearing in the title heading at the beginning of each project have these meanings:

Range of approximate cost:

¢ Low: under $5 or free and found natural materials

$ Medium: about $10

$$ High: above $15

Estimated time to completion for an unskilled adult:

⊠ Hours

🕐 Days

Weeks

Suggested level of experience:

Child alone

Supervised child or family project

Unskilled adult

Specialized prior training

Tools and equipment:
Small hand tools

Large hand and household tools

Specialized or powered equipment

On the cover:
At the shore you can collect fragments of shells that are fine for making collages or even a translucent lamp shade. But if you comb the beach with a discriminating eye, you may find perfect specimens to use in creating jewelry, miniature sculptures, or artificial flowers. Instructions for making these craft items begin on page 1938. Cover photograph by Paul Levin.

**Contents and
craftspeople for Volume 16:**

SCULPTURE
From Pedestal to Patio

Sculpture has long been considered the exclusive province of talented and dedicated artists. It is true, of course, that serious works of sculpture demand a large measure of patience and care in addition to artistic vision. But if you are willing to work with the more tractable of sculptural materials—clay, wood, or soft stone—and will work slowly and patiently on projects that are not too ambitious, there is no reason why you cannot produce interesting, satisfying sculptures for your home and garden.

Three basic techniques are used in traditional sculpture. The choice is largely determined by the material used. Modeling is the technique of giving form to pliable substances, such as clay, whether they are shaped by the hands alone or with simple tools. Subtraction is the process of shaping an object by removing pieces from a larger solid mass, such as a block of wood or stone. These two techniques, taken together, are known as the direct method, because the sculptor works directly on the finished product. There is also an indirect method—called substitution—in which the sculptor uses a mold to cast in one medium a work he has shaped in another.

The projects that follow include examples of both of the direct methods and illustrate the uses of the most commonly worked materials. Projects in indirect sculpture and in assemblage—additive sculpture—will be found elsewhere in *The Family Creative Workshop*, as indicated on page 1937.

Peter Lipman-Wulf, born in Germany in 1905, was apprenticed to a master wood-carver in Bavaria while still in his teens. He completed his training at the State Academy of Fine Arts in Berlin. Since then he has earned an international reputation for his sculptures in bronze, wood, stone, and clay. His works are in public and private collections throughout the world, including those of the Metropolitan Museum of Art, Smithsonian Institution, the Whitney Museum of American Art, and the Museum of Modern Art. He teaches at Adelphi University and lives on Long Island in New York.

Ceramics
A clay figure

$ ☒ 👪 🎨

From what has been learned about primitive man, it seems likely that clay sculpture antedates the making of more utilitarian objects, such as cooking and storing pots. Clay is still ideal for a first sculpture project. It requires few tools and is more forgiving, if you make a mistake, than most other materials.

A finished product in clay can be left to dry by itself, be baked hard in a kiln, or in the ultimate refinement, be made into a plaster cast for a bronze piece. The bronze figure, opposite, was made from a clay model. But the clay original, below, stands on its own and is easy to execute.

Opposite: *Reclining Figure*, by Peter Lipman-Wulf, was cast in bronze from a clay model. The original clay model, pictured at left, is itself a handsome art object; instructions for making it are given here.

Left: Without prior experience in working with ceramics, you can make a modern sculpture like this one from a slab of clay. Modeling clay, simple tools, and the step-by-step instructions from a master sculptor and teacher are the materials you will need.

1: To make the clay slip needed to join elements of the sculpture, first crush a handful of dried clay into small pieces by pounding on it.

2: To ready the slip for use, dissolve the crushed clay in enough water to produce a thick, soupy mixture. It is used like glue.

3: To prepare the clay for modeling, knead it until you are sure you have expelled all the air bubbles; then condense it into a block.

4: Roll the clay block into a rectangular slab ½ inch thick, using a rolling pin. Turn the slab over frequently to keep it from sticking.

5: To make the base that will support the sculpture, use a knife to cut a 4-by-10-inch rectangle from the clay slab. Round off the corners.

6: Carve the rough shape of a tall human figure, somewhat like a gingerbread boy, from the remainder of the slab.

7: Use a knife to score the areas where the figure and the base will be joined, and paint slip onto these points on both elements.

Preparation

To make the clay figure shown, you will need: a 6-inch cube of modeling clay; rolling pin; wire modeling tool (available at craft supply stores); paring knife; spatula; 1-foot length of thin wire; an old cup; and a small paintbrush. When you buy the clay, ask for one with a small addition of medium-sized grog; grog is crushed, fired clay that is added to moist clay to give it texture, body, and strength. When the clay is not being used, keep it in an airtight container so it won't dry out.

Let a small handful of moist clay air-dry overnight. Then prepare some clay slip—a soupy mixture used to join parts of the sculpture—by crushing the dried clay (photograph 1) and dissolving it in enough water to give it the consistency of sour cream (photograph 2). Set the slip aside.

To prepare the modeling clay, knead it on any smooth, clean work surface, squeezing it with your hands and pounding it with your fists to expel air bubbles. This is especially important if you think you might fire the sculpture in a kiln, since trapped air can explode, spoiling the work. Next, form the clay into a block (photograph 3). Flatten it with a rolling pin (photograph 4), turning it frequently to keep it from sticking to the work surface. Roll it out into a ½-inch-thick rectangle as you would roll out pastry dough.

Forming the Basic Shape

Using the paring knife, cut out a 4-by-10-inch piece of clay (photograph 5) to serve as a base for the sculpture, and put it on a separate work surface. I use a square banding wheel (a piece of wood set like a lazy susan on a revolving base), but any smooth, clean area will do. Cut an elongated human shape, like a 3-by-16-inch gingerbread boy, from the remainder of the rolled-out clay. Save the scraps for use later. Arms and legs can be pulled out to the sides after the rough shape is cut (photograph 6).

8: Seat the figure on the base, draw the knees up into an arch, press the feet flat, and hold the back erect.

9: To keep the back upright and add stability, rest the left forearm on the knees, and place the right hand above the left elbow.

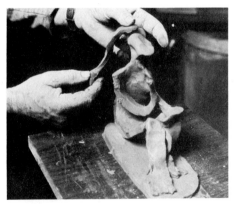

10: Add hair by draping a long, thin, twisted ribbon of clay from the back of the head. Score and moisten with slip if necessary.

In order to attach the figure securely to the base, score a crosshatched pattern with the knife at areas of contact on both clay pieces (the bottom of the feet, the seat, and the corresponding points on the base). Coat these areas with slip (photograph 7). The slip will act like glue.

Bend and shape the figure as you set it in position on the base. Press the feet against the base so you produce a bend at the knees. Hold the spine erect; for the moment, the arms dangle (photograph 8).

Refining the Sculpture

With the basic form in place, a few final manipulations, additions, and subtractions complete the sculpture. Bring the left arm forward, bend it at the elbow, and place the forearm across both knees. Arch the right arm over the torso, and using slip, connect the right hand to the left arm (photograph 9). The arms thus give the figure a plausible pose even as they stabilize the structure and hold the spine erect. To shape the head and make it face upwards, press down on the top of the head with your thumb while holding the neck on either side with index and middle fingers. If the clay is too moist to hold the shape you want to give it, let it dry for two or three hours before going on. Trim the figure by removing unwanted clay with the wire modeling tool; it works something like a cheese slicer. Smooth rough areas with the side of the knife blade. A light, gliding motion with either of these tools should leave the clay quite smooth. If the clay has started to harden, moisten the rough edges with a damp cloth. Add small pieces of clay to the figure to form the hair (photograph 10), the nose, and the eyebrows. As before, score and apply slip to all points of contact. Cut indentations with the knife to represent the mouth, eyes, fingers, and toes (photograph 11).

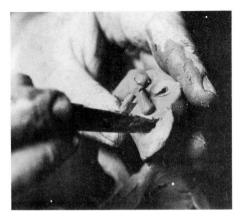

11: Build up facial features with clay scraps, and indent the eyes and mouth with a knife.

Drying or Firing

Let the sculpture dry for a week or more. If leaving it on the work surface for that long is inconvenient, remove it by passing a thin wire—held tautly between both hands and flush with the work surface—under the base from end to end. Lift the sculpture carefully with a large spatula, and move it to another place to dry. Unglazed clay that has been dried in this way is called greenware. It may be left as is, or it may be strengthened by firing it in a ceramic kiln at a temperature of approximately 1850 degrees Fahrenheit (cone 05). Clay objects fired in this way are called bisque. If you do not have a kiln, professional ceramists often will fire work for a nominal fee.

Color

Many people like the natural earth color of air-dried clay. But if you like, you can apply color to greenware with what are called engobe slips—mixtures of clay, feldspar, flint, a flux, and colorants—available at craft supply stores. Bisque can be glazed in a second firing, either with a transparent glaze or with various colored glazes, or it can be colored without a second firing by applying artist's paints or shoe polish. The sculpture shown at right is unfired clay coated with a paint, available at sculpture supply houses, that simulates bronze.

This sculpture by Lipman-Wulf of his six-year-old daughter, Ghilia, appears to be cast in bronze, but it is unfired modeling clay that has been coated with a special paint (available at sculpture supply houses) to make it look like bronze.

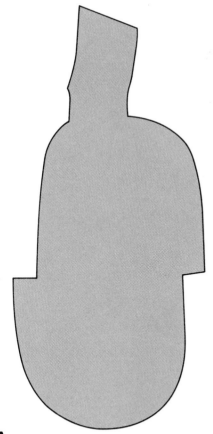

A
Figure A: On cardboard, draw a free-form shape something like this one. Make it the size you want your tray to be, and modify your design to make the best use of your block of wood, rather than copying the figure exactly as it appears above.

A sculptural serving tray, carved from a single block of rosewood, is shaped something like a violin and has a handle carved in the form of two faces. It was shaped with only a few basic wood-sculpting tools.

Carving and Molding
A rosewood serving tray

$ ● 🚶 ⚗

The intricate markings of wood grain are forever an inspiration for an alert sculptor. In the violin-shaped tray shown above, the grain and color of Brazilian rosewood become elements in the design. The exact form such a finished tray will take cannot be foreseen; so if you make such a wood sculpture, be prepared to modify the design as the wood dictates.

Many woods are suitable for sculpture, but the best are fruit, nut, or tropical hardwoods. These are hard enough to resist bruising, and they offer a pleasing variety of grain and color patterns. Do not use green wood or wood that has not been well seasoned or kiln dried; it is too likely to split. Commercially prepared blocks, kiln-dried and sealed with a protective coating of wax or plastic film, are available at

13: Cut out your cardboard pattern, and use chalk to trace its outline onto the block of wood.

14: Use a C-clamp to hold the block on one end of your work table, projecting over the edge, and cut along the chalked outline with a jigsaw, coping saw, or, as shown here, a power saber saw.

12: Wood-carving tools include (left to right) three small wood files known as rifflers, two wood rasps, a mallet, a chisel, two gouges, a C-clamp, and (top) finishing abrasive papers. A power drill speeds open work (like the eye in the carved handle opposite) and, with a grinding-wheel attachment, is used to sharpen beveled tools before they are honed on an oilstone.

sculpture supply houses. Old house or barn beams are also good for carving and sometimes can be obtained at little or no cost. The tray shown here was carved from a 1-foot length of a 1½-by-6-inch board.

Preparation
The tools I used to make the tray include those shown in photograph 12; a mallet (a wooden hammer with a tapered, barrel-shaped head for striking chisels and gouges); a wood chisel (a tool with a sharp, beveled edge at one end for chipping or flaking away a wood surface); gouges (like chisels but curved for making rounded cuts); a file and a rasp (for smoothing surfaces by abrasion); and rifflers (small files with ends curved in various shapes for working in depressions). You will also need a jigsaw or coping saw for making rough cuts, and a vise or C clamps to hold the work. All can be purchased at sculpture supply houses. In addition, I find a power drill essential, both for boring holes and—with a grinding attachment—for sharpening tools before I hone them. You can work with a modest tool collection, but the fewer tools you own the more frequent will be the interruptions for sharpening (see Craftnotes, page 1934).

Forming the Basic Shape
Draw a free-form violin shape—or any other simple shape—on cardboard the size of the block to be carved. Figure A shows the shape I used for my tray, adapted to the individuality of the wood block I had. For example, notice how one side of the handle in my tray leads into the border area between the dark and light tones in the bowl.

Outline the design on the wood with chalk (photograph 13); then clamp the board in place and cut out the design with a jigsaw or saber saw (photograph 14). Be careful not to drop the block; hardwoods such as rosewood are brittle and break easily. Using chalk, mark a ½-inch-wide border around the edge of the block to represent the tray's rim. Be careful not to carve out any wood beyond this line or from the handle area. The handle area can be extended into the bowl area, as shown in the finished work opposite, or it can stop at the rim of the bowl. As you work, the chalk outline will be rubbed off; so redraw it whenever necessary.

Clamp the tray's handle in a vise so the wood will not move while you carve. If you do not have a wooden vise, use C clamps, or improvise a jig by nailing wood strips to the workbench around the block.

15: Clamp the tray's handle in a vise or with a C-clamp, to hold the wood steady, and begin shaping the bowl with a mallet and gouge, making shallow cuts with the grain of the wood.

16: Gouge straight downward, across the grain where necessary, around the chalk outline to keep the horizontal cuts from straying into the rim of the tray.

17: A T shape cut from cardboard, with a 1-inch leg, serves as a gauge to check the depth of the tray's bowl from time to time. The T must be long enough to reach from edge to edge.

18: Invert the tray, clamp it in the vise or with a C-clamp, and round the outer curve of the bowl with the gouge, which has a curved end, or a chisel, which has a flat end.

19: With a wood rasp, round off the rough edges and corners left by the gouge and chisel. Use either the flat or the rounded side, as needed.

20: Use a riffler, which has finer teeth than a rasp, to further smooth off the marks left by the chisel, gouge, and rasp.

Before you start to carve, tap each of your chisels and gouges into a small scrap of the wood to see the effect of each. The mallet pictured should be wielded so it strikes the chisel at a right angle. Practice until you feel you are in control of the tools; then begin hollowing out the bowl of the tray with the mallet and a wide gouge (photograph 15). Use short, crisp strokes, working in the same direction as the grain runs. Remove wood in thin, flaky chips rather than in chunks; do not angle the gouge deeply into the wood. Brace the wrist of your gouge-holding hand against the wood (as shown in photograph 15) for extra control. Work in one direction only.

When you have created a slight depression this way, gouge with nearly vertical cuts all around the chalk outline, across the grain where necessary, to a depth of about ½ inch (photograph 16). Cutting into the wood like this will keep the horizontal slicing cuts from wandering into wood beyond the area to be removed. Continue alternating the series of near-horizontal and near-vertical cuts until the depression is well rounded to a maximum depth of 1 inch. You can test this depth with a T-shaped gauge cut out of cardboard; it needs arms wide enough to span the hollow and a leg 1 inch long (photograph 17). When you are satisfied with the rough shape of the bowl, turn it over and clamp it in the vise so you can work on the bottom. Shape this curve the same way, but here work only with the grain (photograph 18). Use a gouge for rough shaping, inverting it if you want to reverse the curve; then change to a chisel for smoothing out the curve. Test the diminishing thickness of the work from time to time with your thumb and forefinger. Aim for a uniform thickness of ⅜ to ½ inch; this can be estimated by feel alone.

Once the basic shape of the bowl has been formed, use a wood rasp (photograph 19)

21: Following the chalk lines, rough out the handle sculpture with a mallet and chisel, but carve only the top half of the wood. Leave the bottom half of the handle intact.

22: Cut a slot through the handle from side to side by boring a series of adjacent holes with a power drill and ¼-inch bit. Aim the drill carefully for a clean pass through the thin handle.

23: Use a chisel to cut indentations and hollows into the handle sculpture, a drill to make holes. Then refine the contours with rasp, riffler, and sandpaper.

to round off rough edges and corners on the outside. Then smooth over ridges that were left by the chisel and gouge, changing from a rasp to a riffler (photograph 20) as the curvature of the bowl requires. The riffler is more maneuverable in tight areas, as on the concave curves inside the bowl.

The Handle

The handle is the most challenging part of the tray to carve. A design that includes openwork like the one pictured on page 1930 requires extra care as the wood becomes thinner and more brittle. Using chalk, draw an outline of the finished design on the uncarved handle; the faces shown in Figure B could be used as a guide, or you could draw a simple design of your own. A section will be cut away toward the rear of the upper surface, exposing the lower surface for a three-dimensional look.

With a chisel and mallet, chip away wood outside the chalk outline, down to half the thickness of the handle (photograph 21). Then cut the open slot by boring a series of holes through the middle of the handle from side to side. Use a power drill and a ¼-inch bit (photograph 22). Operate the drill with a gentle rocking motion to remove more wood. With a series of holes you will eventually produce a long, thin slot extending from near the outer edge of the handle to its meeting with the rim of the bowl. When the slot is completed, drill holes for the eyes near the top of the handle and a hole at its base.

The rest of the head is easier to make than it looks. Chisel away the indentation for the chin and throat, and gouge a round hollow for the eye socket (photograph 23). Use the wood rasp and riffler as necessary to refine the shape and to remove chisel marks. Then extend the recess downward from the eye socket and past the cheek to form the depression beside and beneath the nose at the left (photograph 23). For convex curves, invert the gouge. Carve out the lip detail with a small gouge. If desired, repeat the sculpting process for a head on the lower surface of the handle at its right. Just the hint of a nose and a drill hole for an eye are sufficient.

Finishing

After you smooth the last of the rough spots with rasp and riffler, sand the entire tray with a medium-grit garnet paper, followed by a fine-grit paper or emery cloth. To enrich the natural luster of the wood and to forestall cracks caused by drying, polish the tray with a mixture of three parts boiled linseed oil to one part turpentine. An even better finish can be obtained with natural beeswax (sold at art supply stores); it is well worth the extra effort needed to apply it. Soften the wax over a radiator, taking care not to scorch it. Then put a small amount in a metal container and melt it in a double boiler. Be careful; melted wax is flammable. Remove the wax from the heat and add enough turpentine (about one part in three) to make a slightly creamy mixture. Apply the mixture to the wood with a soft cloth. When dry, buff it with a clean, soft cloth.

B
Figure B: Use chalk again to draw details of the sculpted handle, such as those of the faces shown above. Keep these features simple and broad enough so they will not chip off later.

Supply sources for sculpting tools and materials

The Craftool Company, Inc.
1421 West 240th Street
Harbor City, Calif. 90710

Perma-Flex Mold Company
1919 East Livingston Avenue
Columbus, Ohio 43209

Sculpture Associates
114 East 25th Street
New York, N.Y. 10010

CRAFTNOTES: SHARPENING CHISELS AND GOUGES

You don't need a complete line of chisels and gouges to do small wood-sculpting projects. Use only a few of each, but keep them sharp. Well-honed tools make carving easier and safer, and they provide more control on fine details. The time spent on sharpening will save time in the end.

To sharpen these tools, you will need a grinding wheel; an attachment wheel on a power drill is adequate if the drill can be mounted securely. Safety goggles are a must to protect your eyes whenever you use the grindstone. You will also need an Arkansas honing stone. Anchor the drill on the workbench so the wheel rotates vertically and away from you. Put on the goggles. As you grind the tool blade, dip it frequently in water to keep friction heat from burning out the temper of the metal, thus making the steel brittle.

At this point, there will be a slight burr on the blade edge as shown above.

Start the grinding wheel and touch the tool's beveled edge on the wheel at about the 30-degree angle shown above. (At this angle, your knuckles come within an inch of the wheel; so be careful not to skin them.) With slight pressure, move the beveled edge steadily back and forth across the wheel. Even with a narrow tool, use all of the wheel's surface so you do not wear ridges in it. Examine the blade from time to time, and continue grinding until the beveled edge is smooth and is twice as wide as the blade is thick. The edge should be sharp, unpitted, and ground at a right angle to the side of the blade. Check for squareness with a try-square.

Remove the burr by rubbing the bevel lightly with a circular motion against an oiled honing stone as shown above. Use a commercial honing fluid or a few drops of household oil. Do not try to break the burr off by pressing hard; hone it down gradually and gently.

When the cutting edge is properly honed, as shown above, the chisel or gouge will be sharp enough to cut paper. Once a tool is properly sharpened, the blade can be touched up on the honing stone several times before it will need regrinding.

The sharpening process is the same for stone-carving chisels except that these should be honed with water rather than oil, since oil will stain stone.

An untitled abstract sculpture in alabaster (above, left), mounted on a hardwood pedestal with a stainless steel rod, gleams with the soft translucency for which this stone is famous. By chipping away and smoothing off a freely formed shape like this one in soft stone, you can ease your way into hard sculpture with a minimum investment in tools and materials. A more representational work (above, right), *Easter Islander*, is an example of what can be done with the same tools and materials, but with developed skills. The polished and expressive face merges into a background of unworked alabaster to suggest the flowing lines of hair.

Carving and Molding
An alabaster sculpture   💲 📅 🧍 🔬

In stone sculpture, as in wood carving, you will find with experience that the shape of your sculpture is dictated by the material itself and can only be realized by careful subtraction.

The harder varieties of stone, such as marble, are difficult to work. Use soft stone for your first projects—soapstone, African wonder stone, or alabaster. The abstract form shown above left—for which step-by-step instructions follow—and the Easter Islander head, above right, were both carved from alabaster, then rubbed with beeswax to enhance the stone's natural luster. Alabaster has been sculpted since ancient times. When smoothly carved, it has a glowing, translucent surface.

24: Basic tools for carving in soft stone include (left to right) a steel hammer; flat-tipped, pointed, and toothed chisels for chipping; steel riffler rasps for filing away rough spots; and No. 600 wet-or-dry sandpaper for final smoothing.

25: Before you start a stone carving, make a clay model in the shape you expect the finished work to be, and mount it on a dowel so you can examine it from all sides as you work on the stone. Include all important details.

26: Wearing safety goggles, chip away major irregularities with the hammer and point chisel; then even off the rough stone with a flat chisel until the surface is relatively smooth and free of blemishes.

27: With pencil or crayon, outline the finished shape as it would appear from each of the surfaces of the stone.

28: Chisel away the areas that lie outside the guidelines until you have reduced the stone to an approximation of its finished shape. The stone is resting on a sandbag on the work table; it is *not* on the sculptor's lap.

Selecting the Stone

Carving stones are sold by sculpture supply houses in blocks or boulders weighing from ten to 50 pounds and are not expensive. The figures on page 1935 were carved from pieces of alabaster of roughly the same shape, size (about 5 by 6 by 10 inches) and weight (ten pounds). When making your purchase, look carefully to see what a stone has to offer in quality and form. Check to make sure it is free of cracks, soft streaks, impurities, and veins that might cause it to fracture while it is being worked. Tap the stone lightly with a steel hammer; if it resounds clearly, it is solid enough for carving, but if you hear a low-pitched thud, pick another stone.

Tools

The tools used to shape stone vary somewhat from those used on wood. The ones I used to carve the alabaster sculptures are shown in photograph 24. You will need flat-tipped, pointed, and toothed chisels—all without handles—and a stone-carving hammer to drive them. Keep the chisels sharp (see Craftnotes, page 1934). Wood rasps and rifflers may be used for smoothing soft stone. In addition, you will need: No. 600 wet-or-dry silicon-carbide papers (used wet) for finishing; a sandbag (or box filled with clean, coarse sand) to absorb the shock of the hammer blows; and a plastic safety mask to protect your eyes from flying stone chips. Modeling clay is useful in visualizing the finished shape before you begin work on the stone.

The Model

From the beginning, it is important to have a clear idea of the finished shape sought. Some sculptors can visualize the end product in the rough stone, but it is a great help to have a model in front of you as you work.

Before starting work on the stone, knead a piece of modeling clay into roughly the same shape as the stone. The model may be the same size as the stone or smaller in scale. Of clay, shape an abstract figure such as the one shown on page 1935. But remember that when you work in stone, you may have to adapt your design to the material. Realistic works should be postponed until you are familiar with the tools of the craft. Your model need not be finished in detail, but it should reflect the volume and rough shape of the finished work. Mount it on a stake so you can rotate it freely, and set it on the workbench at eye level for easy reference (photograph 25).

The Stone

Wearing a plastic safety mask, put the stone on the sandbag and chip off all surface irregularities with a hammer and a pointed chisel. Hold the chisel loosely, midway down the shank, and drive it at a 45-to-90-degree angle to the stone surface, breaking off small chips rather than large chunks. You will need to vary the angle depending on the shape of the chip you want to remove. This is the rough shaping process. (You may want to leave one area in a natural state, as in the head on page 1935, where the uneven surface represents the coarse texture of hair, but in the ab-

29: To bore through the stone, use a ⅛-inch metal-cutting bit on a power drill to make a pilot hole, then change to a ½-inch bit, then enlarge the opening with toothed chisels.

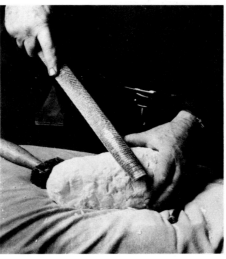

30: When you near the final shape, smooth the stone with a rasp (above) and the smaller, finer rifflers (photograph 24). This final shaping often takes a long time.

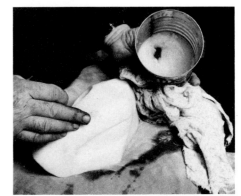

31: Refine the surface with No. 600 wet-or-dry silicon-carbide sandpaper, used very wet.

32: Finally, polish the finished sculpture with warm beeswax applied and rubbed with a soft, clean cloth.

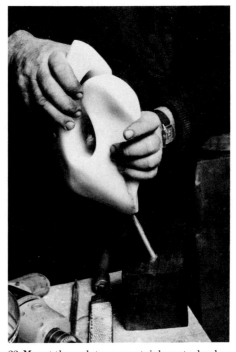

33: Mount the sculpture on a stainless-steel rod and insert the rod into a hardwood base. Drill holes for the rod in the stone and the wood, taking care to bore them at angles that will give you a well-balanced work.

stract shape, I smoothed the entire surface before sculpting.) Next, use a flat-tipped or toothed chisel in a similar way to eliminate blemishes and weak, flaky spots. A flat chisel is best for removing fragments along an existing crack. The stone, when ready for carving, will look like the one in photograph 26.

Using the model as a reference, outline the sculpture with a pencil or crayon on the stone (photograph 27). A three-dimensional shape can best be represented by outlining it as it would appear from each of the four sides of the stone and from the top and bottom as well. Begin removing more stone—the process called subtraction—with a flat or toothed chisel to create a rough approximation of the final shape (photograph 28). After you have worked on one side for a while, turn the stone and work on the next side. That way you can shape the entire piece gradually.

Rotate both stone and model as you work, and pencil in new outlines as old ones are chiseled away. If you come upon a vein in the stone, work around it carefully with light hammer blows; this area will be soft and will tend to crumble. If your design requires that you cut an opening through the stone (as mine did), use a power drill and a ⅛-inch bit to bore a pilot hole (photograph 29). Then enlarge the hole with a ½-inch bit, and finish it with a small, toothed chisel.

When your stone nears its finished shape, do not try to go farther with the chisels. They may remove more stone than you intend. Instead, file the stone down to its finished contours with a wood rasp (photograph 30) and shaped rifflers. To further smooth the surface, use No. 600 wet-or-dry sandpaper with plenty of water photograph 31). Finally, bring out the luster of the stone by buffing it with warmed beeswax (photograph 32).

You can mount your sculpture on a stainless steel rod set in a wooden base (photograph 33). A 4- or 5-inch hardwood cube is a good scale for a ten-pound stone. Decide how you want to display your sculpture and mark the point on the bottom of the stone where the hole for the rod should be bored. Again, drill a pilot hole with a ⅛-inch bit. Then change to a drill bit the same diameter as the rod, and redrill the hole to a depth of 1½ inches. A ¼-inch rod, 6 inches long, suits a ten-pound stone. Make a hole the same size in the center of the wood base. Keep the drill straight while you make both holes, or the sculpture will look lopsided. To steady the stone during drilling, clamp it loosely in a vise, protected by several layers of cardboard and soft rags. Before sliding the rod into the holes, taper its ends slightly with a file, and if necessary to get a tight fit, coat them with epoxy cement. Do not force the rod into the stone; internal pressure could shatter the alabaster.

For related projects, see "Acrylics," "Candlemaking," "Carving," "Casting," "Ceramics," "Foam Forms," "Folk Art," "Enameling Metal," "Kilns," "Mobiles," "Molding Methods," "Pewtersmithing," "Pottery," "Sand Casting," "Whittling," "Wire Sculpture," and "Wood Assemblages."

SEASHELLS

Elegance from the Ocean

These spiny murex shells include one from the Philippines (top) and two from the Mediterranean. The latter were the source of Tyrian purple dye, extracted by the Phoenicians and used to color clothing worn by the elite of ancient Greece and Rome.

Shell collecting and shell crafting are by no means pursuits of recent origin. Shells have figured in art, in religious ceremonies, and as decorative objects since ancient times. Even Neanderthal man was aware of mollusks (the creatures that make the shells and live inside them) as a source of food. Later tribal societies used shells for personal decoration and as money. Tyrian purple, the color worn by nobility of ancient Greece and Rome, came from a dye extracted from the murex shell (pictured above). Italian craftsmen, using the layered shell structure, have produced exquisite shell cameos for centuries. Shells have been used as perfume containers, snuff boxes, drinking vessels, and horns.

Crafting decorative or amusing objects from shells continues today, and the projects on pages 1944 through 1951 will show you how to use shells for making jewelry, collages, representations of flora and fauna, and a luminous lampshade. If your interest lies in collecting shells, pages 1941-1943 will tell you where to find them and what to do with those you find. If you live inland, or if your interest extends to shells found only in distant seas, many kinds are available commercially through shell dealers.

The beauty of the sea and beach is the magnet that usually draws the novice shell collector. Almost anyone walking along the shore beneath a sunny sky stops to pick up shells, marveling at the richness of their shapes and colors. But once you decide to collect shells seriously, you need a more scientific approach. The shells found on the beach are but the empty and weathered houses of dead mollusks. To collect the finest specimens, you must go where the mollusks live. Finding them can be an exciting treasure hunt.

Lustrous, exotic, silky, colorful, and extravagantly varied, seashells have a magnetic attraction for both collectors and craftsmen who see such shells as a new material to be worked. In Japan, some collectors use particularly beautiful seashells as objects of contemplation and meditation.

The Florida conch lives in the sand on the sea bottom. A conch uses its operculum (the door that covers the opening of its shell) as a sort of walking stick as it lurches along. Some conchs grow 2 feet long and weigh five pounds. The word conch comes from the Greek word for shell, and shell collectors are sometimes called conchologists.

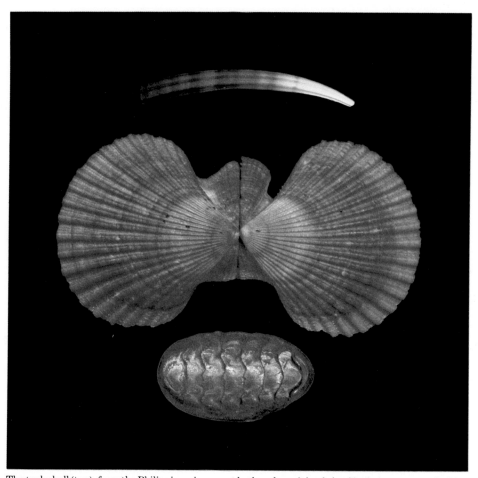

The tusk shell (top), from the Philippines, is open at both ends, so it lends itself to being sewn on clothing for decoration. The noble scallop (center) comes from Japan; scallops can swim by rapidly opening and closing their shells. The chiton (bottom) from California has eight plates in its lustrous shell.

An Environmental Note

Shell collecting is a delightful hobby, but over-collecting is a problem in some popular tourist areas. To ensure the preservation of the mollusk population, always return rocks to their original positions, for small mollusks and eggs are destroyed by sunlight. If you find a cache of mollusks, don't take them all; take only a likely specimen or two and leave the rest to reproduce. Collect only mollusks that are mature. Leave the immature ones to grow and replenish themselves. The only exception comes when you are collecting mollusks that have been thrown up on the beach by the surf and will die anyway.

Shell Shapes and Colors

Scientists who study mollusks do not know why they create shells of such spectacular shapes and colors. Elaborate spines and contortions offer the animal only slight additional protection, and the colors are too bright for effective camouflage. The shell is produced by the mantle, an envelope that surrounds the body of the animal. This mantle simultaneously deposits three layers of calcium crystals: the mother-of-pearl lining, a center layer for strength, and an outer layer of prismatic crystals (photograph, left). It is the diffraction of light through these prisms that gives the shell its luminescence.

The pearl oyster (center) displays the glowing mother-of-pearl shell lining that is valued for its decorative uses. Turban shells are shown before (right) and after (left) a professional acid bath; the latter reveals the inner layer of lustrous shell hidden beneath colored calcium crystals.

The color of the shell appears to be related to the temperature of the water. The brightest shells are found in tropical waters, and the color becomes less vivid in colder climates, fading to pale whitish tones in the polar regions. Bright greens and blues are rarely seen. The body organs of the mollusk itself are often luminescent and change colors as the animal ingests and expels water. The sea slug, which has no shell at all, is considered by many to be more beautiful than any shell.

Where Mollusks Are Found

When you go collecting shells, it is helpful to have some knowledge of the creatures that inhabit them. For a brief description of the classes of mollusks, see the Craftnotes, page 1943. Sources of additional information are listed in the bibliography on page 1942.

Mollusks can be found almost everywhere. They live in fresh water, brackish water, salt water, and on land; in polar regions, temperate zones, and in the tropics. They may be found clamped onto shore rocks, dug into sand beneath shallow waters, or swimming in the depths of the ocean. In general, warmer regions have more kinds of mollusks than cold, but colder regions have more of each particular kind that lives there. Field guides describing the mollusks of specific areas help shell collectors; they tell you what kinds of mollusks you may expect to find and where you are likely to find them.

Looking for Mollusks

Generally, few mollusks live where they will be exposed to the pounding of the surf. They prefer protected areas buffered by coral reefs and forests of submerged seaweed. They like a sea bottom that is a mixture of mud and sand, slopes gently, and has rocks and seaweed for them to cling to.

The sea tide moves in and out twice each day. Tide charts available at Chambers of Commerce and tourist bureaus tell the depth of the tide, and the times that it is at either extreme.

When the tide comes in, it fills holes in the rocky parts of the shore. When the tide goes out, these tide pools are good places to look for mollusks. Mollusks can also be found on shelves of rock where they are somewhat protected from the waves. Few mollusks will be found in the high-tide area where they would have to live for long periods without water.

The best place of all to look is along the tidal flats, sandy and grassy areas between low and high tide lines. Remember that you are pursuing live animals, and learn to catch them where they live. Look under seaweed, break open sponges, turn over planks, pull moss out of tide pools, and check big broken shells for little living ones that may be attached to them. Tunnels and dimples that indicate the presence of mollusks are apparent on the surface of the sand. As the tide is going out, they slow down their activities, but as the tide is coming in, much molluscan motion is visible. In warm waters, look just below the sand where the low tide turns. Periwinkle clams (once used by east coast Indians as money) live in the sand between tide marks. Cockles, conchs, abalones, coquinas, and moon snails live in shallow waters, as do scallops and jingles.

Coral reefs, too, are active with molluscan life. Cowries, the most popular and well known of shells, are nocturnal creatures that move along such reefs in search of food. And cone shells live in the seaweed and sand beside coral reefs.

Occasionally, after a storm, some of the mollusks that live in the depths of the sea will be carried to the shore. Check the beaches after a storm for varieties not usually found there, including rock dwellers torn loose from their moorings.

Equipment Needed

You will need some equipment for serious shell collecting, depending on where you do your hunting. Along sandy shores and in shallow waters, the best tools are a sieve and a water glass—a wooden frame or bucket with a glass bottom used for scanning the sand beneath water. Along rocky shores, a dip net is useful for scooping in tide pools. A knife or chisel and hammer may be necessary to dislodge creatures that have cemented themselves to rocks. Carry cotton bags to hold collected shells, match boxes and other small containers for smaller varieties.

Some gastropods are carnivorous so it is possible to set a trap for them. You can use an open cloth bag containing bits of meat, or you can purchase a lobster or crayfish trap. Set the trap in shallow water, and secure it in place with a rock.

Working in somewhat deeper waters is also possible. You need an air mattress to float on, a face mask to look through, and a long-handled net for dipping. A bushel basket, floating on a life preserver that is anchored with a rock and string, makes a good storage bin for specimens. Collecting while scuba diving in deep water is possible, but only for those who have knowledge of the sport.

This lovely shell is a chambered nautilus from the Philippines; the shell is chambered because as the nautilus grows, it keeps building walls behind it, always living in the outer room of the spiral. When sailors first saw these shells floating on the sea, they thought they were tortoise-shell cats.

Either of these strange creatures can be hazard-ous for the shell collector. The sea urchin (right) can give you a nasty sting if you step on it, though it will avoid you if it can. A few varieties of the cone shell (left), including this one, are also capa-ble of inflicting poisonous stings.

The top mitre still has its skinlike shell covering, while the bottom one has been cleaned. The cover-ing is slightly greenish and can be easily removed with soap, water, and a brush.

For further reading

Art from Shells by Stuart and Leni Goodman, Crown Publishers, Inc.

Collecting Seashells by Kathleen Yeger Johnstone, Grosset and Dunlap

Introducing Seashells by R. Tucker Abbott, D. Van Nostrand Co.

Jewels from the Ocean Deep: The Complete Guide to Shell Collecting by Murray Hoyt, G. P. Putnam's Sons.

Kingdom of the Seashell by R. Tucker Abbott, Crown Publishers, Inc.

Shelling and Beachcombing in Florida and the Caribbean by Gary and Rudi Magnotte, Dukane Press, Inc., Hollywood, Fla.

Shells by William K. Emerson and Andreas Feininger, The Viking Press, Inc.

Shells and Shell Collecting by S. Peter Dance, McGraw-Hill, Inc.

The Collector's Encyclopedia of Shells by S. Peter Dance, McGraw-Hill, Inc.

The Shell: 500 Million Years of Inspired Design by Hugh and Marguerite Stiz and R. Tucker Abbott, Harry N. Abrams, Inc.

The fragile paper nautilus (top, left) and the purple snail (top, right) both live on the high seas, the for-mer clinging to its shell from below, the latter floating upside down on a raft of bubbles. The glorious scallop (center) is from Australia. The orange-spotted mitre (below, left) is from the Philippines, and the spectacular yellow-heart cockle (bottom, right) comes from tropical waters of the Pacific.

Clothing

Wear both shoes and gloves when you collect shells. A barnacle can be as sharp as a knife. Sea urchins (photograph, top left) and sting rays can inflict painful stings. Some collectors recommend walking with a sliding step to alert these animals of your presence; they will avoid you if they can. Watch where you walk among coral reefs, too; avoid stepping into patches of seaweed without first using a pole to as-certain what may be concealed there.

Be particularly careful of cone shells (photograph, top left). Many kinds of cones found in tropical seas can inflict a painful sting. Only a few varieties are truly dan-gerous, but handle all occupied cone shells carefully.

The sun is another hazard. Protect the back of your neck and your legs above the water, where the reflected rays of the sun will be most intense. Creams are avail-able to block the sun, or you can cover up with clothing.

Cleaning the Shells

Collected shells, like fish that have been caught, must be cleaned. There are three ways of doing this, all equally effective. Soaking in denatured alcohol for several hours or overnight is one way. Spiral-shaped gastropods should stand in fresh water overnight before they are put in alcohol; otherwise their flesh will shrivel and be hard to remove. After you have soaked the shells of hinged bivalves, push the flesh out; then rinse and dry the shell. With gastropods, a fish hook is a useful tool for pulling the soft parts out. Cut or pull off the operculum—the covering for the shell's opening—if it is present. Dry it and store with the shell, glued to a bit of cotton; it is a useful aid in identification.

Freezing is a second way to prepare shells for a collection. Keep the shells in a refrigerator for a few hours before and after freezing; extreme temperature changes can cause tiny cracks. Keep the shells in the freezer, in plastic containers lined with paper towels, for at least two days. Thaw them with the opening facing down; then remove the soft parts.

Boiling is the third way to clean the shells. Put each shell in its own cotton bag to protect it from cracking. Use a stainless steel or enameled pan, covering the shells with cold water; then bring the water slowly to a boil over moderate heat. Boil small shells for two or three minutes, larger ones for ten minutes, very large ones for 15. Remove them from the heat and let them cool gradually; then remove the soft parts.

Sometimes it is difficult to remove all the soft parts. Additional soaking in a 10 percent solution of formaldehyde will finish the job.

At this stage, the shells may need additional cleaning. Usually scrubbing the outside with a brush, soap, and water will remove the skinlike covering. Use a knife for scraping if the brush is not enough. If your shells are still not clean, soak them overnight in a mild solution of bleach. Avoid acid solutions, as they are dangerous and damage the finish of the shell. Mineral oil or baby oil can be used to give shells a sheen, but it also gathers dust.

The Collection

If you are going to keep your shells in a collection rather than use them in a crafts project, store them in a dark, dust-free place, and keep accurate locality data. Most collectors label each shell with a number written on the shell. Then they record the same number in a journal, and beside the number, enter locality data. Carefully recorded are such facts as the depth of the water, the type of bottom, the relationship of the shell to the bottom, the type of water, its flow and temperature, whether it was clear or murky, whether the animal was dead or alive, and any other relevant information, together with the date found, and the name of the collector.

For the beginning collector, shoe boxes lined with cotton make good storage compartments. As your collection enlarges, you will need some sort of drawer or shelf arrangement for storage. Shells may be grouped by type, color, size, or shape, as long as they are labeled and indexed in your journal.

CRAFTNOTES: CHARACTERISTICS OF MOLLUSKS

There are more than 100,000 kinds of mollusks. They range in size from microscopic creatures to squid nearly 60 feet long and clams weighing almost 600 pounds. Mollusks are divided into six classes: gastropods, bivalves, cephalopods, scaphopods, amphineura and monoplacophora. Of these, the gastropods and bivalves are the most numerous.

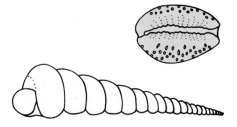

The variety of shell color and shape is enormous. Gastropods can be globular like the cowries (above, top) or long and pointed like the augers (above, bottom). They may be glossy or dull, spiny or smooth, pale or brightly colored, one color or striped, blotched, or mottled in brilliant hues.

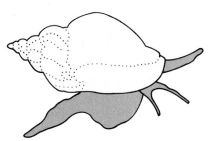

There are some 80,000 kinds of gastropods. They live all over the world, in fresh water, in salt water, and on land. Most gastropods have a one-piece shell, a head with eyes on stalks, and a foot for locomotion (above). A snail is a typical gastropod. Most gastropods, such as the murex, conch, turban, and cone, have a coiled shell. They can close the opening of this shell with a little door, the operculum, attached to the foot. Some, the limpets and limpetlike gastropods, have disk-shaped shells not quite large enough to cover their bodies. These cement themselves to rocks with a substance secreted by the foot. Still other gastropods have no shell at all.

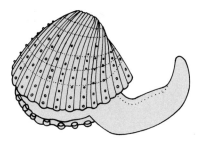

The bivalves, the second largest class of mollusks, have a two-part shell held together with a hinge, no head, and a wedge-shaped foot. This foot is used somewhat like a tongue for burrowing into the sand (above). Like the gastropods, bivalves are found all over the world, but none of

them live on land. Most are wedge- or fan-shaped. Oysters, scallops, and clams are all bivalves. Scallops are able to swim, but most bivalves are more sedentary, attaching themselves with threads or cementing themselves to rocks.

Bivalves vary widely in color and shape. Some are smooth, some spined; some are pale, some brilliantly colored. Some have sculptured ridges in rays; others have raised patterns in concentric circles.

The cephalopods are the most highly developed of the mollusks and the most mobile. These include the mollusks with tentacles such as the squid, the cuttlefish, and the octopus. Some have an external shell like the nautilus, some an internal shell, and some no shell at all.

The sachopods have tusk or tooth shells, open at both ends. They have a flexible foot similar to the bivalves. In the past these shells were used as money by west coast Indians.

The amphineura are the chitons that have eight separate plates in their shell, held together by a girdle; they clamp themselves on rocks with a suckerlike foot. The monoplacophona is a new class designation for mollusks; nearly all its members are fossils.

Leni Goodman, an actress, and her husband, Stuart, a cameraman and director, began collecting seashells while vacationing in the Caribbean. When they returned home to New York after a collecting trip, they wrote a crafts book, Art from Shells. Off stage, they now design and manufacture Gooleni seashell jewelry.

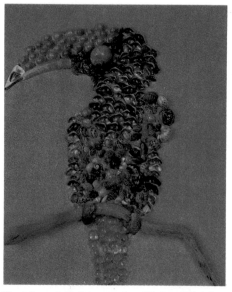

To make a shell picture such as this hornbill, take time to select shells that best represent the various textures of the design—bill, head, chest, wings, and tail—matching some colors and using a random assortment of shells elsewhere.

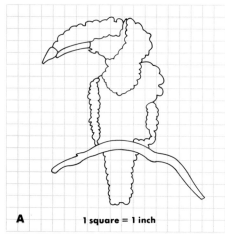

A   1 square = 1 inch

Figure A: To enlarge this pattern for the hornbill pictured above, draw a grid of 1-inch squares on tracing paper. Copy the pattern lines, square by square, from the small grid onto the larger one.

Designs and Decorations
Seashell collage

If you have an assortment of seashells tucked away in plastic bags or jars, as many people do, you may already have enough to make a collage, such as the one of the hornbill perched on a gnarled branch of driftwood pictured at left. If you do not like the bird, you might want to portray a fish, a butterfly, a flower, or an abstract pattern with your shells. Should you need more shells, you can buy them in almost unlimited shapes, sizes, and colors from shell dealers.

In addition to seashells, your collage might include other found materials such as surf-polished sandstone and glass fragments, feathers, bits of coconut shell, palm seeds, pods and cones, netting, or buttons. In addition, you will need: a 14-by-18-inch piece of primed canvas board; acrylic or oil paint for the background color; paintbrush; paint thinner; glass jar; and rags. To transfer the design in Figure A you will need: masking tape; tracing and carbon paper; and a pencil. Or you can use a stick of charcoal to sketch a design directly on the backboard. To fasten shells and other lightweight materials to the backboard, use white glue. Attach heavier accessories, such as the driftwood perch, with epoxy cement. To complete the collage you will need: clear acrylic spray; picture frame; picture hook; and hanging wire.

Transferring the Design
To begin, brush on the background paint with short, even strokes, and set the board aside to dry. Enlarge the design (Figure A) on tracing paper. Tape the tracing to the board, put carbon paper under it, and transfer the outline to the board.

Putting It Together
For the perch, I found a piece of driftwood to balance the angle of the bird's profile. This goes on the board first. Position the branch over the sketch, and mark a guide dot where it touches the board. Then put epoxy cement on branch and board at these points. Hold the branch in place until the cement sets. To fill the sketch with seashells, spread white glue over one area at a time, using a toothpick or ice-cream stick; then press shells in place. A moon snail I found in the Virgin Islands made a prominent eye. To draw attention to it, I surrounded it with miniature cone shells spotted with black and brown. To cover the top half of the bill, I chose small, shiny ring-top cowrie shells. I positioned a long, narrow piece of a razor clam shell across the bottom of the bill. A chunk of surf-worn shell suggested the triangular tip of a beak; so in it went (photograph 1). I outlined the head, neck, chest, and lower back with purple clam shells. Then, to simulate feathers, I used more clam shells in rows covering the head and neck, overlapping curved edges with hinged edges. I filled the area between neck and branch with an assortment of miniature shells; then I layered the tail with pink clam shells (photograph 2). Finally I placed two turkey-wing arc shells on the branch as the bird's feet, gluing them with epoxy.

Once your collage is finished, let the glue harden for a few hours, spray the collage with clear acrylic to make it glisten, and it will be ready to frame and hang.

1: Using epoxy cement, fasten the driftwood on which the bird perches to the mounting board. Then spread white glue evenly over one area of the sketch at a time, and cover that area with shells.

2: To simulate feathers, you can layer clam shells over the head and tail areas of the bird. To do this, work from the top down, covering the bottom curved edge of the shells in one row with the top hinged edge of the shells in the next row.

Designs and Decorations
Seashell jewelry

¢ ⧖ 🚹 🦂

You may like to display your favorite shells in jewelry settings such as the necklaces shown at top right, or the choker and matching earrings pictured at right. You can attach even a delicate shell to a necklace using a metal jewelry finding called a bell cap, so you do not have to drill a hole through the shell. The shell can be suspended on leather lacing or macramé cord, or you can use ribbon or rope, with the shells interspersed with wood, cork, or glass beads. If you make shell jewelry, ready-made chains, metal chokers, earring and cufflink backs, rings, and pins can be found in hobby shops.

Materials
I used ten snake cowrie shells to make the choker and earrings set. You could achieve a similar effect with cone shells, sea urchins, certiths, or olive shells. Starting with cleaned shells (page 1942), you will need: a small block of plastic foam; screwdriver; cotton swabs; wax paper; bonding cement or epoxy cement; eight bell caps, sized to fit the shells; pinch-nose pliers; eight No. 04 jump rings; eight ¾-inch wood beads; scissors; thin leather lacing 36 inches long; and earring findings. If your ears are not pierced, buy screw-back fittings with a hook for attaching shells.

Attaching Findings
To keep track of shells as you work, make holes in the foam block and insert the shells in them. Fit a bell cap over each shell, adjusting its prongs to get a good grip on the shell. Squeeze a few drops of epoxy on wax paper. Dip a cotton swab in the epoxy, and apply it to the inside of the bell cap and each prong. Using the pliers, pick up the bell cap by its tiny loop and slip it onto the shell. Mold the prongs around the shell; then put the shell back in its compartment while the epoxy dries.

After a few minutes of drying time, pry open jump rings with the pliers and attach them to the bell caps. Raise one end of a jump ring and press the other downward, leaving just enough of an opening for the jump ring to pass through the loop in the bell cap (photograph 3). Then press each end of the jump ring back together with the pliers.

Stringing Shells and Beads
To string shells and beads as pictured, tie an overhand knot 13 inches from one end of a thin 36-inch leather cord (photograph 4). Make a single loop knot; then bring the shorter end of the cord through the loop again before tightening the knot. Beginning with a shell, alternate beads and shells until all 15 pieces are strung (photograph 5). Tie another overhand knot to keep shells and beads centered. If you have pierced ears, thread ear wires through the loops at the top of two bell caps attached to shells. But if you use screw-back earrings, use jump rings to attach bell caps to the earring fittings.

The snake cowrie shells that I used were naturally polished, but if you like, you can spray your shells with clear acrylic to make them shine.

A quick way to make a summer necklace is to hang a favorite shell in any of the ways shown here. From left to right are a Babylonian shell on a silky macramé cord; a *cardium cardissa* on a filigree chain; a ramshorn snail on a choker; and a scorpion conch on a macramé cord with a cork bead.

The matching necklace and earrings were made from snake cowrie shells. Bell-cap findings were glued to them with epoxy so they could be suspended from a cord and ear wires.

3: In making shell jewelry, use pinch-nose pliers to separate the end of a jump ring so you can fit it through the loop of a bell-cap fitting. Then pinch the gap between the wire ends closed.

4: To make an overhand knot, tie the cord loosely once, about 13 inches from one end of the cord. Then put the shorter end of the cord through the loop again. Pull the ends to tighten the knot.

5: Alternate shells and beads on the leather necklace cord until you have strung eight shells and seven beads. To keep them centered on the cord, tie a knot after the last shell.

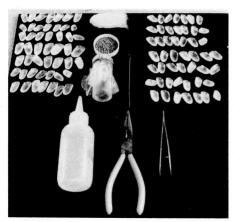

When Marshall and Julia Thomas visited Pompano Beach, Florida, they became interested in the shell collection of a neighbor. They joined the Broward County Shell Club to learn more about shells. When they returned home to Royal Oak, Michigan, Julia began to make shell flowers, and Marshall created shell animals for their grandchildren. Since then they have won many awards for their designs. The Frog Symphony, shown on page 1949, was given a blue ribbon at the Naples, Florida, Shell Show.

6: Sort the proper number of shells needed for the petals of each flower according to right-or-left-hand hinge. Each shell in a row should be about the same size. In addition have these materials on hand (center, top to bottom): a wad of cotton; center decorations such as mustard seeds; a plastic pill bottle with clear plastic wrap and an elastic band; cloth-covered stem wires; bonding cement in a plastic applicator bottle; long-nosed pliers, and tweezers.

The petals on the flowers in this bouquet are lilac coquinas and rose-colored cockle shells. Other natural material can add to the illusion, such as the mustard seeds and the small cones used to decorate the centers of these flowers.

Designs and Decorations
Seashell flowers

Matching bivalve shells were glued together and attached to cloth-covered stem wires to make each shell flower of the bouquet pictured above. Without the stems, these shell flowers could be used to decorate picture frames or jewelry.

Materials
I used seven lilac coquinas or five rose-colored cockle shells as petals for each seashell flower pictured; then I made a center for each flower with yellow mustard seeds or Australian pinecones dyed red. In addition, you will need: plastic pill bottles; clear plastic wrap; scissors; rubber bands; clear-drying bonding cement; tweezers; a roll of No. 18 cloth-covered wire (available at florist or craft shops); wire cutters; cotton; 6-by-9-inch polyethylene sheet; white glue; long-nosed pliers; and clear acrylic spray (photograph 6). To arrange the shell flowers, you will also need: floral clay; plastic foam; knife; filler such as statice or sphagnum moss; and a container.

7: Put a bead of clear bonding cement in the center of the plastic wrap mold. Using tweezers, put the end of each shell in the glue, covering the curved edge of each shell with the hinged edge of the next one so the petals overlap.

8: Before the glue has hardened, sprinkle a few mustard seeds into the center of the shell flower. Use tweezers to arrange the seeds in a rounded shape. When the glue is dry, gently shake away excess seeds.

9: When the glue holding the petals is dry, saturate a wad of absorbent cotton with white glue. Place a loop of cloth-covered stem wire against the base of the shell flower, and hold it there by covering it with the wet cotton ball.

Joining the Petals

Clean all the shells (page 1942). For a natural-looking flower, select an odd number of shells of about the same size, shape, and color. The number of shells needed depends on the width of the shells and the size of the pill bottle used.

Sort the shells into piles with right- or left-handed hinges. Then select matching shells for each flower.

Make a simple, cup-shaped mold to support the shells as you glue them together. Cut a small square of plastic wrap, and put it over the top of a pill bottle. Put a rubber band loosely around the rim of the bottle. Press the center of the plastic to make a depression, and tighten the band. You can make several flowers at one time if you prepare several molds. Changing the depth of the depression slightly will let you make flowers that seem to be at various stages of development.

To fasten the shells into the shape of a flower cup, squeeze some clear bonding cement, about the size of a pea, in the center of the depression in the plastic wrap. Using tweezers, pick up a shell by its wider edge. Lean the shell against the wall of the mold so its bottom edge is in the glue (photograph 7). Then overlap the hinge edge of this shell with the curved edge of another matching shell. Continue until the flower cup is complete.

To make the center of the flower, put half a small pine cone or about 20 mustard seeds into the wet glue that has pooled in the bottom edges of the shells. Use tweezers to position the seeds so they represent the stamens of the flower (photograph 8). Set the pill bottle aside and let the glue dry overnight. Then next day you can lift the shell flower out of the plastic mold. The bonding cement will hold the shells to each other but will not stick to the plastic wrap.

To make a flower of larger shells, you can use a coffee cup covered with plastic wrap for a mold.

Attaching Stem Wires

Cut a 4-inch cloth-covered wire for the stem of each flower. With long-nosed pliers, curl one end of the wire into a ⅜-inch-wide loop at a right angle to the stem. Put white glue on a sheet of polyethylene, and roll a small wad of absorbent cotton in it, using tweezers. Pat the cotton ball on top of the loop of the stem wire (photograph 9). Center the shell flower on the cotton, and hold the assembly in an upright position until the glue sets. Then rest the shell flower on its rim until the glue is completely dry. Coat the flower inside and out with clear acrylic spray to keep dust from penetrating the shells.

Arranging the Design

Cut a 2-inch-thick block of plastic foam slightly smaller than the container selected. Use pieces of floral clay to anchor it in the container. Snip the wire stems of each flower so they are not all the same height; a closed flower that looks like a bud should have a shorter stem than a fully open flower. Push the wire stems into the foam, and add dry plant material to complete the bouquet.

This figurine depicting a shell picker at work on the beach could represent you gathering the shells used to make the shell picker and the pelican watching him.

Designs and Decorations
Shell figurines

Miniature sculptures such as the one depicting a shell picker and pelican at the beach (shown above) and the portrayal of an entire frog symphony orchestra (opposite) can combine a variety of familiar shells picked up while beachcombing. Such figurines can be quite amusing. Fragments of surf-worn shells, spurned by collectors, can be used in piecing together intricate designs. Work in progress will stimulate your beachcombing; sometimes days will pass before you discover just the right shell to add the crowning touch to your composition.

Materials
To support the shell-picker-and-pelican design, I used a 2-by-5-by-5-inch piece of coral as a base. A 1½-inch-long Y-shaped coral stem holds the pelican. A coral base with a smooth bottom and several flat areas on the top contributes to a stable composition. I used matching halves of a small and a large ponderous arc shell for the bodies; one 1-inch and two 1½-inch auger shells for the beak and arms; two 1½-inch olive shells for the legs; four small kitten-paw shells for the hands and feet; one medium-sized yellow cockle shell for the picker's head; and an assortment of a dozen miniature seashells in the pail. Any shell in your collection that resembles one of those listed can be incorporated in this design. You will also need: a pencil; wire cutters; file; clear-drying bonding cement; glue gun with pellets; tweezers; mustard seeds; black acrylic paint; ⅛-inch paintbrush; toothpaste cap; and a 1-inch-long wire wrapped with plastic or floral tape. For detail work, I use clear-drying bonding cement, but when I assemble large joints, I prefer to use a glue gun because the melted adhesive dries almost instantly.

Just how elaborate figurines made of shells can be is indicated by this award-winning frog symphony and croaker chorus. Each frog musician of the orchestra was assembled with cockles, ponderous arcs, augers, certiths, kitten paws, tear-drops, and dosinia shells. A variety of other shell combinations were used to make the individual instruments.

10: To make a pelican figurine, start with the body, using bonding cement on the rims of matching halves of a small ponderous arc shell. Press the shells together until the glue is dry. Then center and glue an auger shell between the valves of the arc shell to make the bird's head and beak.

Standing Room Only

Position the Y-shaped coral stem for the pelican's perch anywhere along the top edge of the base, and use a pencil to mark the place. Locate another flat surface near the center of the base, about 2 inches from the first mark, and pencil two dots 1½ inches apart to indicate where the shell picker's legs will be attached. With a file, smooth any roughness of the bottom edge of the coral stem. Use a glue gun to attach the stem to the base. Remove the pointed tips of the two olive shells with wire cutters; then file their top and bottom edges. (A grinding wheel is more efficient than a file). With the glue gun, fasten the smaller opening in each olive shell to the base.

Making the Pelican

To assemble the pelican, first put bonding cement on the rim of each small ponderous arc shell used in the body. Fit the halves together and set them aside until the glue is dry. Center a 1-inch auger shell between the valves of the body shell so the rounded end of the auger shell extends ¼ inch beyond the hinge of the body shell. Apply bonding cement and glue the beak in place (photograph 10). Paint two mustard seeds black. When the paint is dry, use tweezers to glue the seeds in place as eyes. Using the glue gun, line the V of the coral stem with adhesive, and attach the bottom edge of the body shell to the stem, making sure the beak of the pelican points toward the center of the base.

Finishing the Scene

For the body of the shell picker, glue matching halves of the large ponderous arc shell together, the same way you made the pelican's body. Using the glue gun, put a ring of adhesive on the top rim of each leg. Then fit the valves of the body shell onto the legs (photograph 11). Press until the glue hardens.

For each arm and hand, put glue on the point of a 2-inch auger shell, and attach the valve of a kitten-paw shell. Glue a kitten-paw shell to the base in front of each leg for the feet. Glue the arms to the sides of the body shell (photograph 12) so the outside of the kitten-paw shell faces out.

To attach the head, put glue on the rim of a cockle shell valve; then position the shell on the body shell as shown in the color photograph opposite.

For the shell picker's pail, brush bonding cement inside a toothpaste cap and put in several miniature shells. Make the handle of the pail of plastic-coated wire or a wire wrapped with floral tape. Glue the ends inside the cap. Put glue on the bottom of the pail and position it against the shell picker's right hand, gluing the rim to the hand. To finish the beach scene, glue several miniature shells on the base so the picker seems to be in the process of finding more shell treasures.

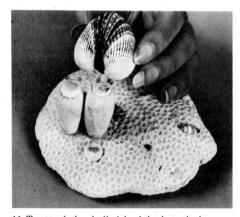

11: To attach the shell picker's body to the legs, use a glue gun to put adhesive on top of the olive shells. Position the valves of the ponderous arc shell over the glue, and press the body on the legs until the glue sets.

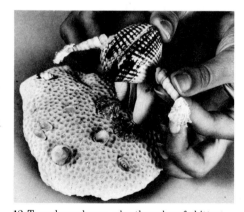

12: To make each arm, glue the valve of a kitten-paw shell over the smoothed end of an auger shell. With a glue gun, fasten each arm onto the body shell ¾ inch from the valve on opposite sides of the seam.

Dick Reagan, a producer of educational film strips, has renovated a brownstone in Prospect Heights, Brooklyn, with the help of his wife, Sheila, and their three children. To restore a broken window there, Dick learned some basic stained-glass techniques from a friend. Using these techniques, he designed lampshades made of seashells to capitalize on their color and translucence.

13: The materials needed to make a lampshade of seashells include: (top) a form such as an inverted stainless-steel mixing bowl; (top row, left to right) cotton swab and copper sulphate for antiquing, ice-cream sticks, solder, flux, watercolor brush, and copper-foil adhesive tape; (bottom row, left to right) suspension chain, shade cap, scissors, shells, and soldering iron.

14: Position adhesive-backed copper foil along the edge of a shell and wrap it over the edge in one continuous motion, overlapping the starting point by ¼ inch. Cut the tape with scissors to leave a squared-off end.

Seashells acquire a jewellike glow when they are joined like bright pieces of stained glass to make a unique but practical lampshade to suspend over a kitchen table.

Jewelry, Lapidary, and Metalwork
Shell shade

Seventy seashells rimmed with copper foil and soldered together over a domed form were used to create the decorative lamp shade shown above. Once the solder had set, the form was removed, leaving the lacy, stained-glass effect pictured. The shade is made of worn shells tumbled by the tide, with smooth, even rims neither too thick nor too delicate. They were selected because they were translucent when held up to the light and because they were curved in such a way that they would conform to the domed shape of the form. Whole scallop shells are ideal for making such a shade, but you might like to add large clam-shell shards, kitten-paw shells, oyster shells, or turkey-wing arc shells.

Materials
The number of shells needed depends on the size of the shells and the shade form. As a shade form, I used an 11-inch stainless-steel mixing bowl with a flat bottom 5 inches wide. A styrofoam lampshade form or a pine or balsa wood block used to shape felt hats could also be used. You will need these materials, some of which can be found at stained-glass suppliers: newspapers; scrub brush; a roll of ¼-inch-wide copper-foil adhesive tape; manicure scissors; zinc chloride flux; small watercolor brush; 60/40 (tin-lead percentage) solid-core wire solder; pliers; ice-cream sticks; a 40- to 140-watt soldering iron with an extension cord and a rest stand; fine sandpaper; copper sulphate antiquing solution; cotton swabs; rags; liquid detergent; and a small jar of mineral oil or linseed oil (photograph 13). You will also need electrical parts to finish the fixture: a 2½-inch-wide threaded brass caplet with a 1¼-inch-wide opening and holes in its surface for ventilation; a standard-sized pull-chain socket; a length of fiber-covered 8/2 SJ wire long enough to run across the ceiling and down the wall to an outlet; two ceiling hooks; an outlet plug; and a 75- or 100-watt clear bulb.

15: An ice-cream stick makes a good tool for pressing the foil snugly against the shell on both sides of the edge. If the shell has ridges, squeeze the foil firmly into the grooves.

16: Use a soldering iron, flux, and solid-core solder to fasten the copper-covered edges of the wrapped shells to the brass caplet and to adjacent shells.

17: To get an antique look, apply copper sulphate to shells and all metal parts using a cotton swab. (Paying special attention to visible solder.) This solution will give a unifying greenish cast to metal and shells. With a mild detergent wash away excess flux and antiquing solution.

Wrapping and Soldering Shells

Clean the shells by scrubbing them with a small brush. Rinse them in warm water and put them on a newspaper to dry.

To unravel the copper-foil adhesive tape easily without tangling it, make a dispenser. To do this, lay the roll of tape flat on a 3-inch-square piece of plastic or hardboard; then evenly space three 1½-inch strips of masking tape loosely over the center edge of the roll (photograph 13) to hold it in place as you pull the tape free. To wrap the edge of a shell, center the copper foil over the straightest edge. Keeping the foil taut, turn the shell as you wrap the tape around it in a continuous motion, overlapping the starting edge by ¼ inch (photograph 14). Use manicure scissors to make a square cut. Fold the foil down over the inner and outer edges of the shell with your thumb and forefinger. Beginning at the overlap, use an ice-cream stick to smooth the foil, and remove any slack or wrinkle that would keep the tape from lying flat against the shell. Use the edge of the stick to squeeze the foil into any grooves on fan-shaped shells (photograph 15). But press gently to keep from chipping edges. Wrap the other shells the same way.

Use sandpaper to remove the finish from the exterior of the brass caplet so the solder will adhere to it. Center the brass caplet on top of the shade form. With a watercolor brush, put flux on the top and edges of the brass caplet and the foil around each shell to induce the solder to flow evenly and freely. Plug in the soldering iron and rest it on the stand. Unwind some solder from the roll, but wait a few minutes before testing to see if the iron is hot enough. You are ready to proceed when the hot tip of the iron, rubbed over the solder, makes it flow evenly. Position a foil-wrapped shell with one of its edges touching the edge of the brass caplet. Tack this joint with solder, either by taking a drop of solder onto the iron's tip and transferring it to the point of contact between shell and caplet, or by placing the solder directly on the contact point and then touching it with the hot iron. Continue to tack shells to each other and the caplet until a band of shells is soldered to the edge of the caplet (photograph 16). Then work down to cover the shade form by soldering on shells wherever shell edges touch. The shade shown is about 6½ inches deep. You can make your shade as shallow or as deep as you wish, depending on how you will use it. Once all the shells are tacked securely, go over all the foil-covered edges on the exterior of the shade with solder to fasten the bindings around and between shells. Then lift the shade off the form, and solder all of the points on the inside of the shade in the same way. To antique the shade, use a cotton swab to rub copper sulphate antiquing solution over the silver-colored solder joints to turn them dark green (photograph 17). Handle copper sulphate carefully; it is caustic enough to cause burns. A similar treatment on the brass caplet and shells will result in a greenish cast. To remove excess flux and antiquing solution that might oxidize and turn the solder powdery white, scrub the lamp with a mild detergent; then rinse with clear water. When the shade is dry, rub mineral oil or linseed oil over shells and soldered areas using a rag. Let the oil soak in; then rub off the excess so you leave only a patina. The oil enhances the translucence of the shells. Wire the shade to make a fixture by following the instructions accompanying Figure B.

For related projects, see "Beachcombing," "Collages and Assemblages," "Flowers, Artificial," "Jewelry," "Lamps and Shades," "Pod and Cone Art," and "Stained Glass."

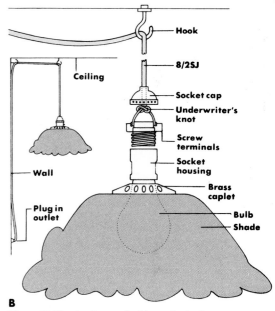

B

Figure B: To wire the seashell lampshade, first measure the amount of cord needed to run across the ceiling and down the wall to the outlet. Disassemble a pull-chain socket. Use a knife to separate the two wires at one end of the cord for about 2 inches. Use a wire stripper to remove ½ inch of plastic coating from each split cord end. Twist each bundle of exposed wire strands tightly. Pass the ends through the socket cap. To reduce tension at the screw connections in the socket, make an underwriter's knot by passing each end of wire through a loop in the other wire. Bend each exposed end of twisted wire into a hook shape. Fit each hook around a terminal screw in the direction the screw will turn, and tighten the screw. Then slip the socket core with connected wires back into the socket housing. Screw a decorative hook in the ceiling directly above the place where you want the fixture to be and another in the ceiling near the wall above an outlet. Attach a plug to the outlet end of the cord the same way that you wired the socket. Screw the threaded bottom of the socket into the caplet at the top of the shade. Insert a bulb in the socket, plug in the cord, and pull the chain to turn the light on.

SEED SPROUTING
The Kitchen Gardener

Stuart Rabinowitz, a reading specialist, combined his interest in gardening with his knowledge of teaching to develop a horticultural education program for the Wavehill Center for Environmental Studies, Riverdale, New York. He has extended this program to many schools and museums in New York, New Jersey, and Connecticut. He is also on the board of the Indoor Light Gardening Society of New York.

If you have tasted oriental cuisine, you may have already sampled sprouts without knowing it. Sprouts, seeds grown in a miniature indoor hothouse until their first green leaves appear, were first cultivated in China about 2000 B.C. They quickly became a diet staple, not only for the Chinese, but for many other peoples in the East. Until recently, sprouting had been most widely practiced by Asians, but now penny-wise homemakers everywhere are learning that they can stretch their budgets by growing their own food from seed. A small cup of dry seed—grains like wheat and barley, legumes like peas and beans, other vegetables like radishes and cranberries, nuts like almonds, and many others—will yield a brimming bowlful of sprouts. As seeds sprout, they multiply vastly in bulk, as shown in the photograph opposite. The whole process, from dry seeds to edible sprouts, takes only a few days, and the result is a crop of tasty and very nutritious food, rich in vitamins, minerals, and proteins. Harvested sprouts can be eaten raw, but they can also be ground and baked into bread, quick-fried as a vegetable, or even used as a dessert topping. From appetizer to dessert, fresher foods cannot be found.

All you need is a wide-mouthed jar, a piece of cheesecloth and an elastic band, plus some seeds, heat, air, and water, to see seeds sprout on your own pantry shelf in from two to six days. Sprouting methods are described starting on page 1954; sample recipes for using the sprouts appear on page 1959.

Greenery and Growing Things
Growing sprouts ¢ ⊠ ♦ 🐀

Everyone knows that seeds are capable of developing into plants, but how this happens often seems mysterious. The process is fascinating—and fairly simple (Figure A). Seeds vary in size, shape, and form, but the basic structure and growth of all seeds are similar. An undeveloped plant (embryo) lies in nutritive tissue (endosperm) that will provide food for the dormant seed when it wakens, a process that occurs when the seed is exposed to water, air, and warmth. (Dormancy can last almost forever, it seems; scientists have been able to sprout seeds 5,000 years old.) Sprouting begins when the seed is soaked in water. If enough moisture is ab-

 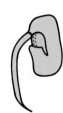 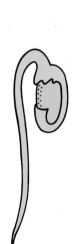 

A

Figure A: The dry seed coat is soaked in water. Gradually the seed breaks its shell, and the embryo begins to develop a root. The first green leaves signal that the seed has sprouted and can be harvested.

When the small cups of wheat, mung beans, alfalfa, and soybean seeds (opposite, lower left to upper right) were sprouted, they multiplied in bulk to fill the four large rice bowls shown. The process took four days; the result, delicious, quick-energy food. To make sprouts go a long way on your dinner table, try the recipes on page 1959.

sorbed, the seed swells and breaks through its covering. The freed embryo then develops roots and leaves. As water is absorbed by the embryo, the food stored in the endosperm is digested, releasing energy for plant growth. Root tips anchor the seed and allow further water absorption, which stimulates the growth of the stem and the first leaves, which in turn manufacture and store food. The seeds are said to be sprouted when their first leaves appear. At this time, the plant can be harvested and eaten, hull and all if you like, adding vitamins, proteins, and variety to any salad or hot meal. The sprouting methods described below tell you how to assemble a miniature sprout garden in your kitchen with materials already available in almost every home.

Seeds for Sprouting

Many health food shops, oriental restaurants, and mail-order houses (listed at left) stock dried seeds, grains, and nuts especially prepared for sprouting. You can also buy dried seeds and beans in supermarkets, but check the labels to make sure the seeds and beans have not been roasted or treated with chemicals. (Most seeds are edible when they are sprouted, but avoid potato and tomato sprouts. They can be poisonous if consumed in quantity.)

Selecting seeds is an art because they come in so many different colors and textures and because each kind can contribute its own special flavor to a meal (see Sprout Table, opposite). Some beans, such as mung beans, have a mild, celerylike flavor. Other seeds, like alfalfa or wheat, are sweet and crunchy.

You do not need a large quantity of seeds to make a lot of sprouts, as the photograph on page 1953 demonstrates. On the average, one pound of seeds will yield about eight pounds of sprouts. Most seeds are inexpensive so you can afford to experiment until you find the ones you like best. Purchase one-pound (or smaller) packages of several kinds of seeds at a time until you find your favorites. If this is your first try at sprouting, I suggest that you start with mung beans, reliable growers that are rich in vitamins and very tasty.

Remove the seeds from their wrappers. Store them by type in containers with tight-fitting lids so they will stay dry—essential until you are ready to sprout them. Metal coffee cans, plastic ice-cream containers, or glass jars make excellent storage containers. Tape the label from the bag of seeds onto the container for sure identification. (Or you might want to soak labels off cans of vegetables and tape these onto the appropriate containers.) If you store seeds for any length of time, record the day of purchase on the container so you can keep track of the seeds' potency. They are best used within three or four months. Once the seed containers are sealed and labeled, store them in a cool, dark, dry place such as a closet or attic. Seeds can also be stored in a refrigerator, but special care must then be taken to ensure that the containers are moisture proof.

Sprouting Containers

The container you use for sprouting should be at least eight times larger than the mass of the seeds that you plan to grow at one time. This will allow air to circulate and give the seeds room to grow. Glass jars and clay pots make good containers, as do bowls. But glazed pottery and metal containers should be avoided, lest lead or rust contaminate the seeds. The mouth of the container should be wide enough for you to remove the sprouts with tongs when they are ready for harvesting.

In addition to a sprouting container, you will need: one-fourth-cup, pint and quart measures; a spoon; a large wire-mesh strainer; and a roll of paper towels. If you are using the paper-towel method, you will also need a large soup bowl for the initial soaking.

Sprouting Methods

The sprouting method that you choose will depend on the amount of moisture and heat that the particular seed needs for growth. (Read the label on each package of seeds before you begin as the seed distributor may offer helpful information concerning the care of those seeds.) The general procedure, however, is always the same. Once the seeds have had a long initial soaking, they are periodically rinsed with water, which is poured into the sprouting container and then poured off. If residual water accumulates in the container, the seeds will rot, so there must be provision for drainage. This can be accomplished with any one of six methods.

Sources of seeds for sprouting

Kwong On Lung Co.
680 North Spring St.
Los Angeles, Calif. 90012

Natural Development Co.
Box 215
Bainbridge, Pa. 17502

Shiloh Farms
Box 97
Sulphur Springs, Ark. 72768

Wing Fat Co.
35 Mott St.
New York, N.Y. 10013

Some of the seeds you can sprout come from flax (far left), radish, wheat, pumpkin, sunflower, peas, millet, and almond.

SPROUT TABLE							
SEED	SUGGESTED METHOD	YIELD SEED SPROUT	SPROUTING TIME *	DAILY RINSINGS	WATER TEMPERATURE	IDEAL TEMPERATURE *	ROOT HARVEST LENGTH
Adzuki	Jar	¼ c. = 1 c.	4 - 5 days	2	Lukewarm	72°	½ - 1″
Alfalfa	Jar/Pot/Towel	1 c. = 2½ c.	2 - 4 days	2	Lukewarm	72°	¾ - 1½″
Almond	Towel	¼ c. = ½ c.	3 - 4 days	2 - 3	Lukewarm	72°	⅛ - ¼″
Barley	Jar/Pot	½ c. = 1 c.	3 - 4 days	2 - 3	Lukewarm	72°	¼ - ½″
Bean (hard)	Jar/Pot	¼ c. = 1¼ c.	3 - 5 days	3 - 4	Lukewarm	72°	1 - 2″
Buckwheat	Jar/Towel	1 c. = 2½ c.	2 - 4 days	1	Lukewarm	72°	¼ - ½″
Cabbage	Jar/Pot	¼ c. = 1½ c.	3 - 5 days	2	Lukewarm	72°	½ - 1″
Chia	Towel	¼ c. = 1 c.	3 - 4 days	4 - 6	Lukewarm	72°	½″
Corn	Jar/Towel	¼ c. = 1¼ c.	3 - 8 days	2 - 3	Lukewarm	72°	½″
Cress	Jar/Towel	1 T. = ¾ c.	3 - 4 days	2	Lukewarm	65°	1½″
Cranberry	Jar	1 T. = 1½ c.	3 - 4 days	3	Lukewarm	65°	1½″
Flax	Towel	1 T. = ¾ c.	3 - 4 days	2 - 3	Lukewarm	72°	1 - 2″
Gourd	Jar/Pot	1 c. = 1½ c.	3 - 4 days	2 - 3	Lukewarm	72°	¼″
Lentil	Jar/Pot	1 c. = 2 c.	3 - 4 days	3	Lukewarm	72°	1″
Millet	Jar/Pot	1 c. = 2½ c.	3 - 4 days	2 - 3	Lukewarm	75°	¼″
Mung bean	Jar	1 c. = 4 c.	3 - 4 days	3 - 4	Lukewarm	72°	2″
Oat (unhulled)	Towel	1 c. = 2½ c.	3 - 5 days	1	Lukewarm	70° - 80°	Same as seed
Pea	Jar/Pot	1 c. = 2 c.	3 - 4 days	2 - 3	Lukewarm	72°	Same as seed
Radish	Jar	1 T. = ¾ c.	2 - 4 days	2 - 3	Lukewarm	72°	½ - 1″
Rice	Jar	1 c. = 2½ c.	3 - 4 days	2 - 3	Lukewarm	72°	Same as seed
Rye	Jar	1 c. = 2½ c.	3 - 4 days	2 - 3	Cold	50° - 68°	Same as seed
Sesame	Jar	¼ c. = ½ c.	3 - 4 days	4 - 6	Lukewarm	72°	Same as seed
Soy bean	Jar/Pot	1 c. = 3½ c.	4 - 5 days	4 - 6	Warm	85°	2″
Sunflower	Jar/Pot	1 c. = 2 c.	5 - 8 days	2	Lukewarm	72°	Less than seed
Other vegetables	Jar	1 T. = 1½ c.	3 - 5 days	2	Lukewarm	72°	1 - 2″
Wheat	Jar	1 c. = 4 c.	3 - 4 days	2	Lukewarm	72°	½″

*Average   * In dark

The chart above includes the most reliable seeds for sprouting. Seeds that require the most moisture should be sprouted in a jar or pot rather than between towels. Sprouting time will depend on the temperature of rinse water and cabinet. Root length indicates when sprouts are ready to be eaten, but give them a taste test. Some get sweeter with age, others turn bitter.

Jar Method

An empty, wide-mouthed quart jar makes a good sprouter for growing about ¼ cup of seeds. For a lid, secure a 5-by-5-inch piece of cheesecloth or nylon over the jar with an elastic band. The cloth will keep the sprouts from drying out and facilitate their daily rinsings. After each rinsing, lay the jar on its side and elevate the bottom edge so excess water will run off (photograph 1). If the jar is transparent, cover it with a brown paper bag, or keep it in a dark place such as a kitchen cabinet, leaving the door slightly ajar so fresh air can enter. Keep the jar tilted until the next rinsing.

Flowerpot Method

Another improvised sprouter can be easily assembled with a clay flowerpot and matching saucer. Plug the opening at the bottom of the flowerpot with a crumpled piece of nylon. The plug can be removed for rinsing the seeds. Cut a piece of cardboard slightly larger than the top of the flowerpot. Leave this on top of the pot so the seeds do not dry out. Tilt the flowerpot against the side of the saucer to keep water from accumulating at the bottom of the pot (photograph 2). Tilting the pot permits air circulation, causing any water that puddles in the corner of the pot to evaporate. (Water can also evaporate through the sides of an unglazed clay pot.) Since the clay container is opaque, the sprouter can be left on a counter, but it should not be placed in direct sunlight unless extra heat is required. Almost any other type of pottery can be used for sprouting, but if a glazed container is chosen, be sure it is high-fired stoneware and not low-fired earthenware, which might have toxic lead sulphate in the glaze.

1: Soybean seeds can be easily sprouted in a wide-mouthed glass jar (left). The jar is laid on its side after rinsing; an inverted ashtray keeps it tilted so excess moisture will drain off. A root length of about 2 inches (right) indicates that the soybeans are ready to be harvested.

2: A porous clay flowerpot and saucer make an ideal sprouting container for alfalfa seeds. An open-weave cloth, such as nylon, is used to plug the hole in the bottom of the pot between rinsings. A cardboard lid permits air to circulate and at the same time keeps out the light.

3: A layer of gelatinous seeds such as chia, or hard-shelled seeds like almonds, can be sprouted between two moist paper towels. If the paper towels lie on an inverted wire basket, air and water can move freely to promote even sprouting. This controls a balance between air and water.

4: Stackable sprouting trays, available at many health food stores, allow you to grow several varieties of seed at one time in separate compartments. Each tray has a ridged bottom with siphon caps that retain enough moisture in the system to eliminate daily rinsings.

Paper-Towel Method

Seeds such as chia, flax, oat and almond require an open-air sprouting system to regulate the amount of moisture directly available to the seeds. This can be accomplished by placing a layer of the seeds between two moist paper towels (photograph 3). Place the towels over an inverted wire tray basket, and put a plastic box underneath the wire to catch any water that drips through. Use a spray bottle filled with water for dampening the seeds.

Spout Method

To sprout large quantities of beans at one time, you can use an old wooden keg (with a lid) that has a spout on its side for drainage.

All-In-One Method

Several varieties of seeds can be sprouted simultaneously in special stackable containers designed for this purpose. These containers, available at many health food stores, have individual trays, siphon holes, and a closed drainage system (photograph 4). Follow the instructions that come with the sprouter to get the best results.

Traveling Method

When you are on the move or camping out, you can sprout seeds in the warm darkness of a backpack. To do this, you need two plastic bags of the same size. Punch a dozen or so tiny holes in the bottom of one bag, and put it inside the other bag. Use an elastic band to suspend the inner bag above the water that will accumulate in the bottom of the outer one. The holes will allow moisture and air to circulate freely while the outer bag will catch water.

Soaking Stage, Day One

All seeds, grains, and beans require an initial soaking period of about 12 hours to soften the seed coat. Measure out ¼ cup of seeds into a strainer for each sprouter you plan to use. (Sprout only as many seeds as your family can consume in a week. Seeds in a sprouter, like kernels of corn in a popper, will multiply in size, and ¼ cup of most dried seeds will yield about two cups of sprout when harvested.) Sift through the seeds with your fingers to remove any that are cracked or discolored. Dead seeds will not sprout, and they can cause good sprouts to decay. Pour the seeds into the sprouting container or a bowl, and cover them with water (photograph 5). Cover the container, and let it stand in a warm, dark place for about 12 hours. Then refer to the chart on page 1955 or read the seed-package directions to determine the sprouting method that is recommended for the type of bean or seed that you have selected. The sprout table also provides you with important information regarding the temperature of the rinse water, the number of daily rinsings, and the ideal temperature for the location of the sprouter for maximum results.

5: To start the sprouting process, soak seeds for about 12 hours, using four times as much water as seeds. If the sprouter is transparent, put it in a dark place.

Day Two

During the soaking period, the seeds begin to soften and take in water, and consequently double in bulk. If you look closely at the surface of the water, you will see gas bubbles, an indication that the seeds are releasing energy and heat in germination. Remove any floating seeds and broken hulls. (If these become soft they will rot, giving off an unpleasant odor.) When the soaking is complete, strain the soak water into a clean container (photograph 6). You can boil this liquid and use it to flavor soups or other dishes.

Spread about ¼ cup of seeds neatly over the bottom of each sprouter, building only a few layers to allow an even circulation of moisture and air. If the seeds on the bottom of the sprouter are weighed down by those above, they may rot. Always leave at least one third of the sprouter empty so air can move freely. Place the covering over your sprouter. When using a jar or pot, be sure to tilt it so water won't accumulate.

Next, set up the conditions recommended for sprouting—the right amount of heat, moisture, darkness, and air. Place the sprouting container in a warm place away from drafts or blasts of heat. A closet or a cabinet is ideal, but be sure to leave the door slightly ajar to admit fresh air.

6: After the soaking, pour the water into a clean container. The soak water, containing vitamins and minerals, can be used for cooking.

Daily Rinsings

As the seeds develop, gases and residues will be given off. To remove waste products that could cause spoilage, it is necessary to rinse the seeds daily, as indicated on the chart on page 1955. Divide 24 hours by the number of rinsings listed to arrive at the approximate time for rinsings. Obviously, you will not want to get up in the middle of the night to do this, but if a rinse is off by several hours it makes little difference in the seed development. In cool weather, soaking times can be doubled and the seeds can be rinsed in warmer water (about 85 degrees Fahrenheit). During each rinse, cover the uppermost layer of seeds with about 1 inch of fresh water. (If the seeds are extremely small or sticky, you can put them in a strainer for the rinsing.) To rinse the seeds simply swirl the water about in the sprouter for a minute or two, so water can circulate among the seeds. Use a spoon or a swizzle stick to gently mix the seeds at the bottom with those on top. This will encourage even sprouting. Then remove the water by pouring it through the mesh covering. If you are using a flowerpot sprouter, remove the nylon plug from the pot to let the rinse water run out; then replace the plug. When using the paper-towel method described on page 1957, simply sprinkle the seeds with water and cover them with a fresh, moist paper towel (photograph 7). Tilt the sprouting container as before, and set it aside until the next rinsing. Be sure to keep jar or pot containers tilted between all rinses. One of the most common mistakes that a gardener makes the first time that he attempts to sprout seeds is to treat them as if they were house plants. For sprouting conditions to be just right there must be a natural balance of heat, water and air. Even if the sprouter is opaque it should not be placed in direct sunlight. Overheating can cause a fungus to develop on the seeds. Use the prescribed water temperatures for rinsing (see the Sprout Table, page 1955), and set the sprouter where air can circulate freely.

Day Three

Continue the rinsings to keep seeds from overheating, molding, or rotting. The outer shell (or husk) of some seeds will fall off and float on top of the water during this stage. Remove them—they may harbor bacteria—as you rinse the sprouts. Any husks that are not shed can be removed when the seeds are harvested, if you like, but many people prefer eating the sprout whole, husks and all. Observe the seed as the root of the plant begins to reach harvesting length. As the root grows, the nutritional value of the plant will also increase.

Day Four

By the fourth day many of the seeds should have little stems and their first leaves. Refer to the root-length chart on page 1955 to determine if sprouts are ready for harvesting. Before removing them from the jar, taste a sample. Although some sprouts (such as sunflower or sesame seeds) become bitter if they are left to sprout too long, bitterness generally indicates that the sprouts are not yet ready. Before harvesting, you may want to expose the sprouts to sunlight for three to 12 hours. This will turn them green and increase their nutritive value. Whether or not you expose the sprouts to light, drain them for three or four hours after the last rinse to remove excess moisture. Then place the sprouts in a jar or a plastic container with a cover and refrigerate them. After one week, fresh sprouts begin to lose their potency; so do not keep them much longer than that before serving them.

From Soup to Nuts with Sprouts

With the wheat, alfalfa, mung bean, and soybean sprouts shown on page 1553, plus a few other items, I was able to fix a four-course meal (see recipes opposite). To alter the flavor of sprouts, you can use them raw in salads, steam or fry them, roast them to make a crunchy snack, or even grind them into flour for baking breads. Aside from being rich nutritionally, sprouts are surprisingly low in calories. One cup of wheat sprouts is eight calories, one cup of sprouted alfalfa or mung beans is 16 calories, and a cup of soybean sprouts is 65 calories. Sprouts are easily digested and are a healthy, quick-energy food. Try some of these recipes to introduce sprouts into your daily menus. Or invent some of your own concoctions.

For related projects, see "Baby Foods," "Breads," "Hibachi and Hot-Pot Cookery," "Organic Gardening," "Sashimi and Sushi," and "Wok Cooking."

7: To rinse seeds when you are using the paper-towel method, mist or sprinkle them with water. Then cover the seeds again with a clean, slightly moist paper towel.

Sesame sticks

To make this you will need a 10-inch plastic mixing bowl and spoon; a grater; wax paper; a towel; large cookie sheet; fork and knife; a pastry brush; a small bowl; and the following ingredients:

¼-ounce packet of powdered yeast
1 cup warm water
1 teaspoon salt
1 teaspoon honey
1 cup wheat sprouts
2 cups wheat flour
½ cup butter or margarine
1 egg
¼ pound sesame seeds

Pour ¾ cup warm water in a mixing bowl and dissolve the yeast. Grind the wheat sprouts with a grater or chop fine. Add the honey, sprouts, 1 cup of wheat flour, and ¼ cup margarine to the dough. Beat all of the ingredients until smooth. Then add another cup of flour to the yeast and mix. Dust an 11-by-14-inch sheet of wax paper with flour. Knead the dough on the paper into a smooth ball; then rinse the bowl and grease it with margarine. Place the dough in the bowl and cover the opening with a towel. Set aside in a warm place for one hour or until the dough has risen and doubled in size. Then press the dough flat on the wax paper with your hands or a rolling pin. Press it into a large square about ¾ inch thick, then cut it into 20 strips. Roll each strip into a stick about 8 inches long. Preheat the oven to 350 degrees. Arrange the sticks about ¾ inch apart on a greased cookie sheet. Beat an egg in a bowl with one tablespoon of water, and brush the top of each stick with the egg mixture. Sprinkle with sesame seeds. Bake the sticks in the oven for 15 minutes or until they are golden brown. Makes about 20 breadsticks.

Mung beans with greens

1 head of lettuce
2 carrots
1 cup mung bean sprouts
½ cup raisins

Shred the lettuce in the salad bowl. Grate the carrots. Mix the carrots, beans, and raisins with the greens. Makes four large portions.

For a sweet, creamy topping, combine ½ cup chopped walnuts and apple slices with 1 cup of your favorite yogurt. For a spicier dressing, beat an egg and add ¼ cup olive oil, ¼ cup cider vinegar, 1 teaspoon mustard, 1 teaspoon rosemary, and 1 teaspoon thyme.

Shredded chicken

3 chicken breast halves, skinned and boned
1 egg
1 teaspoon wheat flour
½ cup sauterne or vermouth
¼ teaspoon salt
⅓ cup oil
1½ cups alfalfa sprouts
1½ cups mung bean sprouts
1 teaspoon sugar or sugar substitute
½ teaspoon garlic powder

Let the frozen chicken thaw partially; then cut it into thin slices, about 2 inches long. Let thaw completely. Then beat the egg in the soup bowl and mix wine, salt and flour. Submerge the chicken in the egg batter and refrigerate for one hour. Pour the oil into the skillet and heat over a low flame. Stir-fry the chicken for five minutes or until thoroughly cooked. Remove the chicken from the pan and drain on a paper towel. Add the sprouts to the hot oil and stir-fry two minutes. Return the chicken to the pan. Fry for two more minutes, adding sugar and garlic. Makes two main-course servings.

Garden gazpacho (alfalfa sprouts)

¼ cup vegetable or olive oil
1 yellow onion
1 green pepper
1 cucumber
2 cups alfalfa sprouts
1 medium-sized eggplant
1 12-ounce can of vegetable or tomato juice
1 teaspoon garlic powder
2 teaspoons white vinegar
1 cup water

Put ½ cup of water in the refrigerator to chill. Peel the onion, cucumber, and eggplant. Dice the onion, green pepper, cucumber, eggplant, and alfalfa sprouts. Line the bottom of the pot with oil and place over a medium flame. Stir-fry the onion, cucumber, and green pepper. Then add the eggplant, alfalfa sprouts, and ½ cup water. Simmer for ten minutes. Pour the vegetable juice over the vegetables and cook for 15 minutes or until the eggplant is thoroughly cooked. Season to taste with garlic and vinegar. When the mixture cools, add ½ cup ice water. Refrigerate the vegetables to make a cold soup for summer, or serve hot as a stew with lamb or veal. Makes three servings.

Soybeans and apple sauce

4 Macintosh apples
½ cup water
¼ pound raisins
2 teaspoons cinnamon
¾ cup red wine
2 teaspoons honey
2 cups soy sprouts
1 teaspoon butter
1 teaspoon salt

Core and peel the apples; then cut them into small chunks. Place the apples in a pot with ½ cup of water and cover. Set on a low flame. After five minutes stir the apples and add wine, cinnamon, honey, and raisins. Stir the mixture every five minutes for a half hour until the apples become soft. Then remove the pot from the heat. Makes four servings.

Spread one layer of soybeans on a greased sheet of aluminum foil and bake at 350 degrees for 30 minutes or until the sprouts are golden brown. Salt to taste. Roasted soybeans can also be used to top ice cream sundaes; and mixed with raisins and shredded coconut they make a fine snack.

The sprouts shown on page 1953 were used to prepare this meal. Ground wheat sprouts were baked to make breadsticks. Raw mung beans were tossed with salad greens, and alfalfa was cooked with vegetables to make a cold soup. Mung beans and alfalfa were stir-fried and combined with shredded chicken for the main dish, and soybeans were roasted to make a tasty topping for applesauce.

SERIGRAPHY
The Silk-Screen Print

Serigraphy, the making of silk-screened prints, is based on the principle of the stencil. By definition, a stencil can be any material with designs cut into it; one familiar type is the alphabet stencil cut in oiled paper. In the case of serigraphy, a piece of silk or nylon, stretched over a frame, has the mesh blocked in selected areas so it acts as a stencil. The unblocked open spaces allow printing ink to pass through the fabric onto the surface being printed (Figure A). The stenciled silk screen, as the frame-and-fabric unit is called, is placed fabric-side down over a piece of paper. Ink is poured along one edge of the screen, then is scraped over the fabric. The result is a serigraph or silk-screened print.

Following the steps in Figure C (page 1962), you can make a print as simple or as complex as you like. For each color, you need to put a different stencil on the screen, but from each stencil you can make as many copies as you want. For example, when I made the garden print shown opposite, I used eight different stencils, one for each color. But before I made a stencil for the second color, I printed 30 copies of the first color so I would have enough prints to cover a wall.

It is this building up of a design, color by color, with an infinite number of copies, that distinguishes serigraphy from most other art forms. But it is the versatility of the art that makes it exciting. Using opaque inks, you can print one color over another without any show-through. Using transparent inks, you can overlap two colors to create a third. Because inks can be mixed to be opaque or transparent, you can create different effects with the same ink. Because the inks can be mixed, you can create many colors from a few. And you can print on materials as diverse as fabric, wood, plastic, paper, or cardboard.

The projects that follow will introduce you to the basics of silk-screen printing—to working with two common stenciling materials, paper and a gluelike filler; printing on various surfaces; and working with designs of varying complexity. Projects range from a simple one-color geometric design printed on fabric (page 1968), to a multihued free-form print done on plastic (page 1970), to the eight-color garden print discussed above (page 1971). The projects begin on page 1963, but first you might like to know a bit about how this art came into being.

How It All Began

No one knows exactly where or when stencils were first used, but we do know that it was in seventeenth century Japan that the forerunner of the silk-screen was invented. There, artists glued loosely woven hair onto parchment stencils, stretching it across open areas. The hair served as a screen for holding additional pieces of parchment that enhanced the design (Figure B). By the late 1800s, woven silk was being used as a printing screen in France, Germany, and England. By the 1930s, silk-screen printing had become a thriving industry in America. Its commercial advantages were readily apparent. From one stencil, thousands of identical prints could be made. Unlike most other types of commercial printing, the silk-screen process could be used to print on any flat surface—wood, tile, plastic, or fabric, as well as paper. Yet its initial success was commercial only; it was ignored as an art form until 1938. Then, as a consequence of a Works Progress Administration art project, artists were commissioned to design posters and other silk-screen prints. As they began exploring this new medium, its popularity grew. By the time the project ended, artists had popularized silk-screening as a fine arts medium and had given it a new name—serigraphy, meaning silk writing. It is now one of the most popular of the graphic arts. Serigraphy did not lose its commercial applications with its acceptance into the world of art. It is still used to print greeting cards, wallpaper, textiles, floor tiles, display signs, and many other items.

Few artists could paint identical copies of a subject as complex as this. But by using silk-screen printing techniques, you can make an unlimited number of identical copies of a print like this—with little more work than it would take to make one copy. Directions for making this print start on page 1971, but try your hand at less complex designs first.

Susyn Berger is a graduate of the Tyler School of Art at Temple University and of the University of Wisconsin, where she received a master of fine arts degree. Ms. Berger has taught print making, design, and painting at the School of Visual Arts in New York, the University of Wisconsin, and the University of Saskatchewan. Her work has been exhibited at the Museum of American Folk Art and the Gallery of Contemporary Crafts, both in New York.

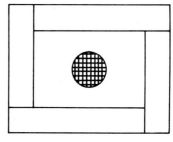

A

Figure A: This silk screen has been stenciled so that only a circle will print. A stencil can be any nonporous material that will block ink or paint except where it has been left open or had designs cut in it. In serigraphy, silk or nylon, stretched over a frame, becomes the stencil when a gluelike filler or tracing paper is added to make parts of it impenetrable. Where the fabric is not covered, it lets ink pass through to the surface being printed.

B

Figure B: Japanese artists used strands of human hair as a screen for stencils. This was the forerunner of modern silk-screening.

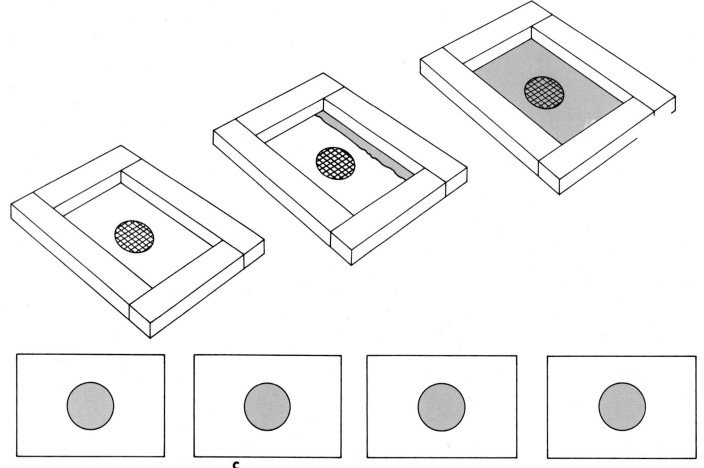

C

Figure C: The final steps in making a silk-screened print are shown above. The stenciled screen is placed over a sheet of paper (left). Ink is poured along one edge of the screen (center), and scraped over it (right). Wherever the fabric is open, ink will be deposited on the paper, resulting in a print. Four prints are shown, but an almost unlimited number of identical copies could be made.

Master Drawing and Registration

If you are silk-screening a design that calls for more than one color, you will need to make a new stencil for each color you add to the design. This does not mean using a different screen; the old stencil is simply removed and a new one applied. What this does involve, however, is creating a single design in many separate steps. The process is something like putting a jigsaw puzzle together; the challenge lies in making sure the pieces fit properly. For example, the simple design used in the first project (opposite) has two green triangles with a yellow triangle fitted neatly between them. There are two means of making sure it will fit—the master drawing and the registration tabs. The first ensures that all the parts of a given design will work with each other; the second helps you position the paper accurately for each successive color application.

Your master drawing will give you an idea of what the finished print will look like. Draw it the same size that your finished print will be, and color it, as shown at left. If a stenciling filler is to be painted on, first trace the master drawing on the screen. If you are using paper stencils, the master drawing will be your pattern for tracing and cutting each stencil.

However, if you put the paper in the wrong position during printing, even just a bit askew, all this work goes for nought. This is where the registration tabs come in. When you have centered the master drawing under the screen, tape it down so that it cannot shift. Then tape heavy cardboard tabs around the drawing (Figure D, opposite). These stay in place until the last color is put on the last print. Before each stage of printing, position the paper accurately between the tabs. Since the screen used for multicolor printing is anchored to the baseboard holding the paper (see Craftnotes, page 1966), this ensures correct alignment of all parts of the print. As a printer would say, it's in register.

The master drawing for a print is the same size the finished print will be. It is often colored to show the design areas clearly. If a painted-on filler is the stenciling material, the design outline is traced directly onto the screen, color by color (it is visible through the fabric). If tracing paper is used, the design is traced—again color by color—onto the paper. The master drawing not only serves as a guide for making stencils, it assures the artist that all parts of the design will be the right size and will print in the right place.

Materials

Few tools are needed for silk-screening. The most important, of course, is the silk screen itself. Such screens can be bought, but the Craftnotes on page 1966 give instructions for making an excellent screen at little cost. The screen, if kept clean, can be used for years. The size of the screen is up to you. To do the projects in this entry in the illustrated size, you need a screen with a 20-by-26-inch printing area. With a smaller screen, simply draw the designs half size.

You also need a squeegee, the long rubber scraper that is used to draw the ink over the screen and force it through the fabric onto the surface being printed. Your squeegee should be 2 to 4 inches shorter than the inside width of the screen.

Other equipment shown (photograph 1) includes: printer's ink; extender base and transparency base (Craftnotes, page 1973); solvents for cleaning the screen; containers and stirring sticks for mixing inks; pencil; straightedge; craft knife; round-tipped paintbrush; heavy cardboard; and masking tape. A rubber spatula, apron, fan, and drying area are also needed. If you have space, simply spread the prints out to dry. If not, any print that has a border of blank paper can be clipped to an indoor clothesline.

Only two types of stenciling materials are used in these projects—a filler that is painted on the fabric and tracing paper that is cut to size. The type of stenciling material, the type of solvent used for cleaning the screen, and the kind of surface you print on will vary from project to project.

Materials used for silk-screening can be purchased from silk-screen supply houses. Art stores also carry some items. Should you have difficulty locating materials, the suppliers listed here will fill mail orders; write to them for catalogs and prices: Advance Process Supply Company, 400 North Noble Street, Chicago, Illinois 60622; Colonial Printing Ink Company, 180 East Union Avenue, East Rutherford, New Jersey 07073; The Naz Dar Company, 1087 North Branch Street, Chicago, Illinois 60622; or Cerigraf, Inc., 359 Chestnut Street, Newark, New Jersey 07105.

Graphic Arts
Poster print

$ 🄳 🚶 🎨

The print shown at right is a three-color silk-screen print made with tracing-paper stencils. The sequence whereby the print was built up, color by color, is shown on page 1965. The finished design, measuring 12 by 13½ inches, is printed on 18-by-19-inch paper to leave a wide white border all around. For this project, in addition to materials listed above, you will need: heavy bond paper for the prints; heavy tracing paper at least 14 by 15 inches for the stencils; matte poster ink or oil paint in three colors (Craftnotes, page 1973); and benzine or a similar paint thinner for cleaning up. If your screen is larger than the tracing-paper stencil, you will also need water-soluble filler to seal the fabric mesh around the edges.

Setting Up

To begin, enlarge the master drawing (Figure E, page 1964) and center it under the screen. Tape it in place; then lower the screen to make sure the design is centered. Lift the screen and put registration tabs around the master drawing (photograph 2, page 1964). Use two or three layers of masking tape to hold the tabs in place.

The printing area of the screen left open must be the same size as the poster design, 12 by 13½ inches. If the stencil tracing paper is too small to cover the entire screen, paint in a border of filler to seal the edges. To use the filler, mix it with warm water—two parts filler to one part water. If the filler is colorless, add a few drops of food coloring so you can see it on the screen. Now lower the screen and trace the border of the design onto it, following the master drawing and using a soft lead pencil. Prop the screen up with the prop bar (Craftnotes, page 1966), and paint filler all around the border of the design (photograph 3, page 1964). Filler is not as thick as printing color and may tend to run down the screen. If that happens, disengage the prop bar and use a shorter object such as a roll of masking tape or a jar lid to prop up the screen. Let the filler dry (a fan will speed this); then check it for pinholes, holding the screen up to a light. If pinholes exist, apply additional filler.

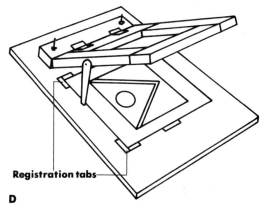

Registration tabs

D
Figure D: The master drawing is centered under the screen and taped in place. Registration tabs, made of heavy cardboard, are placed around it and taped down. The tabs serve as a guide for positioning paper during the printing operation.

1: A silk-screen workshop has been assembled on the oversize baseboard above. At the top, next to the hinged silk screen, are (left to right): paper toweling, extender base, filler, and paint thinner. In the center is a squeegee, used to force ink through the screen. Other materials shown include containers for printer's inks, the ink itself, spoons and sticks for stirring, pencil, paintbrush, straightedges and craft knife, masking tape, and heavy cardboard.

A poster print with bold colors and simple shapes is a good starting point for learning silk-screen techniques. A series of these prints, wall-mounted, makes an exciting addition to the decor of a child's room or playroom.

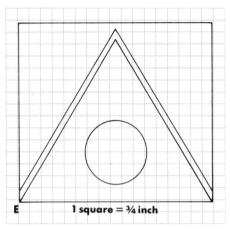

Figure E: To enlarge this design to 12 by 13½ inches, the size of the original, draw a ¾-inch grid on 18- by 19-inch paper. Copy the design, square by square, centering it on the paper. Color it to use as a printing guide. With a smaller screen, you can enlarge the design to half size by drawing a ⅜-inch grid.

Making the Stencils

Three stencils are needed to make this print, one for the two green triangular sections, one for the yellow triangle, and one for the red circle. Each stencil is cut so only the area that is to print is left open.

Leave the master drawing in registration and taped down. Cover it with tracing paper and tape that down as well. Trace the lines that border the green areas of the drawing (photograph 4). Remove the tracing and cut out the outlined area with a straightedge and craft knife. Place this stencil over the drawing again, aligning the cut-out parts with the green triangles of the drawing (photograph 5). Tape it down temporarily. Take four 1½-inch-long pieces of masking tape. Roll them so the tape sticks to itself and provides a sticky surface top and bottom; then place the tape on the corners of the stencil (photograph 6). Remove the tape that is holding the tracing paper to the work surface, and gently lower the screen so it can pick up the stencil. Check through the screen to make sure the stencil has not slipped; then press on the taped corners of the stencil. Raise the screen; the tape will hold the stencil to it (photograph 7). If necessary, add a fifth piece of rolled tape to hold the triangular portion of the stencil against the screen.

Before proceeding, make sure you have all of the necessary materials, including trimmed paper, on hand. (Once you start, it is necessary to print one sheet of paper right after another, without stopping, to keep the paint from drying on the screen.) Then remove the master drawing and prepare to print your first color.

Printing the First Color

Mix the printing ink or oil paint (Craftnotes, page 1973). Prop the screen up slightly, and pour a generous amount of green ink along the ink-well edge of the screen (Craftnotes, page 1967). Then lightly squeegee the ink over the screen while it is still propped up (photograph 8). This process is known as flooding the screen;

2: Center the master drawing under the screen and tape it to the baseboard. Make sure it is centered; then tape registration tabs of heavy cardboard at two corners and along one edge.

3: Paint filler around the edge of the screen up to the outside edge of the design you are stenciling. This will keep the printing inks from penetrating the nondesign areas of the screen.

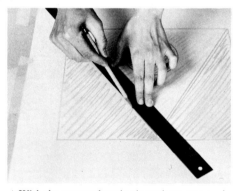

4: With the master drawing in register, use a ruler and pencil to trace the first color you will print, in this case green, onto tracing paper. This will be your first stencil.

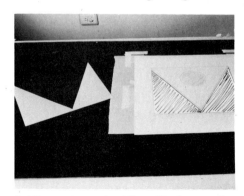

5: After you have cut out the outlined areas, align the stencil you have made with the registered master drawing, and temporarily tape it in place with masking tape.

6: Roll 1½-inch lengths of masking tape so it sticks to itself and will also stick to the stencil and the screen; then put the tape at each corner of the stencil.

7: When the screen is lowered, then raised, the tape fastens the stencil onto the screen in the precise position needed for printing. An additional piece of tape may be needed for the triangle.

the tacky ink serves to attach the tracing-paper stencil firmly to the screen. It also guarantees that you will have adequate ink on the squeegee when you print. Flood the screen each time you are about to deposit printing color on the paper.

Put a blank piece of paper in register, lower the screen, and use the squeegee, held at a 45-degree angle, to print your first color. Move quickly so the ink does not dry on the screen. Make as many copies of the green print as you want, one after the other. Each time you make a print, the excess ink will end up on the opposite side of the screen. To compensate for this, print the next sheet in the opposite direction, pushing the squeegee away from you one time, pulling it toward you the next, but always holding it at a 45-degree angle. Press down firmly on the squeegee as you work; this will ensure a smooth, even coat of ink on the paper.

Adding Colors

Before you can print the yellow triangle, you have to clean the screen to get it ready for the second stencil. Do this while the green prints are drying. First, remove and discard the used stencil and the tape that was holding it. Clean the screen with paint thinner (Craftnotes, page 1973). Next prepare and attach the stencil for the yellow triangle, following the same procedure as before, taping the tracing paper over the registered master drawing, but this time tracing only the lines that border the yellow triangle. Make sure that the green-printed areas of the papers are dry; then flood the screen with yellow ink. Put a green-printed sheet in place, lower the screen, and print as before (photograph 9). Print all of the copies, one after the other, and set them aside to dry while you clean the screen. To print the third color, follow the same procedures to make the stencil for the red circle. Complete the print (photograph 10) and clean the screen again. When all the paint has been removed, take the screen off the baseboard (Craftnotes, page 1967), hold it under the shower or sink faucet, and wash out the border of filler. Stand the screen up to dry.

8: Before printing, lightly coat the screen with ink—known as flooding the screen. To print, lower the screen and rub the squeegee over it in one smooth motion. The result is shown below.

9: To print the yellow triangle, you must clean the screen, change stencils, flood the screen with yellow ink, then squeegee the ink onto the green-printed paper. The result is shown below.

10: To print the red circle, repeat the steps given earlier, but use red ink. The result is shown below. Note that each color must dry before the next one is applied.

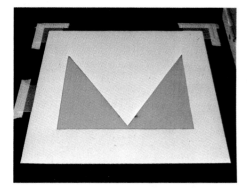

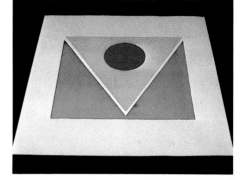

After the first step in silk-screening the poster print shown on page 1963, the paper being printed will look like this. The yellow triangle will be added in the next step.

After the green ink has dried, and the new stencil is on the cleaned screen, the paper is re-registered under it. Yellow ink is squeegeed over the paper to form the yellow triangle of the design.

Once the yellow triangle has dried, the last stencil is applied to the screen and red ink is squeegeed over the paper. The result is the finished design, as shown on the preceding page.

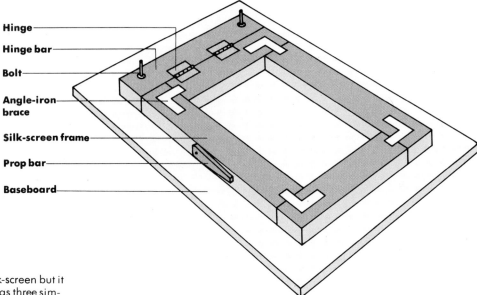

Hinge
Hinge bar
Bolt
Angle-iron brace
Silk-screen frame
Prop bar
Baseboard

You can buy a ready-made silk-screen but it is easy to make one. The unit has three simple elements: the silk screen itself; a baseboard on which the print rests; and a hinge bar connecting the screen to the baseboard (above). The hinge bar is bolted to the baseboard. Sliding-pin hinges connect the screen to the bar so it can be removed for cleaning.

To make a screen with an opening 20 by 26 inches, the size used for the projects in this entry, you will need five pieces of 1-by-2, 2-by-2, or 2-by-4-inch pine, spruce, or cypress, two pieces 26 inches long plus the width of the wood you are using, two pieces 20 inches long plus the width of the wood you are using, and a third short piece, 20 inches long plus twice the width of the wood you are using. This will be used for the hinge bar. You will also need a smooth piece of tempered hardboard or plywood at least 32 by 44 inches for the baseboard, a scrap of wood for the prop bar, monofilament nylon fabric to use as the screen, and the following materials: two sliding-pin hinges with screws; screwdriver; staple gun; hammer and nails; sandpaper; angle-iron braces; square; bolts; a drill with bits the size of the shank and head of the bolt; epoxy paint; white glue; and a paintbrush. The baseboard needs to be ½-inch thick so the bolt heads can be recessed so they do not project on the bottom; thinner hardboard will need to be bolted to a thicker piece of wood.

Begin the unit by making the frame. Fit the lengths of wood together into a rectangle, butting the corners as shown above. Check each corner with a square to make sure it forms a 90-degree angle. Glue the joint with white glue and secure it with nails. Sand lightly to remove any roughness; then reinforce each corner with a surface-mounted angle-iron brace.

Covering the frame

Cover the frame with monofilament nylon, a durable fabric that prints as well as silk and is less expensive. The nylon is graded in numbers which refer to the mesh—the number of threads per square inch. Ask for a double-weight fabric (designated by an xx symbol after the number). A 12xx nylon is recommended, but any monofilament nylon designated 10xx through 16xx will do. This fabric is available at most silk-screen supply houses (page 1963). Wet the fabric under a running faucet just before you begin to staple it down. This causes extra tautness in the screen, essential for successful printing. If the fabric begins to dry before you have finished stapling, wet it with a sponge.

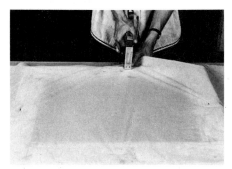

Place the frame bottom side up and lay the fabric on top of it, letting an inch or so overlap on all sides. Align the weave of the fabric so it parallels the frame. Now begin stapling. First staple the fabric to the center of each side (above). Next, starting at the center of one long side and working from the

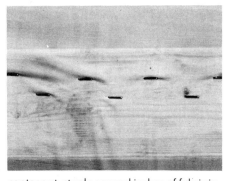

center out, staple several inches of fabric in place. Allow about ½ inch between staples. Use a staggered pattern, so staples alternately are closer to the outer and the inner edges (above). With several staples in place, pull the fabric tightly to the center of the opposite edge (below). Pull hard; nylon is strong and it must be stretched taut. Staple as before; then repeat on the short sides of the screen. Return to the first side and place

THE SILK SCREEN

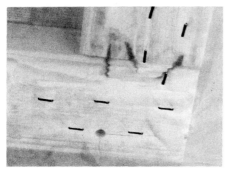

several staples on either side of the center ones. Continue working this way, alternating sides, until all that remains are the corners. These are done last. First make sure that there are no wrinkles in the stretched nylon. If there are, remove the staples and restretch the fabric. Then staple the corners (above). Once this is done, you should be able to tap your fingers on the fabric and feel a resilient, drumlike bounce. To set the staples, go over them with a hammer. Cut away excess fabric with a craft knife, leaving ½ inch outside the staples.

On that side make it 2 to 3 inches wide. This is known as the ink well; it is where you deposit ink before printing. Let the epoxy dry.

The screen fabric will probably have sizing in it. To remove it, use a sponge and a small amount of liquid soap. Wash the screen gently; then rinse it, making sure no soap film remains. Prop the screen up, dry the frame with a towel, and let the fabric dry. A small fan will speed drying.

Assembling the unit

To assemble the silk screen, attach the hinge bar to the baseboard and the screen to the hinge bar. Working on the wider face of the hinge bar, drill holes to accommodate two bolts, about 1 inch in from each end. Place the hinge bar on the hardboard, 4 inches in from one short end and centered between sides. Mark guide holes; then drill through the baseboard. To keep the baseboard level, which it must be, you will need to recess the bolt heads in the bottom surface. Use the larger drill bit, and enlarge the holes in the bottom sufficiently so they accept the heads of the bolts. To attach the hinge bar to the base-

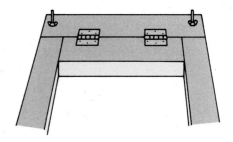

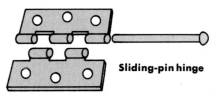

Sliding-pin hinge

board, insert the bolts from the bottom and tighten wing nuts onto the bolts from the top. Put the screen, fabric side down, against the hinge bar and position the hinges that will connect the two. Mark the screw holes on both hinge bar and frame. Remove the hinges, drill pilot holes for the screws, then screw the hinges in place. When you need to take the screen off the baseboard for cleaning, simply slide the pins out of the hinges.

To raise the screen off the baseboard at its free end, as you will need to do during some printing operations, nail a piece of wood to one long side of the frame so it can swing freely with the nail as a pivot. The wood should be about 5 inches long and be placed about 9 inches from the hinged end of the frame. This support is called a prop bar.

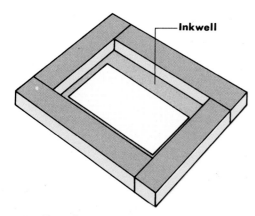

Inkwell

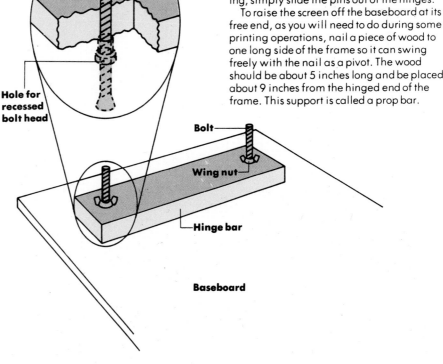

Hole for recessed bolt head

Bolt

Wing nut

Hinge bar

Baseboard

Sealing the screen

To keep ink from leaking out of the frame and to keep the frame from warping, seal it by painting it with epoxy paint. Brown-paper tape can also be used, and some of the frames pictured were made this way. But epoxy paint does just as good a job and is easier to use. With the fabric side up, brush epoxy on the frame. Also paint a ½- to 1-inch-wide border of epoxy on the fabric itself, following a penciled guideline. Let the paint dry. Next, turn the screen so the fabric side is down. Put props under the frame so the screen is not resting on the worktable. Now paint a border of epoxy on the rest of the frame and on the inside of the screen fabric. This border should be ½ to 1 inch wide on all but one long side of the fabric.

Graphic Arts
Wall-hanging catchalls

The pocketed wall hanging shown below was made by printing a one-color design on fabric, cutting the fabric into strips, and weaving the strips together. (The uncut print is shown below, left—weaving makes it possible to get a variety of geometric patterns from a single design.) Each woven unit is sewn to backing fabric and left open on the top, so it can hold any number of things.

The procedure used for making this stencil is known as the liquid frisket method, a two-step process. First, the areas of the screen that are to allow ink to pass through are painted with liquid frisket, a substance similar to rubber cement when it is dry. This protects the silk screen from the filler, which is brushed over the entire screen when the frisket is dry. When the frisket is removed, the design areas are opened for printing while filler closes the rest of the screen.

This design, printed in one single operation, measures roughly 12 by 13 inches and is printed on 18-by-19-inch fabric. I used muslin, but cotton, canvas, or any other smooth, nonsynthetic fabric would work.

For this project, in addition to the materials listed on page 1963, you will need:

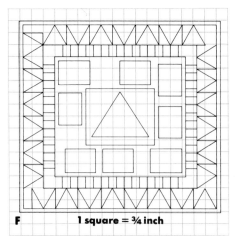

F 1 square = ¾ inch

Figure F: To enlarge this design to make your stencil, draw a ¾-inch grid on 13-by-14 inch paper. Copy the design square by square onto the paper, centering it, and color it. If you use a smaller screen, you can enlarge the design to half size by starting with a ⅜-inch grid.

Silk-screened fabrics are among the most costly of all materials. The design shown here has a homespun effect, and the artist has emphasized this look by cutting the printed fabric into strips and **weaving them into a useful wall hanging (right).**

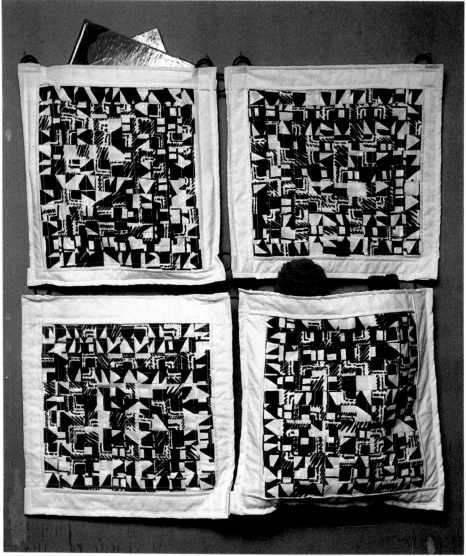

A useful and decorative wall-hung catchall is made of silk-screened fabric with a geometric design. The print was cut into strips and woven randomly so that no two pockets are alike.

oil-based fabric ink; the extender base and solvent recommended to go with it; liquid frisket; water-soluble filler; a straight-edged piece of stiff cardboard about 4 by 5 inches; and a rubber-cement eraser. You will also need a piece of ¼-inch-thick foam rubber, the same size as your silk screen, to cushion the fabric during printing. Finally, you will need approximately five yards of 36-inch-wide fabric, an iron, scissors, and twelve 1-inch curtain rings.

Prepare the fabric for printing by washing it with soap and water. Then iron the fabric and cut it into sixteen 18-by-19-inch pieces.

To make the stencil, enlarge the master drawing (Figure F, opposite. Center it under the screen and tape it in place, following the instructions on page 1962. Lower the screen and trace the design onto it, using a soft lead pencil and a straightedge. Remove the master drawing, prop the screen on its prop-leg, and fill all the design areas that are to appear as color with liquid frisket, applying it with a ½-inch round-tipped paintbrush (photograph 11).

Let the frisket dry. This will take only a few minutes. Keeping the screen propped up, pour a generous amount of water-soluble filler along the ink well (Craftnotes, page 1967). With the cardboard, lightly scrape the filler over the entire screen (photograph 12). Do not use pressure; the filler should coat the screen but not penetrate it. Let it dry (a small fan will speed the process); then add a second coat of filler. Remove any excess filler from the edge of the screen, and let the screen dry thoroughly before you proceed. Then remove the frisket from the screen, using the rubber-cement eraser to rub the frisket away (photograph 13). It will come off easily; the filler will remain on the rest of the screen, making it impermeable. Photograph 14 shows what the prepared screen looks like.

Before printing, center the foam under the screen and tape it in place. Center the master drawing on the foam. For register marks, trace the corners of the drawing on the foam. Each time you print a piece of fabric, make sure it is positioned within these register marks; then tape it to the foam on two sides so it will not slip. To print, place the fabric on top of the foam, mix the ink, flood the screen (page 1965), then squeegee the ink onto the fabric. Print eight pieces of fabric, working quickly so the ink does not dry on the screen; then clean the ink from the screen (Craftnotes, page 1973), using the recommended solvent. Finally, wash the filler off the screen with hot water.

Let the fabric dry; then fix the ink so it will not fade or wash out by sprinkling a small amount of vinegar on each print and going over it with a hot iron.

Such printed fabric can be used in any number of ways. I decided to add variety to the design by cutting each print into strips and weaving the strips together to make the catchalls shown opposite. To do this you will need to use two prints in each woven unit. Working along the length of the fabric, cut each print into 1-inch-wide strips. To weave a unit, align 12 strips vertically on your work surface, and tape them across their top edge to the surface. Over this, lay 13 horizontal strips of

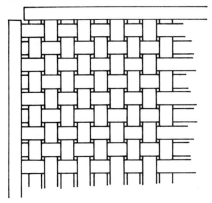

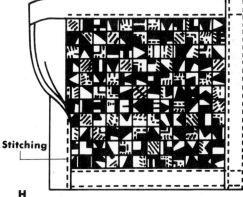

G
Figure G: Interlace the fabric strips in a basket-weave pattern so the first horizontal strip goes over the first vertical strip, under the second, and so on, while the second goes under the first vertical strip, over the second, under the third, and so on across the width of the piece.

H
Figure H: To border the woven fabric, put the backing fabric, wrong side up, on your worktable. Center the woven square, right side up, over it. Fold the backing fabric over the edges of the woven fabric all around, allowing a 1-to-1½-inch border. Sew in place as shown.

Stitching

11: The intricate pattern for the wall catchall is made with a frisket stencil. Start the stencil by painting removable liquid frisket onto the screen, covering just the areas that will appear in color on the finished print.

12: With the frisket in place, lightly scrape the filler over the entire screen with a piece of cardboard. This makes the spaces not covered with frisket impervious to the printing ink, creating a stencil. Let the filler dry thoroughly.

13: Rub the dried frisket off the screen with a rubber-cement eraser. This will leave only the filler on the screen to block the ink.

14: Wherever frisket was painted on the screen, the printing color can pass through.

Transparent sheets of flexible, self-adhesive plastic can be printed with any number of colors, then used to decorate things such as the dishes shown below. In this design, some colors were intentionally allowed to overlap in order that even more colors could be achieved.

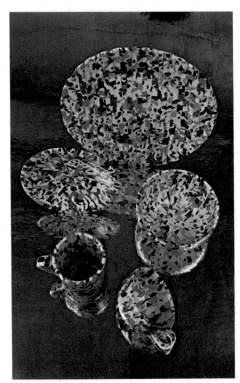

This riot-of-color set of dishes makes an eye-catching display. The dishes, covered with silk-screened self-adhering plastic, are meant for display only. They cannot be used for serving.

fabric and tape them along their left-hand edges. Weave them together with a basket-weave pattern (Figure G, page 1969). Once all four pieces have been woven, hold the strips by stitching the fabric around all four edges.

Each woven unit is backed with two pieces of fabric. One serves as a lining and is folded around the woven edges to form a visible white border. The other piece of backing fabric is sewn to the front piece along three edges, creating a storage pocket. Start by turning the raw edges of the woven pieces under and stitching them down so only the printed area shows. Next, machine-stitch a ½-inch-wide hem all around four pieces of backing fabric. Lay the woven fabric, right side up, on top of the backing fabric, keeping the backing fabric wrong side up. Center the woven fabric on this background; then fold the backing fabric to cover the edges of the woven fabric (Figure H, page 1969), making a 1-to 1½-inch border all around. Machine-stitch as shown. In this way, the weaving is reinforced and no raw edges show. To join a backing piece to the print, trim it to the size of the bordered print, plus ½ inch all around. Make a ½-inch hem; then lay print and backing fabric together with right sides facing, and sew them together along three sides. Turn the fabric right side out and the unit is complete. Finish the other three units the same way; then join all four by sewing 1-inch curtain rings to the corners, as shown in the color photograph. To hang the unit, put hooks or nails in the wall and slip the top curtain rings over them.

Graphic Arts
Printing on plastic

Plastic, as well as fabric and paper, can be silk-screened. If transparent self-adhesive plastic printing stock is used (these are individual sheets of flexible plastic backed with paper), the print can be used in a number of ways. A whole print, wall-mounted, is shown at left. Below, dishes have been covered with strips of the plastic for display purposes. Planters, tabletops, and windows lend themselves to similar treatment.

For this project, you will need: plastic made specifically for silk-screen printing; lacquer-based inks made for printing on plastic; retarder base to slow down the drying time of the inks so they do not clog the screen; and lacquer thinner for cleaning the screen. In addition, you will need tracing paper the same size as the screen for making your stencils, a craft knife, and the materials listed on page 1963.

The print shown here was made with paper stencils in generally the same way as the print on page 1963 was made. A different stencil was cut for each color printed. In this case, however, some of the cutouts were allowed to overlap color areas already printed in order to create different colors. The finished print, trimmed, measures 16 by 22 inches.

Begin with a sheet of tracing paper the size of the plastic you are printing. On this, draw as many small free-form shapes as you like. This will be your master drawing. Center it under the screen, tape it in place, and set up the registration tabs (page 1963). Decide how many colors you will print, and color or code each shape with a letter, indicating the color it will be on the finished print. I used seven colors: gold, magenta, deep green, blue, orange, chartreuse, and violet. Once you have decided how many colors to use, and have keyed the master drawing, tape tracing paper over the registered drawing. Trace only those shapes that will be printed with the first color, working from light to dark. Then remove the tracing and cut out the designated shapes (photograph 15). Put this stencil over the registered master drawing, positioning it so the cutouts correspond to the keyed shapes that are to print in the first color (photograph 16). Attach the stencil to the screen, following the instructions on page 1964 (photograph 17). Remove the master drawing, put a sheet of plastic within the register tabs, flood the screen with the first color, and print as many sheets of plastic as you want, as explained on page 1965.

When you have finished with the first color, clean the screen with lacquer thinner (Craftnotes, page 1973). Once this is done, make your second stencil and print your second color. Follow the same procedure throughout, letting the ink dry thoroughly between printing applications.

15: Make a separate tracing-paper stencil for each color you print. To make each stencil, trace only those shapes that are to print in one color; then cut them out with a craft knife, resting the paper on a cardboard surface.

16: When you place the stencil over the registered master drawing, the cutouts will line up with the color areas that are to print. The other colors, visible through the tracing paper, will be added in subsequent steps.

17: Masking tape, rolled so it will stick to itself, the stencil, and the screen above, is used to attach the positioned stencil to the screen. One piece of tape in each corner is sufficient for this.

Graphic Arts
The garden print

The design shown on page 1972 was printed on two-ply bristol-board paper. Thirty copies were made, then assembled into the wall unit shown on page 1960. Water-soluble filler was used to make the silk-screen stencils, with a method known as reduction printing. In this process, when you begin printing, the open area of the screen is the same size as the material you are printing on. As you add subsequent colors, you gradually reduce the printing area of the screen by adding more filler to it. So, you are not removing filler to make each new stencil; rather, you add more filler to the screen. Each color is laid over the color previously printed, and filler is added to the screen each time only where you want the last color printed to appear as part of the finished design. When I made this print, I covered the entire piece of bristol board with yellow ink. Then I applied filler to the screen only where I wanted the yellow ink to show up in the final design, and overlaid the rest of the bristol board with tan ink. Before printing the third color—a reddish beige—I added filler to the screen only where the tan ink was to appear in the final design.

In using this method, the printing color should be opaque so each color added will totally mask the one beneath it. For the same reason, inks should be applied in sequence from lightest to darkest.

For this project, you will need: 30 pieces of 16-by-16-inch two-ply bristol board; oil paints or oil-based matte poster color in eight colors; paint thinner; a ½-inch round-tipped paintbrush; water-soluble filler; overprint varnish; lacquer thinner; and contact cement, in addition to the materials listed on page 1963.

Begin by painting a border of filler around the screen so the open area in the middle of the screen is the same size as the bristol board, following the instructions on page 1963 and letting the filler dry thoroughly.

Making the Stencils
Enlarge the master drawing (Figure I, page 1972), center it under the screen, and set up registration tabs, following the instructions on page 1963. Remove the drawing and print the square of yellow on each piece of bristol board, following the instructions on page 1964. Clean the paint from the screen with paint thinner (Craftnotes, page 1973). Do not wash the filler out, however—it can be removed only with water. Proceed to stencil and print the next color, following the same procedures. For each color, put the drawing into registration, lower the screen, and trace only the lines that border the color that has just been printed and is to show up in the finished print. Fill these areas in with filler, let the filler dry, remove the drawing, then print the next color. Let each color dry thoroughly before printing the next. Clean the screen thoroughly with paint thinner as soon as you have finished printing a color. But do not remove the filler until the last color has been printed. Thus,

Color key

1 Yellow

2 Tan

3 Light red - beige

4 Dusky red - brown

5 Medium red

6 Deep red

7 Light green

8 Dark green

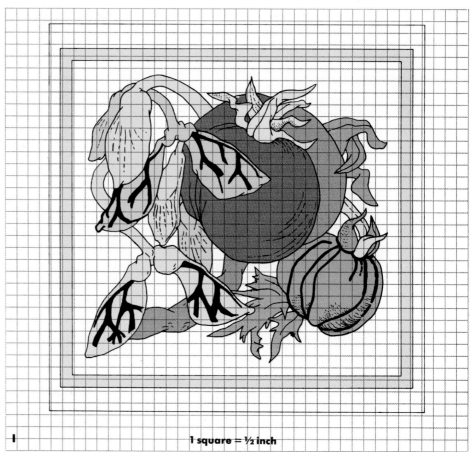

1 square = ½ inch

Figure I: To enlarge the garden-print design to 16 by 16 inches, draw a ½-inch grid on 16-by-16-inch paper. Copy the design square by square and color it. If you use a smaller screen, draw a ⅜-inch grid to get a 12-by-12-inch design. The colors used are indicated above; the numbers on the colors indicate the order in which they were applied. The details, which appear as black lines on the drawing, are all dusky red-brown ink and are printed during the fourth printing operation. Only major details are indicated here; others may be added to suit your taste.

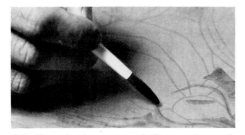

18: In the reduction process of silk-screening used in the garden print, filler is added to change the stencil for each color printed. Here the stencil for the tan ink, the first color applied over the yellow background, is being prepared.

19: The print-to-be has received its second color, tan. In subsequent printings, much of the area that is solid tan will be overprinted with other colors. The parts that remain tan are protected with filler, painted on the screen.

once the yellow square has been printed, put the drawing into register, trace the lines around the areas that are to remain yellow, and add filler to the screen so it covers those areas (Figure I and photograph 18). Let both the filler and the yellow-printed bristol board dry thoroughly before proceeding. Then print the second color, tan. The result is shown in photograph 19. I used the following color sequence: third color, light red-beige; fourth color, dusky red-brown; fifth color, medium red; sixth color, deep red; seventh color, light green; eighth and final color, dark green. These colors and the order in which they were applied are indicated in the master drawing (Figure I). Use other colors if you like; just be sure they are opaque, and add them from lightest to darkest to avoid show-through.

When you finish printing, clean the ink from the screen (Craftnotes, page 1973). Then disengage the screen from the hinge bar and take it to the shower or a large sink. Wash the screen with hot water to remove the filler. Check to make sure all filler has been removed; then let the screen dry. Once this is done, check the screen again to be sure no paint remains to clog it. If any areas are clogged, saturate two pieces of cotton with lacquer thinner, and gently rub both sides of the screen simultaneously. Dry with paper towels immediately.

Before hanging the prints, cover them with a layer of overprint varnish. This varnish, made specifically for silk-screened works, adds a gloss to the print.

To apply the varnish, again reduce the printing area of the silk-screen to a 16-by-16-inch square, following the instructions on page 1963. Put the dry prints one by one into register, lower the screen, and squeegee a thin layer of varnish over each. Clean the screen with the lacquer thinner and let the prints dry overnight.

To mount the prints, measure the space you want to cover with them, and nail sheets of cardboard to the wall to cover this area. Use contact cement to attach the prints to the cardboard, coating the back of each print and the cardboard area it covers with the cement. Let both surfaces dry until tacky—this will take only a few minutes. Then place the prints, one at a time, on the cardboard, smoothing each print down slowly to avoid air bubbles. Position the prints so their edges touch as shown on page 1960.

For related entries, see "Block Printing," "Greeting Cards," "Linoleum and Woodcuts," "Monoprinting," and "Stenciling."

CRAFTNOTES: SOLVENTS, INKS, AND FILLERS

Mixing printing inks

There are many inks that can be used for silk-screen printing. Each is made for printing on a particular surface, so it is important to get the right ink for the material you are printing on. With paper, matte poster-color ink is generally used.

Along with the printing inks, purchase quart containers of transparency base and extender base. The first is used to make ink less opaque; the second makes it go farther. For mixing you will need containers—salvaged jars or cut-down milk cartons. You can improvise covers with plastic wrap and rubber bands. Even after mixing, inks have a long life provided they are kept tightly covered.

To mix matte poster-color inks for an average printing session (20 to 30 prints), pour enough ink into a 2½-by-5-inch container to fill it halfway. Add extender base to this, using approximately one part base to two parts ink. Stir the mixture with a tablespoon or flat wooden stick until ink and extender base are blended.

For printing, the ink should be the consistency of heavy sweet cream. Lift your mixing utensil and let the ink run back into the container. If it runs quickly, the ink is too thin; add more ink or let the mix stand for an hour, uncovered. If the ink is lumpy or thick, add more extender base.

Oil paints, purchased in tubes and mixed with transparency and extender base, are also excellent for silk-screen printing. If you use oils, the color will be slightly more transparent than with matte poster-color inks. To mix oil paints, fill a small container half full of extender base. Then squeeze the paint into the container until you have one part oil paint to two parts extender base. Mix thoroughly.

With either kind of ink, colors can be mixed. You don't need to buy orange ink, for example, if you already have red and yellow ink. You will need both black and white inks, however, as these are invaluable, both in themselves and in changing the tone of other colors.

Varying amounts of transparency base can be added to the ink to get varying degrees of opacity or transparency. If you want to print with truly opaque ink, use matte poster color without adding any transparency base. But if you want transparent color, add transparency base, bit by bit, until you arrive at the effect you want.

Whatever type ink you are using, test it for color and transparency when it has been mixed to the right consistency. Put a small amount of the ink on a scrap of the material you will be printing on. Let it dry for a few minutes; then adjust the ink if necessary.

The same extender base and transparency base can be used with oil paints and matte poster-color inks. When you work with other inks, such as those prepared for printing on fabric or plastic, buy the recommended bases and follow the manufacturer's mixing instructions.

Matching the solvents

Just as you select an ink to suit the surface you are printing on, match the cleaning solvent and the filler (the stenciling material used to block openings in the screen) to the ink you choose. To clean the printing color from the screen, you need a solvent that will not remove the filler, too. (The ink is generally removed several times before the filler is taken off.)

Oil- or lacquer-based printing color can be removed from the screen with, respectively, paint thinner and lacquer thinner. Both are flammable, as are many printing inks; and the fumes can be hazardous, so work in a well ventilated room and do not smoke. A water-soluble filler is used with these inks as the solvents used to remove them will not affect it. With water-based inks, you need a filler that is not water-soluble, such as lacquer. For other inks, use the solvent and filler recommended by the manufacturer.

Cleaning the screen

The silk screen and the squeegee are tools that will last for years—with proper care. Both must be cleaned after each color is printed, and both must be cleaned at the end of the printing session. To clean the screen between colors, first remove excess ink from the inner edges of the frame with a spatula, returning the ink to the container (below, left). If you have used a paper stencil, remove it. Lift the screen, place a thick layer of newspapers on the baseboard, and lower the screen. Pour a generous amount of solvent on the screen to dissolve the ink. Let the solvent soak for a minute; then wipe the screen with paper toweling (below, center). Lift the screen, remove the top layer of newspaper, and with paper towels or rags in each hand, wipe both sides of the screen simultaneously (below, right). Repeat this process until the screen is clean. If stubborn spots remain, soak toweling with solvent and go over the area. Hold the screen up to the light and check for any clogged areas that still remain, other than the stencils. The color of the ink may stain the screen slightly, but if light passes through, the screen is ready for the next color. At the end of the printing session, clean off the ink; then take out the hinge pins so you can remove the screen, and wash away the stencil filler with its recommended solvent.

To clean the squeegee, scrape it with a rubber spatula or piece of cardboard; then rub it with toweling soaked in solvent.

SEWING WITHOUT A PATTERN
Fabric Geometry

Beginning with a rectangular length of fabric—even an attractive bedsheet—you can sew shapes that may seem complicated but are not. The mysteries of a bias-cut apron, of a circular cape that swirls, or of a round tablecloth that completes a bedroom ensemble, are not difficult to solve.

You will not need special equipment. Pins, tailor's chalk, pencil, ruler, and scissors are sufficient for measuring and marking the fabric and cutting out the shapes. A pencil at the end of a taut piece of string makes an adequate compass for describing a circle. If you need to make an adjustment in the size of any of the garments shown here, or if you want to determine the number and size of the sheets you will need for the room ensemble opposite, it may be helpful to work out the proportions on a sheet of graph paper, making each square on the paper equal to an inch.

Eleane Hiller, who describes herself as an instinctive designer, is French. She left her native city of Hyeres to design clothing in Sao Paulo, Brazil, where she lived for 15 years. In 1965, she moved to New York, where she first worked as a sportswear designer. She now owns Elart, a fashion house manufacturing sportswear and accessories.

Needlecrafts
Bias-cut apron-shawl

$ ▣ ⚉ ⚗

A bias-cut fabric triangle with a lace-edged ruffle becomes an apron that molds itself to the body.

The same ruffle-trimmed triangle can also be worn over the shoulders as a casual shawl.

Making the bias-cut calico apron (above, left) is a good investment of time and energy because it can also be worn as a shawl (above, right) or as a beach skirt knotted at one side of the waist.

The triangular shape of the apron is arrived at by folding a length of material on the diagonal, cutting along the fold, and rounding off the opposite tip. The ruffle is then made with two strips of fabric taken from the material remaining after the triangle has been cut. It is trimmed with lace, gathered, and attached. The longest side of the triangle becomes the apron waist. The ruffle begins 12 inches down from the points, freeing them to serve as ties.

The triangle is cut on the bias—the diagonal of the fabric (Figure A)—which is

A

Figure A: To obtain the basic apron triangle, with two sides equal, from a rectangular piece of fabric, fold the fabric diagonally. Measure and mark the desired length (28 inches) from the bottom right-hand corner. To obtain two bias strips 8½ inches wide for the ruffle, measure and mark that width and twice that width along the fold line, connecting the points on the diagonal of the fabric, as shown.

The fresh-looking greenery at the windows, on the bed, and over the night table at right all were stitched from four printed bedsheets and two sheets in a coordinated solid color. These accessories were designed by Judith Hinsch; directions for making them begin on page 1983.

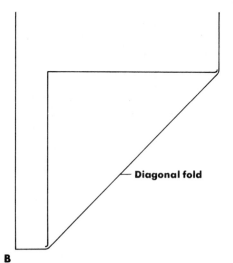

B

Figure B: Fold the apron's triangular section to the left, pin it there temporarily, and cut along the diagonal fold.

not the usual way to cut fabric. Woven fabric consists of two sets of threads, one running lengthwise called the warp and the other running crosswise called the weft. They cross each other at right angles. Usually fabric is cut along these straight thread lines for stability. But when fabric is cut on the bias, angling across the thread lines, it will stretch slightly when pulled. The bias cut of this apron lets it cling and mold itself to the body as it is tied into place.

You will need 1⅔ yards of material for the apron and 3¼ yards of ½-inch-wide lace for the trim. In order to cut a fabric triangle 28 inches long down the center front, not counting the ruffle, you will need material at least 45 inches wide (Figure A, page 1974). The long side of the triangle measured diagonally is 56 inches.

To cut a perfect triangle from the length of fabric, fold the fabric as shown in Figure B and cut along the fold. Round off the tip, as shown in Figure A, by measuring 3 inches in from the tip on either side and cutting a freehand curve.

Ruffles are gathered strips of fabric used for trimming. By cutting them on the bias (Figure A), you can make them produce softer folds than they would if cut along the lengthwise or crosswise threads. To make a ruffle of average fullness, use a strip of fabric 1½ to 2 times the length of the edge to be trimmed. For the apron, cut two strips, each 8½ inches wide and 56 inches long. Round off one end of each strip by measuring 3 inches in from a corner and cutting a freehand curve. Join the two strips end to end with a French seam (Figure C) so the raw edges will not be

1: To attach the lace trimming, turn up the raw edge ⅛ inch to the right side of the apron and stitch it. Then sew the lace on top.

2: With right sides facing, stitch the lace-trimmed ruffle to the apron triangle ½ inch inside the latter's raw edge.

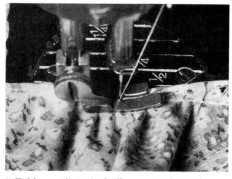

3: Fold over the ½-inch allowance twice, so its raw edge and the raw edge of the ruffle are enclosed. Then stitch close to the edge of this fold.

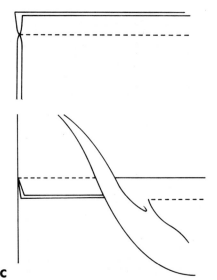

C

Figure C: A French seam encloses raw edges to provide a neat finish. First, machine-stitch the two pieces, wrong sides facing, ¼ inch from the edge (top). Trim the seam allowance to ⅛ inch. Fold along the stitched line, right sides facing, and stitch again ¼ inch from the fold to enclose the raw edges (bottom).

visible on the wrong side of the ruffle. With the wrong side of the two strips facing, stitch ¼ inch in from the edge. Trim the seam allowance to ⅛ inch, turn the fabric so the right sides are facing, and stitch ¼ inch in from the seamed edge to encase the raw edges of the seam allowances.

Making the Ruffle

It is not necessary to hem the raw edge of the ruffle before sewing on the lace trimming. Simply turn up the raw edge ⅛ inch, right sides facing, and stitch it down with invisible nylon thread (photograph 1).

To gather the ruffle, loosen the tension on the sewing machine slightly, and sew a row of stitches along the raw edge of the ruffle opposite the lace, ¼ inch in from the raw edge. Knot one end of the threads, pull the bobbin thread at the other end with one hand to reduce the length from 112 inches to 52 inches, and arrange the fullness evenly with the other hand.

Finish the raw edge of the triangle across the top and 12 inches down on each side before attaching the ruffle. If your sewing machine has a hemming foot, it will double-roll the edge for you. If not, fold under ⅛ inch of fabric and then a second ⅛ inch and stitch.

Join the ruffle to the triangle so the seam on the wrong side will have a clean finish. With right sides together, place the ruffle ½ inch in from the edge of the triangle, pin it in place, and baste it with a loose running stitch before sewing a row of permanent stitches right over the basting and gathering stitches (photograph 2). Then turn under the ½ inch of fabric twice, and stitch it down so it encases the raw edge of the ruffle (photograph 3).

Needlecrafts
Man's kimono coat

$ ◻ ♟ ♟

The kimono, worn traditionally by men and women alike, is a loose, wrap-around robe distinguished by its wide, straight sleeves cut in one piece with the bodice, and by its sash. The word is Japanese, from *ki*, to wear, plus *mono*, meaning person or thing; the literal translation is "thing for wearing."

The kimono originated not in Japan, however, but in China. Visual documentation dates back to the third century B.C., but it is probably much older. Known to the Chinese as a *p'ao*, it was worn by them until the end of the Ming dynasty (1644). The Japanese adopted it in the eighth century. Westerners have modeled countless bathrobes, lounging robes, and beach jackets after the comfortable kimono style.

Traditional kimonos were made of exquisitely woven and patterned silks, a textile art which the Chinese discovered and began to develop more than 4,000 years ago. The most beautifully decorated and colored Japanese silk kimonos date from the seventeenth and eighteenth centuries. The kimono's style lends itself not only to silk but to any type of fabric that is supple enough to drape well, and even to some fabrics with more body.

The short kimono coat (below, right) is made of machine-washable, drip-dry cot-

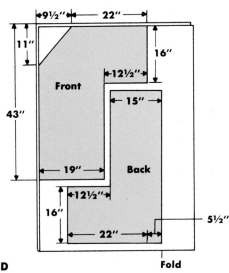

D

Figure D: Kimono sleeves are cut at right angles in one piece with the body of the coat. To cut both back and front pieces from doubled 45-inch-wide fabric so you have two of each, place the bottom of the back section in the space below the sleeve of the front section so they nest together.

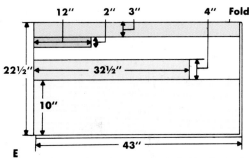

E

Figure E: To reduce the amount of stitching in the facings and sash, fold the material lengthwise and draw the front neckline facings (yellow) along the selvage side so the woven edges serve as the inside hem. Place the sash (green) along the fold so only one side need be stitched. Fit sleeve facings (blue) and back neck facing (orange) between.

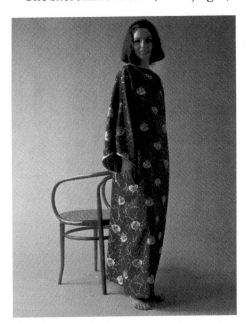

The caftan is similar in shape to the kimono but is slotted at the neck for slipping over the head.

The right-angle sleeve is the key in making a kimono coat suitable for men or women.

ton with a bold, colorful stripe, suitable for lounge wear or beach wear. It has a V-shaped neckline and a front closing with a generous overlap that is faced with the same striped cotton fabric as the coat. The sleeves stop short of the wrist and are also faced so they can be turned back. The striped pattern in itself provides an attractive border and sash. This design is only a starting point for many variations that you can make by changing the neckline, making the kimono longer or shorter, using other fabrics, binding it instead of facing it, or adding trimmings.

This kimono was made for a man according to his measurements: width of neckline across the front, 10 inches; length of arms, 25 inches, less 3 inches for adjusted sleeve length; desired coat length finished, 42 inches. Before you start this project, read the directions on page 1978 for measuring accurately.

A kimono of this length requires 4 yards of 45-inch-wide material to make the two front and two back sections (Figure D) and an additional 1½ yards to make the facings and the sash (Figure E). The fabric width is sufficient for small, medium, or large sizes, providing that you lay out the pattern pieces for cutting with a minimum of waste.

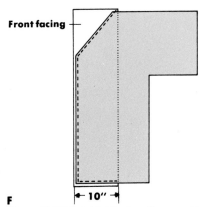

Front facing

F

Figure F: With right sides together, sew the raw edges of the facings to the front sections of the kimono. Turn the kimono right side out and sew another row of stitches 2 inches from the edge—to frame the front overlap and to keep the facings flat inside. Trim off the excess fabric.

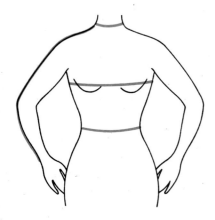

G
Figure G: To hem a raw edge by machine, fold it under ⅛ inch; then fold it again to make a hem of whatever depth you want, and stitch it along the inside fold.

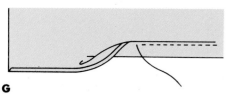

Body measurement guide

Neck: Measure around the top of the collarbone, past the point where the neck joins the shoulder, and around the most prominent vertebra at the back of the neck. The width of the neckline across the front is half of this total.

Sleeve length: Measure the length of the arm from the neckline atop the shoulder to the place where you want the sleeve to end.

Bust: Measure under the arms around the fullest part of the bust and across the shoulder blades in back; then add 2 inches for ease.

Waist: Measure from the base of the neck to a point just above the bottom curve of the spine; then measure horizontally around the torso. Hold the tape measure loosely so the finished garment will fit comfortably around the waist.

Cut off a piece of material 43 inches long for the facings and sash. Fold the remaining 4 yards in half across the width (for cutting two back and two front pieces), and pin the selvages to prevent the fabric from slipping while you are marking and cutting it. Be sure to include ¼-inch seam allowances.

Starting in the upper left corner, measure for the V-shaped neckline (Figure D, page 1977). To find the sleeve length, measure along the fold from the neck point and mark off the length desired. Draw a line 16 inches long perpendicular to the shoulder to establish the depth of the kimono sleeve. Mark a second point 16 inches down parallel to it so you can rule off a straight line 12½ inches long for the bottom of the sleeve. Next, starting at the upper left-hand corner, rule off 43 inches down the left selvage for the length, then 19 inches across the bottom for the front width. Connect the points for the side seam. The back is identical to the front of the kimono in all but two respects; the neckline is measured 5½ inches straight across the base starting in the lower right-hand corner, and the bottom is only 15 inches wide. Cut out two of each piece.

The Facings and Sash
You can avoid sewing extra seams by the way you mark and cut the facings and sash pieces. Fold the remaining material in half, matching the selvage edges (Figure E, page 1977). Take the front facings from the selvage side, letting the woven edge serve as the inside finish. Use the shape of the kimono neckline as a pattern for the facings, which are 10 inches wide and 43 inches long. Pin the strips, right sides together, beneath the front pieces of the kimono, with their raw edges flush against the closing edge, and cut out the neckline (Figure F, page 1977). By taking the belt from the folded side, you will have only one long edge seam to sew later.

Sewing the Kimono
Sew the center back seam of the kimono (right sides facing as with all seams). If you are working with stripes, be sure to match them. Sew the front to the back at the shoulder seams, from neck edge to edge of sleeves. Join the front facings and back neck facing at the shoulder seams. Pin the right sides of the kimono and facing together. Sew a row of stitches all around the edge and trim the excess fabric (Figure F). Turn right side out and sew a second row of stitches on the right side, 2 inches away, to frame the closing and to keep the facing lying flat on the inside. Face the sleeves with the 4-inch strips of fabric. Pin the right sides together, sew around the edge, and turn; then fold the raw edge under twice and stitch around the inner edge of the facing (Figure G).

Match the angle of the underarms; then pin the front and back together completely before sewing the underarms and side seams. Carry the row of stitching from the edge of the sleeve to the underarm, and reinforce it by sewing around the curve over the first row of stitches before continuing all the way down to the hem. Turn up the hem, double roll the raw edge, and machine-stitch it (Figure G). Join the belt strips with right sides together to obtain a length of 60 inches; then sew the raw edges together along the length, leaving an opening of 1½ inches for turning it right side out. Iron the belt flat and stitch the opening closed by hand.

Needlecrafts
Contemporary caftan

The caftan is a long, loose, shirtlike garment with long, wide sleeves, usually fashioned of striped cotton or silk. It is derived from garments common throughout the eastern Mediterranean and North African countries and, coincidentally, resembles the Japanese kimono in its basic outline. The word caftan, common to the Turks and Persians, was used originally to describe a type of luxurious coat worn by men in the eleventh century. Features of the Moroccan man's djellaba, a full, long-sleeved woolen cloak with a hood, also enter into the styling of westernized caftans.

The caftan shown on page 1977 is essentially the same shape as the man's kimono coat pictured next to it, but its greater length and softer fabric give it a different look. Instead of being a coat style, sashed at the waist, it is designed to be slipped over the head. The neckline, high and round, has a deeply cut center opening in front. Bias binding is used for ornamental trimming.

The ankle-length caftan shown was made for a woman 5 feet, 6 inches in height who wears a dress size 8. Her measurements: neckline, 14½ inches; length of arms, 22 inches; desired length finished, 54 inches. (Refer to instructions on taking body measurements, opposite page.)

Making this caftan requires 4 yards of material, 45 inches wide, and at least 3 yards of ½-inch-wide, double-fold bias binding, available in any notions department. If you choose a printed fabric, allow enough extra yardage to match the repeat of the pattern. Match the print while folding the fabric to assure a continuous flow of the design across the front and back seams (photograph 4). Save the extra fabric for cutting out the facing of the neckline.

The procedures for folding and pinning the fabric, making the diagram for the caftan (Figure H), and using the neckline as a pattern for the facing are similar to those described for the man's kimono coat (page 1977). To locate and measure the neckline for the front (the upper left-hand corner in Figure H), measure a distance of 4 inches across the top and 2 inches down along the left selvage. Connect the two points with a diagonal line (Figure I). Then draw a continuous curve freehand, close to the diagonal line. To ensure a smooth curve you can draw a rectangle as shown; then draw a second diagonal line in the opposite direction. Using the point where

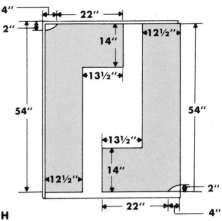

H

Figure H: The sleeves and body of the caftan are similar in shape to those of the kimono coat (page 1977). The neckline, however, is rounded. The extra inches gained by eliminating the front overlap make it possible to lay out front and back sections along the selvages of 45-inch-wide material.

4: To make a caftan that has the pattern matched at the seams, match the pattern of the printed fabric (it will be repeated at regular intervals) when you fold the fabric before cutting it.

5: Use commercial bias binding to enclose the raw edges of the caftan and its neckline facing. With wrong sides together and the bias binding face down on top, stitch ¼ inch from the edge.

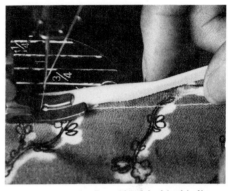

6: After sewing the first side of the bias binding (photograph 5), fold the binding over the raw edges of fabric, turn the binding edge under, and stitch along this fold, as shown.

the diagonals intersect, measure ⅜ inch down along the first diagonal line (this will be the deepest point of the curve). Draw a curve connecting this point with the upper right corner and the lower left corner. Cut out the neckline, allowing 8 inches for the center front opening. To make the back neckline, start in the lower right-hand corner, and follow the directions for the front neckline. Although the distance from the neckline over the shoulder to the tip of the sleeve is 22 inches, the same as for the man's kimono, this garment when finished seems to have longer sleeves because the woman's arms are shorter than the man's. The cut of the garment under the armpit controls the width of the garment and its comfort. As the right angle moves up and closer to the body, the width of the sleeves and the width of the sides diminish. Conversely, as it moves down and away from the body, the widths of the two increase. If the caftan sleeves are cut too skimpily, the sides of the garment will pull up whenever the arms are raised and extended horizontally. There should be no problem with a sleeve that measures at least 14 inches in depth along a line perpendicular to the shoulder line. This line corresponds to the distance between the neck point and a point about 2 or 3 inches below the bottom of the bust in average women's sizes. It is easy to make the garment smaller without narrowing the sleeves by bringing the side seams closer to the body. If you have any doubts about the measurements you want, work out the proportions on graph paper before marking the fabric.

Lay the back sections of the caftan right sides together, and stitch the center back seam; then sew the front seam in the same manner, leaving not only the neckline opening unstitched but also a few inches extra below it. Then, after you have

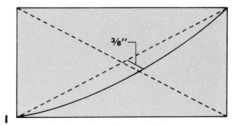

I

Figure I: To draw the caftan neckline curve smoothly, draw a diagonal line connecting the neckline marks (top left, Figure H). Draw another diagonal crossing the midpoint of the first, as shown above, and mark a point ⅜ inch below the intersection to locate the center of the curve. Join this point to the upper right and lower left marks with a curved line.

bound the front of the neckline, you will be able to catch the raw edges of the binding in the center front seam and avoid having to square off this binding at the point where it finishes off the neckline. Join the front of the caftan to the back, right sides together, at the shoulder seams; then pin and sew the under-sleeve seams and the side seams, using the same two steps described for the man's kimono on page 1778. Join front and back facings at the shoulder seams, and finish the outside raw edge by double folding and machine stitching.

Double-fold bias binding comes ready made with one fold slightly wider than the other. The wider portion goes on the inside of the garment. Baste the facing in place along the raw edge of the neckline, wrong sides facing (photograph 5, page 1979). Sew around the front closing first. Then when you finish sewing the front seam up to the neckline, you can catch the raw ends of the front binding underneath. Turn the caftan right side out, fold the binding over the raw edges of the neckline, and topstitch the binding close to the edge to completely encase the raw seams (photograph 6, page 1979). To keep the front opening closed, add ties.

To make these 15-inch-long streamers from the binding material, keep the binding folded, and stitch along the open edge. Attach at the top front of the neckline. Bind the sleeves and finish the garment by turning up the hem (Figure G, page 1978). Notice that the caftan can be worn backwards, as it is in the photograph on page 1977), because there are no bust darts to interfere with the flow of the fabric.

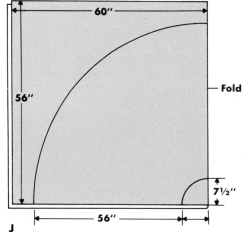

This semicircular cape was cut in one piece from a 112-inch-long rectangle of wool, 56 inches wide. An angled hood can be fashioned from the remnants of the wool rectangle.

Needlecrafts
Semicircular cape with hood

The cape, a type of ancient sleeveless cloak, is at its most fashionable in periods when loose garments are popular or when they are worn in layers for reasons of warmth.

To make a semicircular cape like the one shown at left, you need a rectangular piece of fabric at least wide enough to accommodate the length of the cape (the radius) and at least twice as long (the diameter).

This hooded semicircular cape, 54 inches long plus 2 inches for the seams, required a rectangular piece of fabric (wool and mohair) measuring 112 inches in length and 56 inches in width. After it was sewn, the raw edges were encased decoratively with ¾-inch-wide flat double braid. Ten yards of braid are needed to edge the cape and hood and make the ties at the neckline.

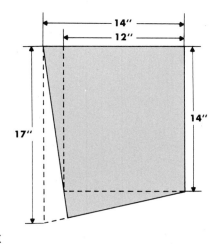

J

Figure J: To make a semicircular cape, use fabric wide enough to accommodate the cape's desired length (the radius), and at least twice its radius in length to accommodate the full sweep of a semicircle. Fold the fabric in half as shown, and mark the quarter circles with a pencil on a string, using the fold as the center line of the cape's back and the woven selvages at the bottom as the front closing of the cape.

K

Figure K: To draw one side of the hood, make the top and back lines, plus three temporary lines (dashed lines above). To establish the neckline, connect the bottom right corner with the end of the 17-inch temporary line. To mark the front edge, connect the upper left corner with the intersection of the two dashed lines that meet at a right angle; then continue to the neckline. Allow a ½-inch seam allowance along top and back.

In preparation for drawing the semicircle, fold the fabric rectangle in half along the width, and pin it along the selvages and down the center to prevent the two layers from slipping. The positioning of the cape with its center back on the fold eliminates construction seams (Figure J). The selvages at the bottom of Figure J serve as the center front opening. The curve of the neckline and that of the hem fan out from the center point. The material left over after the semicircle is cut provides material for the hood, detailed in Figure K.

If you choose a napped fabric (any fabric with a one-way design, or a pile or texture that runs in one direction), the nap will run in opposite directions when you fold it, so you must then cut along the fold line and turn one of the squares upside down so all the nap runs in the same direction. Then place one square on top of the other, right sides together; pin and mark. Instead of having the seamless center fold, you will now have two raw edges to sew together to make a center back seam.

With the fabric folded as shown in Figure J, measure a distance of 7½ inches from the bottom right corner up along the center fold. Make a compass with a pencil or tailor's chalk tied on the end of a 7½-inch length of string. Hold the end of the string at the corner, and with the string taut, draw a quarter circle. Follow the same procedure to mark the hem, measured along the center fold; in this case it is 56 inches from center point to hemline. Then cut out the cape. Baste along the seam line of the neck edge to keep it from stretching out of shape.

7: With the raw edge of the cape against the fold of the braid trim, stitch the cape to the braid ½ inch from the edge, starting at the neckline.

8: Fold the braid trim over the raw edge of the cape and stitch along its edge, thus securing it to the right side of the cape.

9: Fold under the raw edge of the braid trim where it meets the starting point of the braid, at the point where the neckline and hood are joined.

The Hood

The only right angle in the side of the hood is the one formed by the top and back which are the same length—14 inches (Figure K). You will have to make three temporary lines (shown in dashed lines in Figure K) to get the correct angles for the front and neckline. Rule off the top and back lines and the three temporary lines as shown. Next, rule a line that connects the bottom right corner with the bottom of the lower temporary line—to establish the neckline of the hood. To make the front opening angle, connect the upper left corner with the intersection of two temporary perpendicular lines, and continue the line to meet the neckline of the hood. Allow an additional ½ inch at the top and back for seams. Cut two identical pieces.

Join the sections of the hood across the top and back with a French seam (Figure C, page 1976); then pin the neckline of the hood to the cape, right sides together. There is always some extra fullness when an inside curve is being fitted to an outside curve; so pinch in the fullness as you pin and baste it into place before sewing a French seam for a neat finish.

The cape is bound all around with ¾-inch flat double braid in eggshell color. Such braid can be machine stitched to both sides of the garment, using colorless nylon thread. Place the cape right side up. Starting at the neckline, lay the edge of the cape along the inside fold of the braid, and stitch it ½ inch from the edge (photograph 7). Fold the free edge of the braid on top, and stitch it along the edge (photograph 8). Finish off by folding the braid under itself at the neckline where it meets the starting point (photograph 9); it will be least visible here. Hand stitch it so it lies flat (photograph 10). Stitch on the ties by hand or machine.

10: Stitch the folded end of the braid to the starting braid, making small stitches by hand.

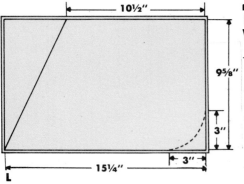

Figure L: To make a wraparound skirt with elasticized waist, two shaped rectangles are stacked right sides up and trimmed as shown in the diagram. The slanted left edges are then stitched together. The bottom corners at the right are rounded off. Measurements shown are for a child's size 4, but the proportions can be adjusted to fit any size.

Needlecrafts
Wraparound skirt with tube top ¢ ▯ 夫 ⚘

The wraparound skirt with bound edges, bottom left, is proportioned for a small child, but it can also be made in women's sizes. The elasticized waistline can be tied at the side or front. The skirt is made of two rectangular scraps of cotton calico, left over from another sewing project, using these miniature measurements: 21 inches around the waistline and 9 inches long, finished. Elastic ½-inch wide makes the waistband.

Take two rectangles, each measuring at least 15¼ inches wide to provide hem and seam allowances, and 9⅝ inches long to allow the waistline casing (Figure L). Lay the rectangles wrong sides together and pin. Measure 10½ inches across the top for the waistline, and draw a line connecting this point with the bottom left corner of the rectangles. Mark off 3 inches on both edges adjacent to the lower right-hand corner. Draw a line connecting the points to round off the tip. Cut out the skirt and join the two sections with a French seam. Sew on the red bias binding, following the directions on page 1979.

Measure 2 inches in from each side of the waistline, and mark each point to indicate where the elastic begins and ends. Fold the raw edge under ⅛ inch; then make a second fold to enclose the elastic (photograph 11). After stitching down one end of the elastic, sew the casing with the elastic inside. (Be careful not to stitch over the elastic.) By following this method, you will avoid having to pull the elastic through the casing after it has been sewn. Gather in the casing to fit the waistline, and stitch the elastic down on the opposite end. Sew a hook and eye to close the skirt. Stitch two ties made from the red bias binding to the front flap and at the waistline, where the flap meets the skirt.

A tube top sewn with elastic thread and a wraparound skirt elasticized at the waistline fit perfectly without a need for darts. This summer outfit could be made in any size.

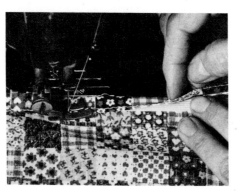

11: To enclose the elastic and make the casing for the waistline of the child's skirt, fold the fabric over the elastic, as shown, and stitch.

12: To stitch the tubular top with elastic thread, hold your index finger behind the presser foot, and press down firmly against the fabric.

Elasticizing the Tube Top
To make the pert matching top, one length of fabric 42 inches long and 9 inches wide was sewn with elastic thread. The fabric's long dimension circles the torso and is seamed down the center back. Row upon row of elastic thread running around the tube gives it its stretch. The tube is 6 inches long finished; the other 3 inches were turned up to make the top and bottom hems. The red shoulder ties are made from extra pieces of the bias binding used for the skirt.

Thread the bobbin with elastic thread, winding it tightly by hand, until the bobbin is almost full. The elastic thread should come off the bobbin with plenty of stretch; so be sure the tension is tight enough. Leave your regular sewing thread on top, but set the machine for a long stitch in order to give the elastic thread as much play as possible. Turn under the raw edge 1½ inches for the top hem, and catch it in the first row of stitches. Sew the rest of the rows 1 inch apart except for the bottom which is hemmed in the same manner as the top. As you sew, hold your index finger right behind the presser foot, and press down hard against the fabric to hold it taut (photograph 12).

Needlecrafts
Quilted coverlet

💲 ⧗ 🧍 ⚗

Bedspreads can have a tailored look with straight sides or a frilly look with flounced sides; they can be formal or informal, snug-fitting or throwlike, floor length or short on the sides. Short, loose covers, called coverlets, are often coordinated with separate skirts, called dust ruffles. The ruffle conceals the box spring. The coverlet covers the mattress on top plus overlapping the top of the ruffle by 3 inches. Printed sheets can easily be turned into coverlets.

Like any quilt, the coverlet pictured on page 1975 has three layers: the top fabric, the filling or batting, and the backing. The top of the quilt was made from a twin-sized plaid sheet, the backing from a twin-sized sheet in solid green. Quilt battings are sold in standard sizes, including 72 by 90 inches, the most practical size to use for a single bed. Lightweight polyester batting is easy to work with and will remain fluffy through many washings.

To assemble the quilt, pin the three layers together on a flat surface. Place the backing wrong side up, spread the batting smoothly over it, then cover it with the fabric, right side up. The first step is to hold the batting in place with pins. Pins placed every 3 inches are not too many. Use T pins or safety pins if you find that straight pins do not hold. Begin at the center and work out towards the edges in rows parallel to the lengthwise and crosswise grains, checkerboard fashion, smoothing the surface as you pin. Then baste the layers together, using the same procedure as you did for pinning.

The design of a patterned fabric often suggests the placement of the quilting lines; here, the plaid provided the answer. Use the longest stitch on your machine for quilting. Usually eight to ten stitches to the inch set at a looser than normal ten-

Judith Hinsch has been sewing since the age of seven, when she made doll clothes. She was taught to sew by her grandmother, a professional seamstress. Judith was awarded a Homemaker of the Year award when she was graduated from high school. With additional instruction in advanced sewing techniques, she now sews all of the clothes that she and her two children need. She also designs and sews children's clothing for a shop near her home in Holliston, Massachusetts.

13: To quilt a coverlet by machine, push down on the three layers—the fabric, batting, and backing—as they go under the presser foot.

14: To prepare the dust ruffle for gathering, stitch three rows of long machine stitches (about six to the inch) inside the ½-inch seam allowance.

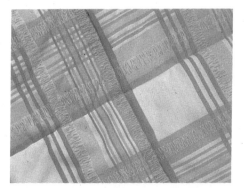

This coverlet was quilted by following the lines of the plaid. Working out from the center, first the lines were sewn in one direction, then the other.

sion take care of the bulk. Begin stitching in the center of the coverlet and move out towards the edges. First sew all the lines in one direction; then do all the cross lines to correspond with the lines in the plaid pattern. As they move under the presser foot, press the fabric layers down to lessen their bulk (photograph 13). (A coverlet larger than twin size may be too cumbersome to quilt by machine; stitching by hand is recommended.) After the coverlet has been completely quilted, lay it evenly on the bed and trim to size, 3 inches longer than the mattress on each side. Bind the raw edges together with medium-width (⅞-inch) bias binding in a contrasting color, in the manner shown in photographs 5 and 6, page 1979. Be sure to enclose the edges of the batting as you stitch.

The Dust Ruffle

The dust ruffle on the bed has a center section made from an old sheet; unbleached muslin could be used. The ruffle itself, a three-sided one because the head of the bed is against a wall, was made from a twin-sized sheet. What remained from the sheet was used for the pillow cover, page 1985.

15: To gather the dust ruffle, pull the ends of the three bobbin threads with one hand while gathering the ruffle with the other hand.

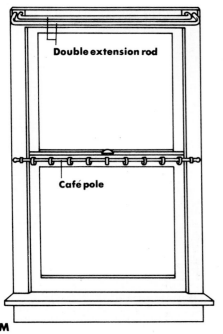

M

Figure M: Accurate measurements are the key to well-fitting café curtains. Mount the curtain rods first; then measure for each section of the curtain.

Two sets of café curtains topped with a valance, all created from printed bed sheets, make a distinctive window treatment.

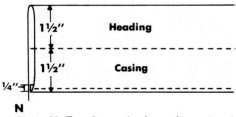

N

Figure N: To make a casing for a café curtain rod, allow 3 inches for the top hem. Fold and press it. Turn under the raw edge ¼ inch and hem it. Make a second line of stitching along the center of the hem. Slip the rod into the casing and gather the curtain along the rod.

To make the center section for the dust ruffle, spread the sheet over the box spring, taking advantage of the 1-inch finished hem by placing it at the head flush against the edge. (If you are using muslin, finish this edge with a double-stitched hem.) Cut the sheet to fit the perimeter of the box spring, allowing an extra ½ inch for seams on both sides and at the foot of the bed. Round off the corners.

Measure from the top of the box spring to 1 inch from the floor to establish the finished length of the dust ruffle. (The one pictured is 14 inches.) Allow an extra ½ inch for the top seam and 2 inches for the bottom hem. Measure the perimeter of the box spring on the three sides to be ruffled and allow 1½ times its length for the dust ruffle before gathering. Cut out enough sections of solid-color sheeting to equal this total.

Sew three rows of long running stitches along the top of the ruffle material, instead of the conventional two rows, to prevent the thread from breaking under the weight of the fabric (photograph 14, page 1983). Keep rows inside the ½-inch seam allowance. Join the sections but be careful not to catch the ends of the gathering threads in the side seams because you will need to pull them later. Hem the raw edges at each end, as described on page 1978, making two ¼-inch folds.

Starting at the head end of one long side of the bed and with right sides together, pin the dust ruffle to the center section, following the rounded corners at the foot. Pull up the gathering stitches (photograph 15, page 1983) until the ruffle fits around the box spring and the fullness has been distributed evenly all around. Sew the ruffle and center section together. Trim the seam allowances and press them towards the center section so they will lie flat when the dust ruffle is placed on the box spring. Place the dust ruffle on the box spring again, pinning up the hem to clear the floor. Take it off the bed, turn under the raw edge of the hem ¼ inch, then stitch the finished hem as indicated by the pinning. The hem will be a little less than 2 inches deep.

Needlecrafts
Café curtains with valance $ ◻ 🧍 ⚱

Café curtains (left) are short, straight-hanging rectangles or squares of material designed as window treatments for casual room settings. When used to curtain double-hung windows, they are commonly hung in tiers of two or more pairs, one tier covering the upper half of the window, another the lower. A valance usually completes the ensemble. A valance is a very short borderlike curtain hung at the top of a window frame to provide a decorative heading for the tiers. When the top of the window is treated with tiers and a valance, a double extension rod is used to accommodate both. To hang correctly, both valance and the top tier should cover the curved ends of the rods and reach the wall. Each lower tier is suspended on a single rod which is slipped through rings sewn onto the top of the curtain.

Measuring and Cutting
Two sets of café curtains and a valance were made to decorate the standard double-hung window pictured. A double extension rod supports the valance and top tier, and a café pole and rings support the lower tier (Figure M).

One double sheet provided enough material for the window pictured, as well as the top pair of cafés for another window, not shown. The bottom set of cafés came from a twin-sized sheet needed in part for the ruffle described above. The other valance came from the remnants of the double sheet used for the tablecloth described opposite. Windows vary so much from house to house that you will need to plot the measurements for your windows on graph paper to get the most out of each sheet.

Allow the following measurements for each of the curtains: 1-inch side-seam allowances, 2-inch bottom hems, and a width equal to that of the window itself. Each pair of café curtains will therefore be twice as wide as the window, enough to make them hang with generous folds. When you are making two or more tiers of curtains, add 3 inches to the vertical measurements to allow for the tier above to overlap the one below. Since each piece will vary in proportion only slightly, write the position of the piece in pencil on the back of the fabric.

To make a top hem with a casing, allow 3 inches. Fold along the 3-inch line, wrong sides together, and press it. Turn under the raw edge ¼ inch and stitch it (Figure N). Make a second line of stitching halfway along the center of the hem. The rod slips into the casing and the curtain is shirred along the rod, creating fullness and a decorative heading. The valances, 11 inches deep when finished, and the top tier of curtains have casings made the same way.

When curtains are hung from rings that have either been clipped on or sewn, only a 1-inch hem allowance is needed on top. Check the length of the curtains by hanging them up and pinning the hem before sewing it.

Needlecrafts
Ruffled pillow cover

A sham is about the easiest type of decorative pillow cover to make and its closure is just a simple overlap in the center of the back. The material for the front and two back sections of the sham, at right, was left over from the green sheet used to make the dust ruffle on the box spring (page 1983). The sham's plaid ruffle is a remnant of the twin sheet used to make a pair of café curtains (opposite).

Measure the length and width of the pillow to be covered over the fullest part, and add 2 inches extra for ease and seam allowances. Cut one piece to these measurements for the front of the sham. To make the back, measure two sections of the same length, but only half the width, and add 1¾ inches to allow for the center hem. Cut out the two pieces. Hem one side of each small piece by turning the raw edge under ¼ inch, stitching it, then turning and stitching again to make a 1½-inch finished hem. Pin the sections together with hems overlapping so that the total area of the pillow back measures the same as the front piece.

A 3-inch ruffle of pleasing fullness is twice the perimeter of the sham. The strips for it should be cut on the bias (Figure A, page 1974). Cut strips 4 inches wide, including 1 inch for seams. Join the strips to make one continuous ruffle piece, using French seams to enclose the raw edges (Figure C, page 1976). Now turn up the bottom edge of the ruffle ¼ inch, then another ¼ inch, and hem it. Sew two rows of gathering stitches along the top of the ruffle, keeping both rows within the ½-inch seam allowance. Then gather the ruffle to fit the perimeter of the sham.

To assemble this pillow sham, sandwich the ruffle between the front and back sections of the sham (Figure O). First, place the front section right side up and pin the ruffle on top, matching raw edges. Then place the back pieces on top of them, face down. Pin them all together and sew around the perimeter ½ inch from the edge. Turn the finished sham right side out and insert the pillow through the back opening.

Needlecrafts
A round tablecloth

To find the measurements of a floor-length tablecloth, measure the diameter of the table top, and measure the drop from the edge of the table top to the floor. Double the latter measurement, add the table's diameter, and you have the diameter of the circular cloth. Divide the diameter in half to obtain the radius. The radius of the tablecloth shown in the room setting on page 1975 is 37 inches. You can eliminate seams entirely by using a sheet. To gain a little extra material, open the sheet's hem and press with a steam iron to remove the creases.

To cut out the circle, fold the sheet carefully into quarters and pin the edges to prevent them from slipping. Starting in the corner (Figure P), measure and mark the radius, allowing an extra inch for the hem. Using a pencil held taut at the end of a measured piece of string, draw the curve. Cut along this line through all four layers of sheeting. Finish by machine hemming (Figure G, page 1978).

For related crafts and projects, see "Fur Recycling," "Machine Stitchery," and "Recycling Clothes."

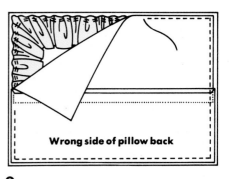

Wrong side of pillow back

O

Figure O: To match the right sides of the ruffle and pillow cover, sandwich the ruffle, face down, between the front and back sections of the sham, which are placed right sides facing. After the sham is sewn and turned right side out, the front of the ruffle will frame the front of the sham.

The pillow cover, made from remnants of the other projects described here, coordinates the printed and solid-color fabrics of the bedroom ensemble.

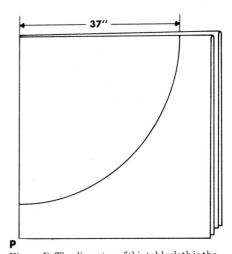

P

Figure P: The diameter of this tablecloth is the diameter of the table top plus twice the height of the table. Half this total is the radius. Fold the sheet in quarters, mark the radius, draw a quarter circle with a pencil compass, then cut all four layers along that line.

SHADOW THEATER

Puppets Made with Light

If you have ever cast shadows on a wall by putting your hands in front of a light, you already know something about an ancient and unique form of puppetry called shadow theater. The principle employed is a simple one. An object held between a light and a surface casts a shadow. If the shadow is cast onto a translucent screen, it can be seen from the other side (Figure A). If the object is opaque, it will cast a silhouette; if it is transparent or translucent, the shadow will be shaded or colored. In shadow theater, puppets held against the back of a screen are used to act out stories. The puppeteer, standing behind the light, is invisible to the audience, while the puppet, pressed against the screen, is clearly seen. To permit this distancing between puppet and performer, long rods are attached to the back of the puppet. Using these rods, the puppeteer can manipulate the puppet without going near the screen.

Traditional shadow puppets, such as the beautiful Chinese puppet pictured opposite, are fashioned from thin, translucent materials, intricately pierced, and delicately colored. Though they are two-dimensional, these shadow puppets are extremely flexible and in the hands of a skilled puppeteer, capable of many deft movements and lyrical gestures.

The Chinese Shadow Theater

Shadow theater is said to have originated in China in 121 B.C. when the Han emperor Wu-ti, overwhelmed with grief at the death of his favorite concubine, commanded the court magician to summon her back. The crafty magician produced Wu-ti's true love by casting her shadow on a screen, and the emperor's grief was lightened. (The ancient Greeks had a similar tale about the origin of silhouettes.)

There are some 300 traditional Chinese shadow-theater plays. They depict scenes from daily life or well-known historical and religious tales. Cycle stories—plays casting the same characters in different adventures—are frequently performed. The White Snake Lady, opposite, is one such character, and her adventures are depicted in several dramas. In one, *The Theft of the Miraculous Grass*, she must find the stolen grass to cure her lover's ailment. In another, *The Flooding of the Monastery of Golden Mountain*, she must oppose the gods in heaven who have taken her husband away. Music is important in all Chinese shadow theater, and traditional music accompanies each story. The plays are performed at night, and the entertainment sometimes lasts until morning.

Other Countries

Indian shadow puppets, which also date from ancient times, are similar to Chinese puppets but much larger—often 4 or 5 feet tall. (Chinese puppets rarely exceed 1 foot in height.) The tales Indian puppets tell are drawn from the great Sanskrit epics, the *Ramayana* and the *Mahabharata*. These colorful dramas in verse are fraught with heroes and heroines, villains, gods and demons. A shadow theater production in India, as in China, might continue all night; people of the audience (who know all the stories and every note of the music by heart) come and go as they please.

Shadow theater spread to Indonesia, Java, Greece, and Turkey. The hero of the Turkish dramas, Karaghioz, is a pugnacious ne'er-do-well, constantly in love and out of funds. He is repeatedly bailed out by his friend and straight man, Hachivat. The characters are so well known that their mere appearance on the screen excites applause.

Shadow puppets first became popular in Europe in eighteenth-century France. *Ombres chinoises* (Chinese shadows), as they were called, were smaller than the

Sandra Robbins is both a performer and a teacher. She founded The Shadow Box Theater in 1967 after discovering that puppets, particularly shadow puppets, draw children like a magnet. Led by Ms. Robbins, the company of half-a-dozen presents shadow plays frequently at the Riverside Church in New York City. All puppets used in the productions are designed and built by artists and members of the group. The music that accompanies the plays—a traditional part of shadow theater—is composed by Sandra Robbins.

Figure A: When a shape is held in front of a light and behind a translucent screen, its shadow is visible on the other side of the screen. This is the principle of shadow theater. Above, a puppeteer is manipulating a rabbit silhouette with a long rod. Because the puppeteer stands behind the light, only the rabbit's shadow is visible to the spectators.

The White Snake Lady, a major character in Chinese mythology, is an intricate example of a shadow puppet. Rods (the shadows are visible through the screen) are attached to her collar and to each of her hands. By manipulating the appropriate rod, the puppeteer can make the Snake Lady appear to run, sit, gesture, or perform almost any action sought.

Eastern puppets, only 6 inches high, and were intricately cut from opaque black paper or cardboard. Some had movable parts, others had none. All were manipulated by means of a tab at the bottom of the figure.

Shadow Theater Today

From time to time, shadow theater has been in danger of becoming a lost art, but presently it is having a revival. In the countries of its origin, particularly China and Turkey, the governments are protecting this traditional art form by supporting shadow theater companies. In Western countries, shadow theater is being created by professional puppeteers offering ingenuity rather than traditionalism.

Projects that follow will introduce you to the art of making shadow-theater puppets from cardboard, paper and glue, or plastic. Included are instructions for making scenery and several types of screens. The Craftnotes on pages 1994 and 1995 will tell you how to make pivots so the puppets can have moving parts, how to make rod assemblies for working the puppets from a distance, and how to make the puppets move the way you want them to. With these basics in hand, you may be surprised by the productions you can stage.

There is a great deal of room for creativity in shadow theater. The basic elements are simple: a screen, a light source, and a puppet; the result can appear almost like a bit of animated film. For the most part, a shadow theater and shadow puppets can be made from common household materials. With imagination, a story line, and perhaps some music, you can produce a shadow play for your own enjoyment and the entertainment of your friends.

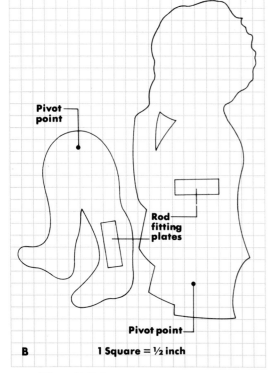

Pivot point

Rod fitting plates

Pivot point

B   1 Square = ½ inch

Figure B: Enlarge the two pattern pieces for the little-boy puppet by copying each square onto paper ruled into ½-inch squares. Cut out the pattern and trace it onto black cardboard. The location of the two horizontal rod fittings and of the pivot point are indicated above.

Performing Arts
Silhouette puppets $ ▯ 👫 ✈

Simple silhouette puppets can be as charming as those that are brightly colored or intricately made, as demonstrated by the little-boy puppet opposite (top). This puppet has but two parts, the legs and the torso. The legs, pivoted to the body and controlled by a separate rod assembly, can be manipulated so the body seems to stand or sit. To make the puppet, you will need: heavy black cardboard; scissors; two horizontal rod assemblies; a pivot assembly; and clear lacquer or varnish (optional).

Transfer the pattern for the little boy (Figure B) onto cardboard and cut it out. To make the puppet more durable, you can coat it with clear lacquer or varnish. Attach the legs to the body at the pivot point (Craftnotes, page 1995); be sure to attach the legs to the back of the body. After joining the sections, make two rod fittings (Craftnotes, page 1994), one to manipulate the head and torso, the other to manipulate the legs. Attach them to the puppet at the points indicated (Figure B). Because this is a heavy, stiff puppet, use horizontal rods, which are stronger than the flexible vertical rods.

Sandy Robbins manipulates the little boy and balloon puppets. She is standing behind the light that casts the shadows. To make sharp shadows, the puppets must be held against the screen.

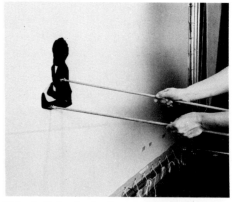

Using both hands, Sandy moves the little-boy puppet into a sitting position. How the puppets appear from the viewer's side of the screen is shown opposite.

This is how the little-boy and balloon puppets appear from the viewer's side of the screen. Though both of these puppets are easy to make, they can be manipulated quite effectively.

A jellyfish takes center stage while a fish striped in three colors swims to the right. It is easy to introduce color into shadow theater with the use of cellophane paper, special plastic crystals, and other media. The scenery, cut from tissue paper (left) and plain brown paper (right), is given color with felt-tipped pens.

CRAFTNOTES: THE SHADOW BOX

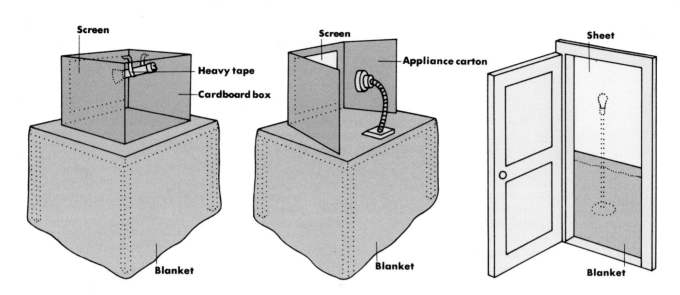

To create shadow plays, you need a shadow box. A shadow box is not necessarily an actual box, but it is the arrangement of two essential elements of shadow theater: a translucent screen and a strong, single light source. The latter is essential. A shadow will be cast by every light source present; more than one light produces multiple shadows, a situation to be avoided.

The sketches above illustrate three light-box arrangements. At left, opposite ends of a cardboard box have been removed, and a piece of white paper or sheeting has been stretched across one end and taped in place. A light inside the box (here, a powerful flashlight) provides illumination for the puppets, which are manipulated with long rods against the screen in front of the light. The audience views the shadow play from the opposite side of the screen. Alternatively, you can make a large, three-sided screen that is easy to store using an appliance carton (above, center). Cut the top, bottom, and one side of the carton, leaving three joined panels. Cut away part of the center panel for your screen, leaving enough cardboard at the top, sides, and bottom to maintain the strength of the structure. Stretch sheeting or paper over the opening. A very large carton, such as those used for refrigerators, would yield a walk-in shadow-box theater. The three-paneled shadow box gives the puppeteer a little more room and lets him work closer to the screen. The light source illustrated is a goose-neck desk lamp with a 60-watt bulb. A sheet taped across a doorway (above, right) also makes an excellent screen. It gives the puppeteer almost unrestricted room for manipulation, and the light can come from any floor or table lamp.

When you decide to make a more permanent shadow box, consider using a frame on a stand. Canvas stretchers or a picture frame could be used to hold and stretch the translucent screen material.

Placement of the light

The source of light and its placement are determined by the size and position of the screen. If the light is too near the screen, a hot spot—a very bright, almost glaring section of the screen that is hard on the viewer's eyes—will be created on the viewing side. But if the light is too far away, it will not produce dark, sharp shadows. Experiment with the placement of the light—it can be directed toward the bottom, top, or center of the screen—until you produce a clear, distinct shadow with your puppet. You will be manipulating the puppets from behind the light; so place it where your movements will not be restricted. The puppeteer always operates from behind or beside the light; anything in front of the light source, including any part of the puppeteer, will cast a shadow on the screen.

Light sources and mounts

In ancient times, a puppeteer hung a lantern over his head to light his shadow play. Today, there are more convenient and effective lighting devices. A small shadow box can be lighted with a standard two-cell flashlight, taped to the top with masking tape, or with a 60-watt bulb in a small gooseneck lamp. Frosted bulbs are recommended because they yield a softer, more diffused light than clear bulbs. For larger screens, you may need bulbs of higher wattage, but be sure that any bulb larger than 100 watts is mounted in a fixture so

designed that it will not overheat. Some floor and table lamps are rated for bulbs up to 300 watts. Such bulbs should be kept outside the back of the shadow box to eliminate any danger of setting it on fire. An inexpensive substitute is a clamp-on reflector of the type used by photographers. These are especially convenient, since they can be hung or mounted anywhere and are easily angled. They can be purchased at camera stores. Reflectors also keep the light efficiently directed toward the screen, while keeping the glare out of the puppeteer's eyes. They can be used with powerful photoflood bulbs (up to 500 watts) which are relatively inexpensive but short-lived. Also short-lived, but very effective for a shadow theater production, is the fan-cooled bulb in a slide-film projector. This will produce a very sharp shadow unless a light-diffusing slide is inserted in the projector. To make such a slide, mount a piece of frosted acetate in a glass slide frame.

Hiding the puppeteer

The illusions created by moving shadows are worth your audience's full attention, so you will want to hide your movements completely. Hang opaque fabric, such as a blanket, anywhere that part of your anatomy might be seen by the audience. If you are using a cardboard shadow box on a card table, for example, drape the table to hide your feet and legs. If you are using a sheet in a doorway as a screen, hang a blanket across the bottom portion to limit the size of your screen. If you want your shadow box to resemble a theater, you can put gathered cloth at the sides of the screen, or even hang a small curtain that can be opened and closed across the front.

Performing Arts
Silhouette with color inserts $ ☒ 👫 ✈

To add color inserts to a silhouette puppet, first cut the shape from black cardboard; then remove sections of the body and replace them with colored cellophane. To make the striped fish shown on page 1989 (bottom right), you will need: cardboard; scissors; cellophane in one or more colors (available at hardware, variety, and art-supply stores); masking tape; a rod assembly (Craftnotes, page 1994); and clear lacquer or varnish (optional).

Enlarge the pattern (Figure C) and transfer it to the cardboard. Cut it out; then recut the holes as indicated (photograph 1). Cut pieces of cellophane slightly larger than the holes in the body, and tape them over the holes (photograph 2). To strengthen the puppet, you can cut a duplicate and glue it on top of the first, so the cellophane is sandwiched between the two. To further strengthen the puppet, cover the cardboard with clear lacquer or varnish. Attach the rod to the puppet (Figure C and Craftnotes, page 1994). Either a rigid horizontal rod or a flexible vertical rod can be used, depending on how you want the fish to move, but the pattern is marked for the attachment of a rigid horizontal rod.

1: After enlarging the fish pattern below, cut it out and trace it onto black cardboard. Cut out the cardboard pattern and the three holes, using scissors or a craft knife.

2: Tape pieces of colorful cellophane over the three holes in the fish. To make this shadow puppet stronger, you can cut out a second identical fish and glue it on top of the cellophane.

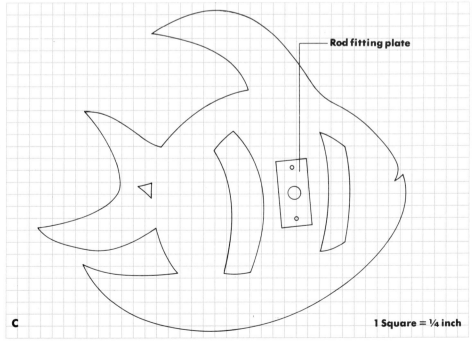

Rod fitting plate

C

1 Square = ¼ inch

Figure C: To enlarge the fish pattern, copy it a square at a time onto paper ruled in ¼-inch squares. The location of the rod fitting is indicated near the center of the pattern.

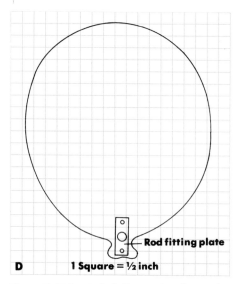

Figure D: Enlarge the balloon pattern by copying it, square by square, onto paper that you have ruled in ½-inch squares. The position of the rod fitting is marked on the pattern.

D **1 Square = ½ inch**

← **Rod fitting plate**

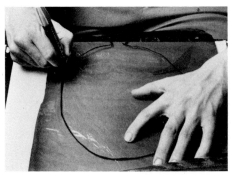

3: Place colored cellophane over the enlarged pattern and trace it, using a felt pen. Then cut out the cellophane balloon.

4: With a few drops of rubber cement, anchor the cellophane balloon to a clear piece of rigid vinyl; then cover the balloon with flexible, transparent, self-adhesive plastic. When you cut through both layers of clear plastic, leave a ½-inch border around the cellophane to hold it in place.

Plastic puppets

$ ▨ 👥 ✈

Shadow puppets made of stiff plastic are durable and allow much color variation. The red balloon shown on page 1989 is very simple, but the method used to make it can be used to create more complex puppets, such as the lady, opposite. The balloon is cut from a transparent piece of rigid vinyl plastic, 20- to 30-mil weight—thin enough to cut with scissors. It is manipulated with a rigid horizontal rod at its base (Craftnotes, page 1994). You also need colored cellophane, transparent self-adhesive plastic, and rubber cement. The rigid vinyl is available at variety, hardware, and specialty stores that stock plastics; the other materials can be found at variety, hardware, and department stores.

Enlarge the balloon pattern (Figure D) and trace it on a sheet of colored cellophane (photograph 3). Cut out the cellophane and lay it on the rigid clear vinyl, securing it with a few dabs of rubber cement to hold the cellophane flat as you work. Cover the cellophane balloon with a piece of clear self-adhesive plastic, cut at least 1 inch larger all around than the balloon (photograph 4). Work slowly and carefully to avoid wrinkling the cellophane. Peel the paper backing from the plastic gradually; do not remove it all at once. When you have covered the cellophane with the transparent plastic, cut around the cellophane balloon, leaving at least a ½-inch border all around the balloon and allowing slightly more room at the bottom for the rod fastener. When cutting through the clear plastic above and below the cellophane, cut near the back of the scissors with short strokes; if you cut near the tips, the plastic may crack. Attach the rod assembly (Craftnotes, page 1994) at the point indicated on the pattern.

Jellyfish

$ ▨ 👥 ✈

The multicolored jellyfish shown in the center of the aquatic scene on page 1989 was made from plastic crystals that fuse when baked in an oven. The crystals are available in most craft stores in many colors.

To use the crystals, line a pan with aluminum foil. The crystals spread slightly as they bake; shape the foil into a mold if you want the edges of your puppet to be well defined. Pour the crystals onto the foil, and if you are not using a mold, shape them with your fingers (photograph 5). If you mix several colors, as I did, they will blend as the crystals are baked. Follow package directions for baking the crystals.

Let the jellyfish cool; then attach its tentacles with clear plastic tape. These are made from ribbons dipped in clear lacquer, then encased with two sheets of plastic wrap (photograph 6). Attach a rigid horizontal rod to the top of the jellyfish as described in Craftnotes, page 1994, except make the bolt holes with a heated nail, awl, or ice pick. (Without heat, the tool may crack the fused shape.)

5: To make a colored jellyfish, spread plastic crystals on a piece of aluminum foil on a pan, shaping them with your fingers. Use whatever colors you wish; they will fuse together when they are baked in an oven.

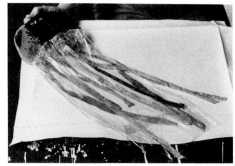

6: The jellyfish's tentacles are made from ribbon dipped in lacquer, then wrapped in two sheets of plastic wrap. A rod fastener is connected to the top. Holes can be poked through the fused plastic quite easily with a heated nail, awl, or ice pick.

The old lady who swallowed a fly (and a lot of other creatures) is both puppet and scenery for a shadow theater production. Her figure is attached to the back of the screen with masking tape. The various things she swallows are puppets manipulated from behind.

A cardboard silhouette can be encased in self-adhesive plastic for durability, instead of being lacquered or shellacked.

Yarns, tissue paper, and ribbon can be encased in the same kind of plastic to add color and texture to the scene. Rigid plastic can be cut to shape, then colored with a felt-tipped pen. Translucent press-on color sheets, which are self-adhesive, can also be used to give color to puppets.

In making scenery, plain brown paper is translucent when held up in front of a light. It can be colored with felt-tipped markers or watercolors.

Colored tissue paper is also translucent when used in scenery.

Performing Arts
A shadow play

$ ▨ 🕴 ⏋

One nice quality of shadow theater is that it invites innovation. For example, in one production of The Shadow Box Theater—based entirely on the folk song, "There Was an Old Lady Who Swallowed a Fly"—the old lady is both puppet and scenery. Her outline and features were drawn on a sheet of 3-mil flexible vinyl (shower-curtain weight) with a felt-tipped marker. Such a vinyl is available at specialty, department, or hardware stores. Other materials, such as yarn for her hair and colored paper for her clothes, were placed on the vinyl and held there with an overlay of transparent self-adhesive plastic. The lady's big skirt was left clear, and she was taped against the screen like a piece of scenery.

As the song goes, the old lady swallowed a fly. Next, she swallows a spider—to catch the fly. With each verse, the lady swallows increasingly larger creatures—bird, cat, dog, and cow—all in an attempt to catch the one previously swallowed. In The Shadow Box Theater production, each creature is a puppet worked behind the lady. One by one they are swallowed and appear inside her wide, transparent body, as pictured above.

All of the puppets used in this production are plastic puppets. The fly and the spider were drawn with a felt marker on small pieces of rigid vinyl and then cut out. The bird was made of tissue paper, colored with a felt marker and overlaid with clear plastic in the same way. To make these and similar puppets, use the technique outlined for making the balloon (opposite).

Songs that tell a story provide an excellent basis for shadow plays, especially since music has traditionally been so much a part of shadow theater performances. If you can't sing or play an instrument, use a recording to accompany your play.

There are two types of rods used to manipulate shadow puppets: flexible vertical rods and rigid horizontal rods. The flexible vertical rods work better with light-weight, multijointed puppets or puppets that respond well to a springy, flowing, loose kind of motion. Because these rods are loosely attached, small movements on the part of the puppeteer produce considerable motion in the puppet. These flexibly attached rods, though usually vertical, may assume any position from vertical to horizontal so that the puppets can be moved around the screen with little change in the puppeteer's position. With the flexible rod in a vertical position, the puppet can change direction briefly (with the rod against the screen) if the action of the story demands it.

Rigid horizontal rods are stronger than flexible vertical rods and are better for heavy puppets. The rods are not flexible at the point they are attached to the puppet, hence must remain always in a horizontal position. While a certain bounce and range of movement is lost (the puppeteer must raise and lower his entire arm to move the puppet up and down), quick and decisive action is gained. This more definite movement works well with one-piece puppets and uncomplicated jointed puppets. These puppets cannot change direction, but they can be moved in complete circles or turn somersaults.

Rigid horizontal rods
The rigid horizontal rod is made from a ⅜-inch dowel, joined to half of a curtain-rod fitting (above). The other half of the fitting is bolted to the puppet; then the capped dowel is screwed onto it.

The curtain-rod fitting is available at hardware stores. It comes with wood screws which must be replaced by two bolt, nut, and washer assemblies of the same size. You will also need one tiny wood screw to hold the dowel in its cap.

Tools needed are: a screwdriver; pliers; saw (to cut the dowel rod); drill; masking tape; and scissors. You may also need a small piece of rigid plastic to shield plastic puppets from marring.

Bolting the plate to the puppet
Place the curtain-rod fitting plate against the puppet where you wish to attach the rod.

Mark the two screw holes on the puppet with the point of the scissors (above).

Then punch the holes with the scissors (above), working first from the front and then from the back until the holes are large enough to accommodate the bolts.

Bolt the fitting plate to the back of the puppet (above), using washers on the front and passing the bolt through from front to back, so the bolt head is on the front of the puppet.

Use a screwdriver to tighten the bolt, holding the nut steady with a pair of pliers (above).

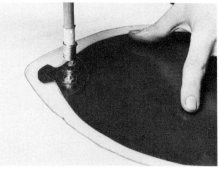

When you use this method with plastic puppets, you can keep the nuts from scratching the plastic by placing a plastic shield under them (above).

Attaching the rod
Cut a piece of ⅜-inch dowel long enough to let you stand comfortably behind the light source while you manipulate the puppet. If the part of the curtain-rod fitting that caps the end of the dowel is too large, wrap the dowel with masking tape to tighten the fit (above). Screw the dowel into the fitting; then drill a tiny hole through the base of the fitting. Insert the wood screw and turn into the dowel. As a set screw, this keeps the dowel from coming loose. The rod may be used with any puppet that has a fitting plate.

SHADOW PUPPETS

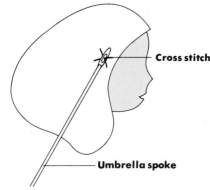

Cross stitch

Umbrella spoke

Flexible rods

The second type of rod used is the flexible rod, jointed at the point where it is attached to the puppet. Cast-off umbrella spokes have holes at either end and can be sewn to the puppet (above). If a single spoke is not long enough, use masking tape to join two spokes together.

To sew an umbrella spoke to a puppet, make four evenly spaced holes through the puppet, with a needle or scissors, at the point of attachment. Using a single cross-stitch, sew the rod in place with buttonhole or nylon thread. When manipulating, hold the rod horizontal and pivot. This puts pressure on the cross stitches and moves the head up and down. When packing, hold the rod down, flat against the body.

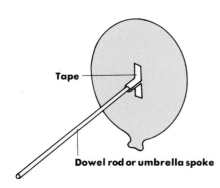

Tape

Dowel rod or umbrella spoke

Tape hinges

There are two quick and easy (though not very durable) methods of attaching rods. In the first (above), masking tape is used to fashion a flexible hinge to attach a dowel or an umbrella spoke.

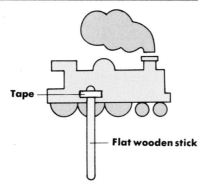

Tape

Flat wooden stick

In the second (above), a flat wooden stick is simply glued or taped flat onto the puppet; this makes it necessary to manipulate the puppet from below the screen.

Joining multisectioned puppets

Shadow puppets are often designed with movable parts. Depending upon what the puppet is made of, the sections may be joined with either a bolt or a tie pivot.

Knotted thread or cord can be used to join parts of lightweight cardboard or reinforced paper puppets. But nut-and-bolt joints should be used with puppets made of heavy cardboard or plastic.

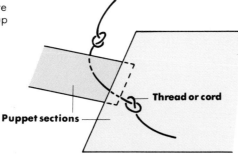

Thread or cord

Puppet sections

To make a string pivot (above), determine where the sections should be attached and pierce both pieces with a needle or scissors. Thread a short length of thread, or cord, or fishing line through the two pieces. Fasten them together by knotting the ends of the line, but not so tightly that the pieces cannot pivot freely. Secure the knots with glue.

To make nut-and-bolt joints, which are stronger and hence suitable for puppets made of rigid plastic or heavy cardboard, you will need: one bolt; two nuts; three metal washers; and a lock washer for each pivot. Determine where the joint should be made; then pierce through the sections to be joined with scissors, an awl or ice pick, or a drill. Lift the puppet from the table and gently enlarge the hole, working slowly and from both sides to prevent tearing or cracking the puppet.

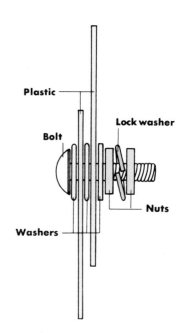

Plastic

Bolt

Lock washer

Nuts

Washers

Assemble the joint (above) by slipping the puppet sections and the hardware over the shank of the bolt in the following sequence: washer, front puppet piece, washer, second puppet piece, washer, first nut, lock washer, second nut. Holding the first nut in position, tighten the second nut against the lock washer and first nut.

The function of the lock washer is to let you tighten one nut against another but not against the puppet pieces that must move freely. The inside nut may be positioned to allow as much space as you want between the puppet pieces.

Arranging the pieces of the puppet

The head of a puppet is always held against the screen. The torso, therefore, should be joined to the back of the head. All pieces subsequently added should also be joined to the back of the previous piece. A hand, for example, is joined to the back of the forearm, which is joined to the back of the upper arm, which, in turn, is joined to the back of the torso. The hand and arm can then be moved by a rod attached loosely to the hand.

*Penny Jones has worked in the field of pup-
petry as an artist, performer, and teacher.
She is director of the Penny Jones and
Company Puppet Troupe, specializing in
puppetry for younger children. Ms. Jones
became involved in shadow theater when the
American Museum of Natural History in
New York asked her to demonstrate puppet
manipulation during an exhibition of
oriental shadow puppets. As part of the exhibition, Ms. Jones duplicated several authentic Chinese puppets, and in the process
developed a paper-and-glue technique for
puppet construction.*

Performing Arts
Paper shadow puppets $ ◼ 🏃 🐭

Though constructed with jointed arms and free-swinging legs, like complicated
Chinese shadow puppets, the puppets depicting a little girl and a witch (below) are
easily made from readily available materials. All the parts are made from bond
paper (not construction paper), coated on both sides with white fabric glue that becomes invisible when it dries. For each puppet you will need: bond paper; felt-
tipped markers; two umbrella-spoke rods (Craftnotes, page 1994); and several
pivot joints (Craftnotes, page 1995). In addition, you will need: a sewing needle and
thread; manicure scissors; regular scissors; and a small paintbrush. The instructions that follow are for making the little-girl puppet. By modifying the pattern slightly, you can also use them to make the witch.

Trace the pattern (Figure E) onto white paper. Hold the paper against a window,
place a sheet of bond paper over it, and trace the pattern onto the bond. Use pink
paper to make the head, two hair pieces, arm, and hand pieces. Use blue paper for
the dress and white for the legs. Stir a mixture of white fabric glue and water that is
just thick enough to flow smoothly from a brush. The mixture is used throughout
the project; any leftover can be saved in a covered jar for later projects. Before cutting out the tracings, paint one side of each with the glue-and-water mixture and let
it dry. A pan placed on top of a radiator makes a good drying rack. Paint the reverse
sides of the tracings, and let dry; then cut out the shapes. Use manicure scissors to
cut the tiny comma-shaped openings for the eyes. Glue the two hair pieces on either
side of the head, making a triple layer. When the glue has dried, use a needle to
poke small holes in the pattern pieces at all pivot points, and where the rods will be

In *Eartha the Good Witch*—a shadow play with an ecological theme, a little girl watches as Eartha
grows a tissue-paper tree. (The puppeteer, of course, slowly slides the tree up into the visible portion of
the screen.) The tree is made from rectangles of blue and green tissue paper glued to a stick.

attached to the head and the hand (Figure E). Join all pieces with a needle and thread, using the tie-pivot method, and sew the umbrella-spoke rods to the head and the hand (Figure E and Craftnotes, page 1994). Sew the rod loosely to the hand for maximum flexibility.

When making paper puppets, design all major sections so that they widen at the bottom (here, the skirt and leg pieces). This gives these puppet parts enough weight for good balance. When such construction is not possible, you can weight the lower pieces with additional layers of glue or by adding decorative trim on the bottom edges. Where the main rod joins the puppet (the head in the case of the little girl), the paper must be several layers thick for added rigidity. In other places, a single layer of paper is sufficient. When you plan colors, remember that layering the paper affects color. The little girl's hair, made with three layers of pink paper, becomes auburn on the screen, whereas her face and arms, single layers of pink paper, remain pink. You can hold sheets of paper up to the light to gauge the strength of a color. It is not essential that you use colored bond paper to achieve these color effects. White typing paper of good quality can be used. Coat and layer the pieces with glue and water as described above; then color the finished puppet with felt-tipped ink markers.

For related entries, see "Music Making," "Puppets and Marionettes," and "Stagecraft."

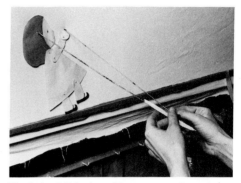

The little girl's body and legs move as the main umbrella-spoke rod, attached to the head, is manipulated. The arm is moved by a second umbrella spoke, joined loosely to her hand.

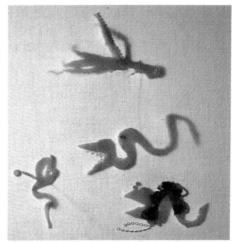

These squiggly germs from *Eartha the Good Witch* were cut from foam rubber and decorated with bits of dressmaker's trim (sequins, buttons, and fringe). They are manipulated with umbrella-spoke rods. Use your imagination when you make shadow puppets. Cotton makes an effective cloud when glued on cardboard and teardrop earrings could be raindrops.

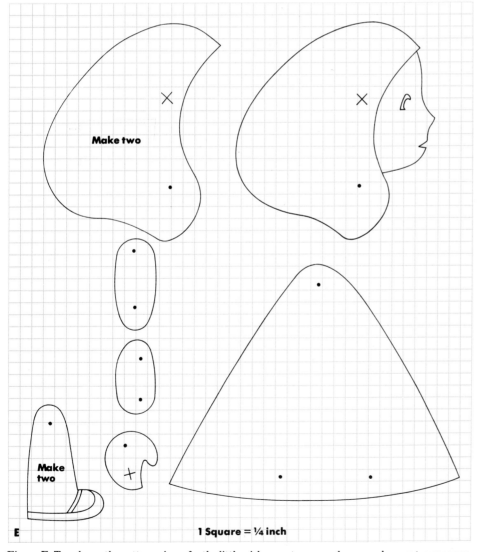

Make two

Make two

E

1 Square = ¼ inch

Figure E: To enlarge the pattern pieces for the little-girl puppet, copy each square above onto paper you have ruled in ¼-inch squares. Make two hair pieces (top, left). Also cut two leg pieces. The Xs indicate where the control rods are to be attached; the dots mark pivot points.

SHAKER FURNITURE
Hands to Work, Hearts to God

The beauty and simplicity of Shaker furniture are tangible manifestations of a religious philosophy that spanned more than two centuries. During the summer of 1774, a small band of Quakers fled England, seeking religious freedom in America. They were then known as the United Society of Believers in Christ's Second Appearing. Later they became known as the Shaking Quakers, or simply the Shakers, because ritual dancing was a part of their worship.

The Shakers grew in numbers (to more than 6,000 in 1850) and in communities (18 in New England, Ohio, and Kentucky). As they grew, their faith gave them a life-style that made their convictions a part of everyday existence. The Shakers believed that everything one did was a religious expression, a belief most apparent today in their designs of buildings and furniture.

Functionalism was a guiding principle for the Shaker craftsman. To make something that was needed, that would fulfill the purpose intended, and that would last was considered a worthy expression of one's love of God. To this end, the Believers used the best materials available, avoided worldly decorations, and pared each design to the simplest possible form.

It must be noted, however, that the sparsest designs are often the most difficult to do well. In woodworking, pieces that look very simple usually call for the highest level of skill, because you don't have surface decoration to conceal ill-fitting joints. That is not to suggest that only an expert should attempt the projects that follow—only that a novice should not be surprised or discouraged if he is unable to approach the perfection of the furniture pictured. If your skills are still in the formative stage, you may well find that the doweled joints of the table base will not fit exactly because the drilled holes are slightly askew, or that you need to resort to wood plastic to close gaps between the edge-glued boards of the table top (page 2003) or the hand-cut dovetailed joints of the candle box (page 2009). If you do use a filler, test to be sure you can hide it with the finish you have selected.

Opposite, top: Eldresses Gertrude Soule (left), and Bertha Lindsay (right) are two of the remaining Shakers at the Canterbury, New Hampshire, village. The meeting house in the background, where religious services were held, had separate entrances for the Brothers and the Sisters. *Above and opposite, bottom:* Interior views of the village buildings show how sparsely furnished and uncluttered the rooms were; yet the overall feeling is one of warmth, not austerity.

Douglas Noren, president of the Guild of Shaker Crafts in Spring Lake, Michigan, supervises the work of a small but dedicated group of craftsmen that makes replicas of Shaker furniture and accessories. As training, he spent a five-year apprenticeship as a wood and metal patternmaker. Doug's wife, Gwen, is also involved in Guild work, especially the publication of a quarterly newsletter, The World of Shaker.

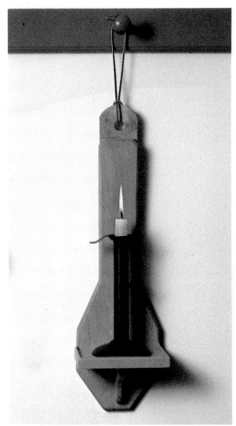

Candle sconces such as this one hung from wooden pegs in Shaker rooms. The wood parts pictured are stained with a color known as meetinghouse blue; the hanging plate is tin.

Materials needed for one candle sconce

Clear white pine, ½ inch thick, sufficient to cut:
one 6-by-18-inch piece (back),
one 4⅛-by-5⅝-inch piece (shelf),
and one 3-inch-square piece (brace)

Pine facing strip, 3/16 by ¾ by 18 inches

Sheet tin, at least 1/64 inch thick, sufficient to cut:
one piece 2½ by 6½ inches
(hanging plate)

Five ¼-inch No. 8 round-headed wood screws

Finishing nails, 4-penny and 8-penny

Woodworker's resin glue

Wood plastic

Wood-toned or colored oil stain

Semigloss lacquer or satin-finish polyurethane varnish

Simply having the right tools has much to do with woodworking success. Chisels you know how to keep razor sharp, a fine-toothed saw with a reinforced back, the right clamps, a solid workbench with a wood vise—all will help you work more skillfully. The directions that follow call only for hand tools. If you have power tools, by all means use them. But even if you have power tools, you will need a great deal of skill, as well as care and patience, to make Shaker furniture as warm and clever and pleasing to the eye as the originals.

Furniture and Finishes
Candle sconce

Candle sconces of the type pictured at left were used in the meeting house of the Shaker village in New Lebanon, New York, around the beginning of the nineteenth century. The tin hanging plate at the top makes the sconce unusual. The sconce has a back, a shelf, and a brace of ½-inch-thick clear white pine, the tin plate, and wood facing strips around the shelf's edge (see the list of materials needed, below left).

With a pencil, draw the back on a 6-by-18-by-½-inch piece of pine, following the lengthwise grain of the wood. Dimensions are given in Figure A. Cut out the back with a handsaw (photograph 1). Plane the edges to smooth them and to bevel the front angles slightly (photograph 2). (Bevel the front of all edges before assembly except those of the shelf that will be faced.) The inner angles at the neck of the back are hard to reach with a plane, but you can round them with a pocketknife (photograph 3) or coarse sandpaper.

The shelf is a rectangle, 4⅛ by 5⅝ inches. Cut it with a handsaw, and position it against the back so its bottom is 3⅝ inches above the bottom edge of the back (Figure A). Square it and draw lines on the back edges at the top of the shelf (photograph 4). Put woodworker's resin glue sparingly on the back edge of the shelf. Position the back against it, and drive three 8-penny finishing nails through the back into the shelf (photograph 5). Hold the two pieces together with C-clamps until the glue sets. Then countersink the nails, and fill the holes with wood plastic.

Smooth the edge joints between shelf and back (and any other rough spots) with coarse sandpaper wrapped around a wood block (photograph 6). Then finish by sanding edges and bevels with fine sandpaper wrapped around a padded wood block or a blackboard eraser (photograph 7). Use a light touch, and sand face surfaces only with the grain to avoid scratches.

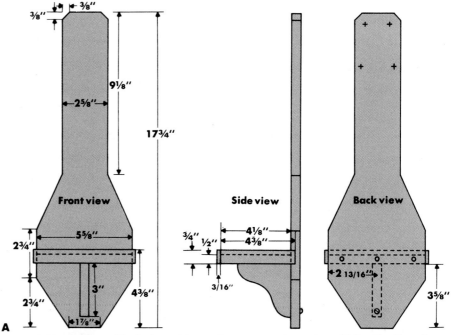

Figure A: Front, side, and back views of the candle sconce are shown above. Follow the dimensions given as you cut out the back, shelf, and facing strips. A pattern for the shelf brace is given in Figure B, page 2002.

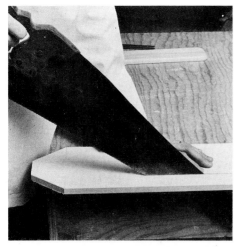

1: Use a handsaw to cut out the back piece of the sconce. The grain of the wood, which is clear pine, should run the length of the piece.

2: Use a block plane to bevel the front edges of the back piece and to smooth them to the exact dimensions in Figure A.

3: Inner corners, where the plane cannot reach, can be beveled with a pocketknife. Make several short, shallow cuts rather than one deep one.

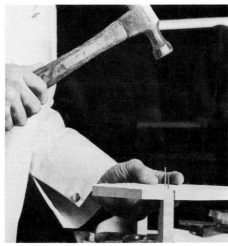

4: Position the shelf on the back, square it, and mark the position of its top surface on the edges of the back.

5: Join the back and shelf with woodworker's resin glue, reinforced with three finishing nails spaced evenly across the back.

6: Use what is called a hard block—coarse sandpaper wrapped around a block of wood—to smooth the shelf joints and any rough spots.

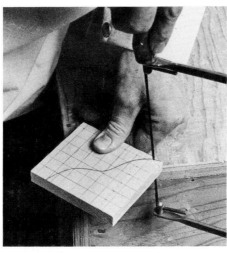

7: Then use a soft block—fine sandpaper wrapped around a padded block of wood or a blackboard eraser—to smooth curved or beveled edges and other surfaces.

8: Enlarge the pattern for the brace (Figure B, page 2002) on a grid drawn on a square of wood. Cut out the brace with a coping saw; then sand off the pencil marks.

9: Center the brace below the shelf and glue it in place. Keep the glue off any exposed wood; it would prevent the finishing stain from penetrating the wood.

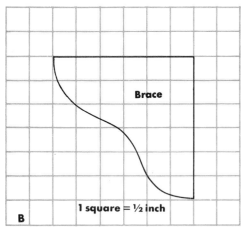

Brace

1 square = ½ inch

B

Figure B: To enlarge the pattern for the brace, draw a grid of ½-inch squares on a piece of wood; then copy the pattern square by square. Remove the grid marks with fine sandpaper after the shape is cut.

To make the brace, enlarge the pattern in Figure B on a piece of wood; cut out the brace with a coping saw (photograph 8, page 2001). Bevel both sides of the edge that will face forward, and sand off the penciled grid marks. Center the brace, with the wood grain running vertically, on the back below the shelf (photograph 9, page 2001, and Figure A, page 2000). Mark its position lightly with a pencil, put wood-worker's resin glue sparingly on the flat edges, and position the bracket. Clamp with a C-clamp until glue sets. Avoid smearing glue on exposed surfaces; it would keep stain from penetrating the wood.

Next, cut three facing strips—two pieces 4⅜ inches long and one piece 6 inches long. Bevel the top lengthwise edges of the strips with a hand plane (photograph 10). Using glue and 4-penny finishing nails, attach the side strips to the shelf so their bottom and front edges line up with the bottom and front edges of the shelf. The back edges will extend ¼ inch onto the back piece (photograph 11 and Figure A). Countersink the nails and fill the holes with wood plastic. Sand the edges smooth, being careful not to distort the beveled edges. That completes the assembly of the wooden part of the sconce.

Finish the wood with a wood-toned or colored oil stain (photograph 12). Shaker stains are available from The Guild of Shaker Crafts, 401 West Savidge, Spring Lake, Michigan 49456, and Shaker Workshops, Inc., 42 Bradford Street, Concord,

10: With a hand plane, bevel one edge of each of the three facing strips. That edge will be on top when the strip is attached to the shelf.

11: Use finishing nails to attach the strips to the shelf; countersink the nails. The side strips extend ¼ inch onto the back piece.

12: When the wooden parts of the sconce are assembled, use a soft cloth to rub on a finishing stain in a wood tone or color.

13: Enlarge the pattern for the hanging plate (Figure C) and scribe the outline on the tin. Cut out the shape with tin snips and sand the edges.

14: Clamp the tin between pieces of scrap wood to keep it from slipping while you drill the five holes. Start the holes with a nail.

15: Attach the tin plate to the back with four round-headed wood screws. Another screw, near the bottom of the sconce, lets it hang evenly.

Massachusetts 01742. You can mix your own colored stain by thinning an oil-based paint with paint thinner. (Use more paint than thinner; a 50-50 mixture is too thin.) Rub the stain on with a soft cloth and let it dry overnight. Complete the finish with two coats of a semigloss sealer such as clear lacquer or polyurethane varnish.

Enlarge the pattern for the hanging plate (Figure C), and scribe it on 1/64-inch-thick tin. Mark the positions of screw and hanging holes. Cut out the plate with tin snips and sand the edges (photograph 13). Clamp the plate between two pieces of scrap wood to keep it from slipping as you drill the holes (photograph 14). Start the holes with a nail, then drill, using a 3/16-inch bit for the four screw holes and a larger bit for the hanging hole.

Attach the tin plate to the back piece with ¼-inch No. 8 round-headed wood screws (photograph 15). A single screw, the same size as those holding the plate, should be screwed through the back into the bottom of the brace so the sconce will hang vertically (Figure A).

Hang the sconce with a leather thong from a wooden peg, Shaker style, or from a metal hook. Buy a simple black candleholder to set on the shelf. If the sconce is hung from a peg, make sure holder and candle are short enough to avoid scorching the peg when the candle is lit.

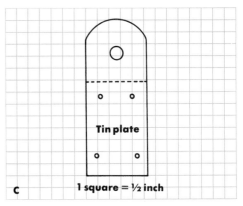

C   1 square = ½ inch

Figure C: To enlarge the pattern for the hanging plate, draw a grid of ½-inch squares on stiff paper; then copy the pattern square by square. Cut out this pattern and scribe its outline on a sheet of tin with a nail or awl. Mark the positions of the screw holes and the larger hanging hole.

This side table is a generous size—23 inches wide, 30¾ inches long, and 28 inches high. It would be useful in a bedroom, dining room, or entrance hall.

Furniture and Finishes
Sisters' side table

💲 ⏱ 🧍 🛩

The original of the Shaker table pictured above was found in the Upper Canaan family branch of the New Lebanon, New York, Shaker community. It is made entirely of clear white pine. The extended top has breadboard ends to conceal the end grain, and the slender legs are gently tapered on the two inner faces (Figure D, page 2004).

To shape a leg, start with a 27¼-inch length of 1½-inch-square pine. Taper it from 1⅜ inches, starting at a point 4¾ inches below the top of the leg, to ¾ inch at the bottom. The top of the leg is left square so it fits snugly against the skirts. Taper only the two inside faces of each leg; the outer faces remain straight. If you cut the taper with a hand plane, mark the finished shape of the leg on the wood with a pencil

Materials needed for one side table

Clear white pine, four pieces, 1½ by 1½ by 27¼ inches (legs)

Clear white pine, ¾ inch thick, sufficient to cut:
two 4¾-by-24-inch pieces (side skirts),
two 4¾-by-14⅞-inch pieces (end skirts),
and two 1⅜-by-23-inch pieces (breadboard ends of top)

Clear white pine, ¾ inch thick and 28 inches long, of any widths to total 23 inches (table top)

Pine strips, ¾ by 1 inch, and 6½ feet long (screw cleats)

Eight pine blocks: four ½ by 1 by 4¾ inches, and four ⅝ inch by 1½ by 4¾ inches (glue blocks)

Eight ⅜-inch wooden dowels, 1⅞ inches long

Metal dowel centers

Ten 1¼-inch No. 8 round-headed wood screws

Twenty 2½-inch flat-headed nails

Woodworker's resin glue

Wood-toned or colored oil stain

Semigloss lacquer or satin-finish polyurethane varnish

A close-up view of the table top shows how nails can be used to visibly join it to the base. If you prefer, an invisible joint can be made by screwing the base to the top from beneath.

as a guide. Plane from the wide end to the narrow end (photograph 16). (If you have a table saw and know how to use a tapering jig, you can cut four identical tapered legs in short order.) Plane the uncut inner edges enough to smooth them; then sand all the surfaces with fine sandpaper.

Next, cut one end skirt from ¾-inch-thick pine, following the dimensions in Figure D. Into the edge of one end, drill two holes, 1 inch deep and at right angles to the surface, for the connecting dowels. The center of the top hole should be 1 inch below the top edge; the center of the bottom hole should be ¾ inch above the bottom edge, as indicated in the end view in Figure D. Start drilling the holes with a ⅛-inch bit, since a small bit is easy to guide and center; then switch to a ⅜-inch bit. Wrap a piece of masking tape around the bit as a depth guide. Put ⅜-inch metal dowel centers into the holes and, on a flat surface, butt the skirt against one inner plane of a leg so the top edges are even. The points of the plugs will mark the centers of the holes to be drilled in the leg (photograph 17). Drill the holes in the leg, also 1 inch deep. Join the skirt to the leg with ⅜-inch dowels, 1⅞ inches long, and woodworker's resin glue (photograph 18). Dowels should fit snugly; they can be sanded lightly if they do not slip in easily. Repeat for the other leg. Clamp the skirt and two legs together with bar clamps until the glue dries. Use cushioning blocks to avoid marring the legs (photograph 19). Cut the other end skirt and join it to the other two legs in the same manner.

Cut two side skirts from ¾-inch-thick pine, following the dimensions in Figure D. Drill dowel holes in the side skirts, staggering these holes ½ inch higher than the holes in the end skirts, as shown in the side view in Figure D. With dowels, join the side skirts to the legs (already attached to the end skirts) and glue as before, using the dowel centers for marking and turning the assembled sections as necessary. Square the joints and clamp the assembled base until the glue dries.

The table top will be attached to ¾-by-1-inch wood cleats that rim the insides of the skirt tops rather than directly to the skirts (see underside-of-top-view, Figure D). These screw cleats are shorter than the skirts. The spaces between them and the table legs are filled with glue blocks, two in each corner, which reinforce the skirt-to-leg joints (photograph 20). These small blocks are as deep as the skirts; glue them in place before attaching the screw cleats. No. 8 flat-headed wood screws, 1¼ inches long, are used to attach the screw cleats to the skirts (photograph 20). Three countersunk screws on each long side and two on each short end will be sufficient. Drill starter holes for these screws, being careful not to penetrate the skirts with the drill. At the same time, drill vertical holes through the screw cleats for the screws that will attach the table top to the base (photograph 20). Sand the entire base with fine sandpaper before attaching the top.

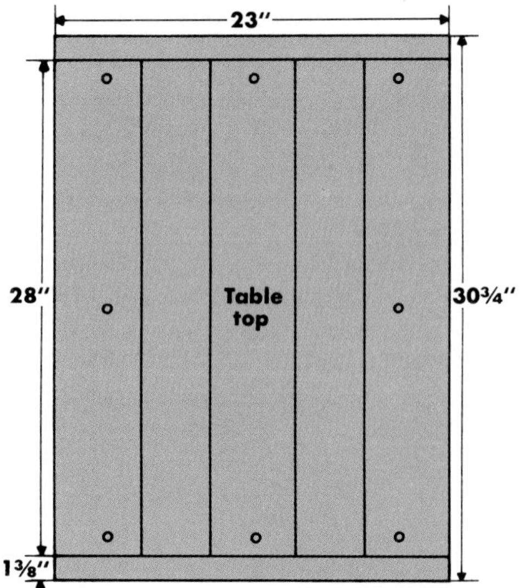
23"
28"
Table top
30¾"
1⅜"

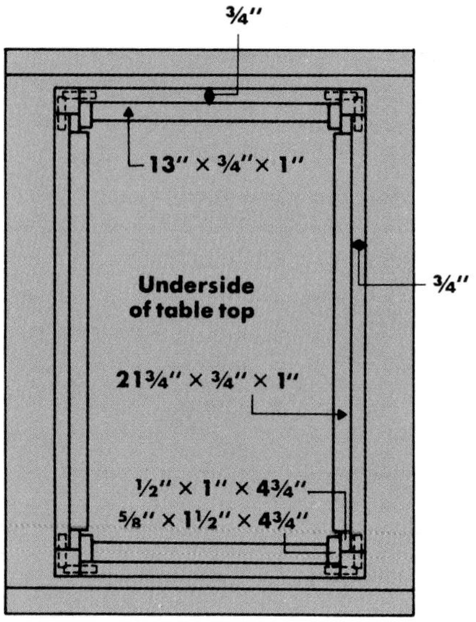
¾"
13" × ¾" × 1"
Underside of table top
¾"
21¾" × ¾" × 1"
½" × 1" × 4¾"
⅝" × 1½" × 4¾"

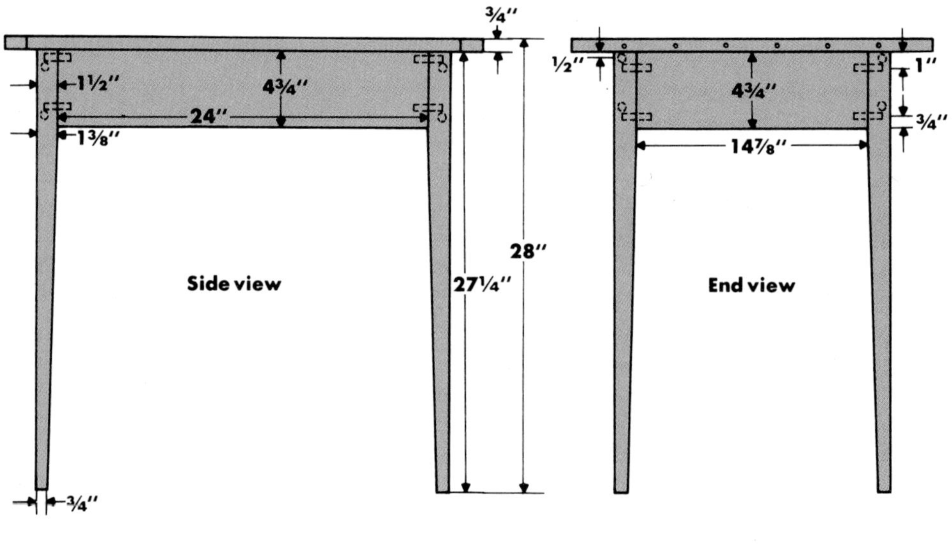
¾"
1½"
4¾"
24"
1⅜"
28"
Side view
27¼"
¾"
½"
1"
4¾"
¾"
14⅞"
End view

D

Figure D: Four views of the side table are shown above. Follow them to obtain dimensions of individual pieces and details of hidden construction.

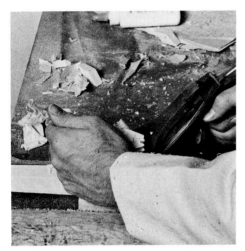

16: With a hand plane, taper the two inner faces of each table leg. Start the wide end of the taper the width of the skirts below the top of the leg.

17: Insert metal dowel centers in the holes in the skirt piece to mark the centers of the corresponding holes to be drilled in the leg.

18: Connect the skirt and leg pieces with 1⅞-inch-long dowels and woodworker's resin glue. The dowel holes in each piece are 1 inch deep.

19: Hold the skirt and legs together with a bar clamp until the glue dries. Use blocks of scrap wood to keep the clamp from marring the legs.

20: A detail of the inner construction of the table base shows the screw cleats attached to the skirts and the glue blocks in the corner.

21: The table can be assembled invisibly, with screws from the underside (above) or visibly, with decorative flat-headed nails.

The table top is made up of edge-glued 28-inch-long pine boards plus two end pieces running crosswise (see top view, Figure D). Cut the center strips from ¾-inch-thick boards; they can be whatever widths you have available as long as the total width is 23 inches, but cut them slightly long to allow for trimming. Sand the edges to be joined until they are straight and square. Glue the edges of the lengthwise boards together; clamp (with bar clamps) until the glue is dry. The ends are two 23-inch strips 1⅜ inches wide. With the saw, trim the cut ends of the lengthwise boards square with the end pieces; then glue and nail the end pieces in place. Use six 2½-inch-long flat-headed nails evenly spaced on each end; countersink them with a nail set. Clamp the ends to the center until the glue dries. Sand the table top with progressively finer sandpaper (photographs 6 and 7, page 2001) until it is smooth and free of cross scratches and nicks.

To mount the table top on the base, drive No. 8 flat-headed wood screws, 1¼ inches long, through the holes previously drilled in the screw cleats (photograph 20) and into the underside of the table top (photograph 21), working from the underside of the table. An alternate way, shown in the color photograph opposite, is to nail the top onto the base with a total of eight flat-headed nails. Figure E shows how to make such nails look hand wrought.

Finish the table with a yellow varnish or lacquer, or a saffron-colored stain, and two coats of semigloss clear lacquer or satin-finish polyurethane varnish.

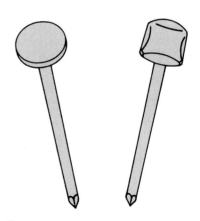

E
Figure E: To make nails with a hand-wrought look, lay a flat-headed nail on a metal surface and hammer the side of the head four times, turning it a quarter turn between hits.

Materials needed for one utility bench

Clear white pine, ¾ inch thick,
sufficient to cut:
one 9⅝-by-48-inch piece (top),
two 9⅝-by-15-inch pieces (legs),
and four 2 5/16-by-17-inch
pieces (braces)

Woodworker's resin glue

Twenty-two 1¼-inch flat-headed nails

Wood-toned or colored oil stain

Semigloss lacquer or satin-finish
polyurethane varnish

Shaker restorations and museums

The two Shaker communities still occupied are Shaker Village, Inc., Canterbury, New Hampshire (near Concord) and the Shaker community at Sabbath Lake, Maine (near Portland). Two former Shaker communities, now historical restorations, are Hancock Shaker Village, near Pittsfield, Massachusetts; and Shakertown at Pleasant Hill, Kentucky (near Lexington). Two museums near or on the sites of former Shaker communities are The Shaker Museum at Old Chatham, New York, near the Mount Lebanon community; and the Shaker Museum in the Center Family House of the South Union, Kentucky community.

Other museums featuring Shaker furniture and artifacts include The Henry Francis DuPont Winterthur Museum, Winterthur, Delaware; Western Kentucky University Museum, Bowling Green, Kentucky; The Fruitlands Museums, Harvard, Massachusetts; The Henry Ford Museum, Dearborn, Michigan; The Shelbourne Museum, Shelbourne, Vermont; Smithsonian Institution, Washington, D. C.; Shaker Historical Society Museum, Shaker Heights, Ohio; Warren County Historical Society, Lebanon, Ohio; Western Reserve Historical Society, Cleveland, Ohio; the Philadelphia Museum of Art; the Boston Museum of Fine Arts; and the Milwaukee Art Center.

This handsome utility bench is light enough to be easily moved; yet it is surprisingly strong because four angled braces are half-dovetailed into the legs and top. The ingenious middle-lap joint appears to be a unique joint devised by Shaker craftsmen.

Furniture and Finishes
Utility bench

The pine utility bench pictured above is a replica of a piece from the Hancock, Massachusetts, Shaker community, where it had a variety of uses, principally for seating at the dining table. Similar benches, longer but with the same half-dovetailed braces, were used in the meeting house of at least one other Shaker village.

To make such a bench, first cut out the legs and the top. With the length following the grain of the wood, cut the pieces as indicated in the materials list (above, left). Do not cut the notches, indicated in Figure F, in either legs or top at this time.

Enlarge the pattern for the leg arch (Figure G, page 2008), and transfer its outline onto the wood. Then cut out the arch with a coping saw (photograph 22).

Position the legs on the underside of the top, 6 inches in from the ends, and hold them in place with bar clamps, but do not glue or nail them at this time. Square the joints (photograph 23). On the edge of a leg, draw a line 4⅞ inches down from the arched end (the top as you are working).

Cut a brace 2 5/16" by 16½ inches, and hold it so it diagonally spans the leg and the bench top. Line up the bottom edge of the brace (the top edge as you are working) with the 4⅞-inch mark on the leg, and position it at a 45-degree angle with a combination square (photograph 24). The brace will extend beyond the leg and the top at both ends. Mark the position of the bottom edge of the brace on the side of the leg. Then mark the outside edges of the leg and the top on the brace (photograph 25). Also mark the brace to indicate the inside edges of both pieces (photograph 26). With a handsaw, cut off the ends of the brace that extend beyond the top and leg (pink in the side view of Figure F); the brace will now have diagonal ends. On the inner side of the brace, draw a line 5/16 below (and parallel to) the shorter edge, starting at the diagonal end and ending at the mark that indicates the inside of the leg. Do the same at the other end of the brace that will fit into the top. Cut out these small sections (yellow in the side view of Figure F) with the handsaw (photograph 27). Now the brace has notches at both ends on the shorter side. Hold the notched brace against the top and the leg as before, with the notches on the inside of the triangle formed by the brace, top, and leg. Check to make sure the brace is still at a 45-degree angle (photograph 28, page 2008). Then mark the placement of the notches on both the leg and top pieces. Repeat with the other braces.

22: Trace the enlarged pattern for the leg arch (Figure G, page 2008) onto the bench leg; then cut out the shape with a coping saw.

23: Square the joint of the leg and top and clamp them together temporarily. Do not nail or glue the leg to the top at this time.

24: Position the brace so it spans the top and leg diagonally at a 45-degree angle, 4⅞ inches from the arch end of the leg.

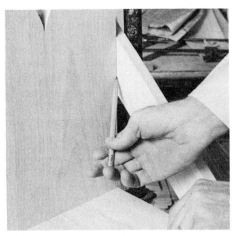

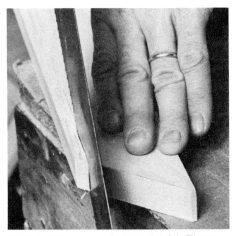

25: On the end of the brace that extends beyond the leg, mark the outside edge of the leg. Do the same for the end that extends beyond the top. These ends will be cut off later.

26: With the brace still held at a 45-degree angle, mark the inside edge of the leg on the brace. Also mark the inside edge of the top on the opposite end of the brace.

27: Cut off the ends of the brace (pink in Figure F); then make a cut 5/16 inch below the top edge of the brace between the diagonal end and the mark for the inside of the leg (yellow in Figure F). Repeat at the opposite end of the brace to the mark that indicates the inside of the top piece.

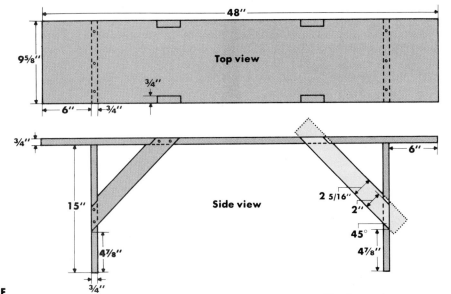

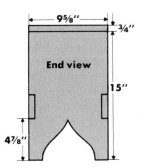

F

Figure F: Top, side, and end views of the utility bench are shown above. Use them to determine the dimensions of individual pieces and the assembly techniques. The pink and yellow tints on the brace indicate wood that will be cut away in two separate steps.

28: Position the notched brace at a 45-degree angle against the top and the leg. Use the brace to mark the location of the notches to be made in both pieces. Mark these cutting lines carefully.

29: Put the leg lengthwise in a vise and clamp two scrap blocks ¾ inch below the edge to serve as a depth guide. With a handsaw, cut along the marks for the ends of the notch.

30: Make additional cuts between the first two; this makes it easier to cut out the notch with a sharp chisel. Cut shallow indentations along the bottom of the notch first, to prevent splitting.

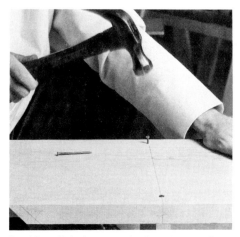

31: After all the brace notches have been made, glue and nail the top to the legs. Use flat-headed nails (Figure E, page 2005) for an antique look; countersink them, but do not fill the holes.

32: Fit each brace into the corresponding notches in top and leg. Glue with woodworker's resin glue; then nail with flat-headed nails. Countersink the nails but do not fill holes.

33: Round the edges of the top with a hand plane. Or with a special molding plane, make the rounded thumb-nose edge shown in the color photograph on page 2006.

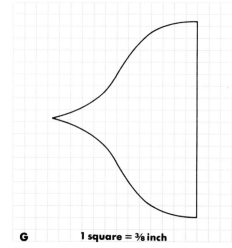

G   1 square = ⅜ inch

Figure G: To enlarge the pattern for the cut-out leg arch, draw a grid of ⅜-inch squares on stiff paper; then copy the arch, square by square. Cut out the enlarged pattern and trace it onto the two leg pieces.

Unclamp a leg and put it lengthwise in a vise. Use C-clamps to hold two blocks of scrap wood ¾ inch below the edge of the leg piece to serve as a guide for the depth of the saw cut. With the handsaw, make two diagonal cuts into the leg—one at the mark indicating the bottom edge of the brace, one at the mark indicating the notch (photograph 29). Make several more cuts between these two, not more than an inch apart, to make removal of the wood in the notch easier. With a sharp chisel, make indentations across the bottom of the notch, just above the cushioning blocks, to forestall splitting. Then chisel out the sections of wood between the cuts (photograph 30). Cut out the notches on both sides of each leg and on both sides of the top.

Put woodworker's resin glue on the top edge of the leg, and position it again against the underside of the top. Reinforce the joint with three flat-headed nails (Figure E, page 2005) driven through the top and into the leg (photograph 31). Do the same with the other leg.

Next, glue the braces, one at a time, into the notches in the legs and the top, and reinforce the joints with flat-headed nails (photograph 32). Use a nail set to drive all nail heads below the surface of the soft pine; do not fill the holes.

Smooth all rough edges and surfaces with sandpaper, and bevel the top edges of the top piece with a hand plane (photograph 33). A special molding plane will give you the shaped edge shown in the color photograph on page 2006.

Finish the bench with a yellow varnish or lacquer, or a saffron-colored stain, and two coats of a semigloss clear lacquer or satin-finish polyurethane varnish.

This simple but handsome candle box has the dovetailed corner joints so typical of Shaker construction. In addition to giving strength and durability, they provide a pleasing pattern. A warm burnt-orange paint stain adds color but lets the wood grain show.

Furniture and Finishes
Dovetailed candle box   💲 🕐 🧍 🪚

The candle box was considered essential by the Shakers. Each room of the community had a small box such as the one pictured above to hold hand-dipped tallow tapers. Larger candle boxes were made for storing candles in the meeting rooms. Box corners have multiple dovetail joints; such joints, carefully crafted, are perhaps the most obvious marks of Shaker furniture. They provide exceptional strength as well as beauty.

To make such a box, start by cutting four pieces of ⅜-inch-thick clear white pine, two for the sides (4¼ by 11¾ inches) and two for the ends (4¼ inches square). These pieces will be joined with corner dovetails; then the bottom and lid will be added. All dimensions are given in Figure H.

A full-sized template for the dovetails on the end pieces is given in Figure I. These are not identical with those on the front and back pieces. On the end pieces, the dovetails narrow at the inner corners; those on the front and back do not. However, you need to cut only one template, that for the end pieces. Corresponding dovetails on the front and back pieces can then be marked by using the cut dovetails of the ends for a pattern. This assures a precise fit.

Carefully trace the template onto stiff paper, and cut it out with a sharp craft knife, guided by a metal ruler. Careful marking and cutting, starting with the template, are essential in making precise, snug-fitting dovetailed joints.

Place the template on an end piece so that the dovetails are aligned with one end-grain edge. Score the outlines of the dovetails on the wood (photograph 34, page 2010). (Once the five smaller sections are removed, four full dovetails will remain.) Score guidelines on front, back, and edge of the end piece. The knife blade gives a more precise line than a pencil, but if the cuts are hard to see, lightly fill them in with a sharp pencil (photograph 35, page 2010). Use a light touch so you do not distort the score marks. With Xs, mark the five sections to be removed.

Clamp the end between blocks of scrap wood, lining up the tops of the blocks with the bottom of the dovetails. The blocks serve as a depth gauge for the saw.

Using a fine-toothed backsaw, make eight vertical cuts just inside—not directly on—the lines outlining the sections to be removed (photograph 36, page 2010). It is important to cut inside the lines to allow for the width of the saw cuts and the hand fitting to come. With a sharp chisel, score, then cut through the bottom of each marked section, just above the scrap blocks; scoring helps prevent the wood from

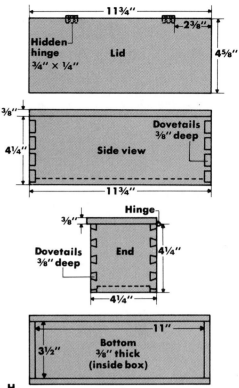

H Figure H: Four views of the candle box give the dimensions of each piece and show the dovetails.

Materials needed for one candle box

Clear white pine, ⅜ inch thick, sufficient to cut:
two 4¼-inch-square pieces (ends), two 4¼-by-11¾-inch pieces (sides), one 4⅝-by-11¾-inch piece (lid), and one 3½-by-11-inch piece (bottom)

Two ¾-inch brass butt hinges

Four ⅜-inch No. 3 flat-headed brass screws

Four ¼-inch No. 2 flat-headed brass screws

Woodworker's resin glue

Wood-toned or colored oil stain

Semigloss lacquer or satin-finish polyurethane varnish

I Figure I: Trace this full-sized pattern to make a template for the dovetails of the two end pieces.

34: Score the outlines of the dovetails on the end piece with a sharp craft knife. The blade makes a more precise mark than a pencil line.

35: With a very sharp pencil, lightly fill in the scored marks to make them more easily seen. Mark the sections to be removed with Xs.

36: Clamp the end piece between scrap blocks that serve as a depth guide, and make vertical cuts with a backsaw just inside the lines outlining the sections marked with Xs.

splitting when you chisel out each section (photograph 37). Push on the chisel to cut out the marked sections, a little at a time, using gentle but firm pressure. Use your hands, never a hammer. The two sections at the outer ends can be cut with a saw.

When one set of dovetails has been cut on the end piece, clamp that piece on top of one end-grain edge of the front piece, at a right angle (photograph 38). Support the end piece from underneath with a piece of scrap wood; you need two sets of clamps to do the job. With a sharp craft knife, score the outlines of the four dovetails onto the edge of the front. Mark the lines at the base of each dovetail slightly higher than indicated to allow for cutting and chiseling (photograph 38). Mark the four inner sections to be cut out (those corresponding to the four dovetails) with penciled Xs. Pencil in the scored lines with a light touch, as before. As a reminder when you match them later, mark the end and front pieces with Xs at adjacent corners.

Chiseling Techniques

As you did with the end piece, clamp the front piece between two blocks of wood so the bottom lines of the marked sections match with the top edges of the blocks. With the backsaw, make eight vertical cuts inside—not directly on—the lines outlining the sections to be removed (photograph 39). Because these sections are larger than those in the end piece, you can also make several more cuts inside the marked sections to make removal easier (see photograph 30, page 2008). Cut through along the bottom lines of the marked sections with a very sharp chisel. Chip away the marked sections with the chisel, a little at a time. Hold the chisel horizontally (photograph 40), then vertically (photograph 41) to remove the chips. Work from the front to a midway point, then from the back, rather than pushing straight through from one side to the other.

Fit the dovetails of the front and end pieces together. They should interlock only when the two corner Xs you marked earlier are adjacent. Apply pressure evenly across the entire width of the piece as you push the dovetails together with a firm hand. Do not force them, however; you may need to chisel the inside edges of the dovetails a bit to achieve a snug but easy fit (photograph 42). Work the two pieces apart if necessary, and chisel the inside edges very carefully so you do not distort the shapes of the dovetails.

Make the dovetailed joints on the three remaining corners in the same manner. When all the dovetailed corners have been cut and fitted, use woodworker's resin glue to join them. Square the inside corners; then clamp them evenly, using cushioning blocks to avoid marring the wood. Cushioning blocks should extend only to the inner points of the dovetails. Keep the corners clamped until the glue is dry (photograph 43).

Cut the bottom piece of ⅜-inch-thick clear white pine, 11 by 3½ inches, adjusting the size if necessary so the bottom fits inside the four walls. One way to be sure of an accurate fit is to place the walls of the box on a slightly larger piece of the ⅜-inch-thick wood, tracing as close as possible to the inside perimeter of the box. Cut or plane the wood just outside this line; then hand plane the piece lightly until it fits. Put the bottom piece inside the walls of the box and glue it in place with woodworker's resin glue. Sand the outside edges when the glue is dry.

The lid is attached to the box with two ¾-inch brass butt hinges mortised into the top edge of the back piece. Place a closed hinge on the back edge with its round section extending outside the edge, as indicated in Figure H, page 2009. With a sharp craft knife, score the outline of the hinge on the edge. With a sharp chisel, remove that section (photograph 44). But do not chisel quite to the full thickness of the closed hinge; let the hinge sit a little high in the mortise. Repeat for the other hinge.

Cut out the lid piece as shown in Figure H; place it on top of the box with the back edges flush. Let the front edge of the lid extend slightly, approximately ¼ inch, beyond the front of the box; plane the edges smooth (photograph 45).

Before attaching the lid to the box with the hinges, finish the box pieces with a wood-tone or colored stain and two coats of semigloss clear lacquer or satin-finish polyurethane varnish.

Screw the hinges onto the lid with No. 2 flat-headed brass screws ¼ inch long and into the box with No. 3 screws ⅜ inch long. The hinges are mortised only into the box; they lie flat on the inner surface of the lid.

For related crafts and entries, see "Rockers and Cradles."

37: With a sharp chisel, cut a bit into the base of a section to be removed. This cut will prevent the wood from splitting when you chisel into the section from above the cut.

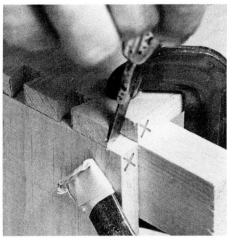

38: Use the cut dovetails of the end piece as a pattern for marking the sections to be cut from the front piece. Use a knife for precise marks; then fill them in with a pencil.

39: Use the same technique for cutting out the sections in the front piece as on the end piece. The blocks of wood tell you how deep to cut with the backsaw.

40: Gradually chisel away the sections marked for removal. Use gentle but firm pressure. Work from both sides to the middle—do not push through from one side to the other.

41: Hold the chisel vertically to remove chips, bracing it against your other hand to keep it from slipping. Pay special attention to the corners; angles must be well defined.

42: Interlock the two sides of one corner, applying pressure evenly across the dovetails. The joint should fit snugly, but if force is needed, check for spots that need to be chiseled slightly.

43: When you are sure that all dovetails fit perfectly, apply woodworker's resin glue and clamp the box walls together. Check to see that the inner corners form right angles.

44: The two butt hinges that hold the lid to the box are recessed into the top edge of the back piece of the box. Chisel out the hinge mortise as indicated in Figure H, page 2009.

45: Place the lid on the box and align the back edges. Let the lid extend beyond the front of the box about ¼ inch. With a hand plane, smooth and round the edges of the lid.

SHELTERS AND TENTS
The Great Cover-Up

Roger "Strider" Coco is one of a new breed of mountain men. As much at home in the wilderness as in Elmhurst, New York, he's a skilled hunter, trapper, and prospector. When he is not leading back-packing expeditions into the mountains of the American and Canadian west, he maintains shelters and trails for the New York/New Jersey Trail Conference and draws maps for Walking News, Inc.

If you are like most people today, you spend three-quarters of your time under a roof of some sort—at home, on the job, shopping, or traveling. Less of life is lived under the sky than ever before. The need for protection from weather is only occasional—it might be satisfied almost casually by ducking under a rock ledge in a thunderstorm, or by throwing up a few poles and thatch covering. But many people, if left to their own devices, would be hard pressed to make any kind of shelter for themselves.

There is a special satisfaction in building and using a simple shelter. One type, such as a tepee, would be enjoyable in the backyard, and some are handy on a camping or fishing trip. Each of the shelters described on the following pages has its own special virtues, depending on weather conditions, available materials, and the work required to make them. Every outdoors enthusiast should know at least those shelters that can be made with a tarpaulin and a length of rope.

What and Where to Build

The first and most important step in shelter making is to consider whether a shelter is necessary and if so, what kind would be most feasible. Under favorable conditions, there is no better canopy than the open sky. If a light rain is the only problem, a tall evergreen tree will keep you dry, and in many areas you can find sheltering rock ledges like the one pictured opposite. Where natural protection is not available, any number of simple shelters can be improvised.

The first three examples show how to keep dry with only a lightweight, waterproof tarpaulin and some nylon rope. These are easy to tote and should be standard equipment for all hikers. The suspension tarp-tent (page 2014) is the best bet where trees are plentiful, and the tarp lean-to (page 2016) where woody growth is scarce. The pup tent (page 2017) is a more secure arrangement in downpours or high wind, requiring only two trees or posts to support the tarp. (In areas where you might have difficulty finding even short posts, you can make the tarp lean-to or pup tent if you carry a couple of light aluminum poles with you.)

If you're caught without a tarp, you can build a traditional branch-and-thatch lean-to (page 2018). When oriented properly, this simple structure will afford good protection against wind.

In desert conditions, where shade is needed in the middle of the day, you can use any of the tarp shelters, or dig a sand trench (page 2018).

But don't expect to heat a tarp shelter or lean-to with a fire in cold, rainy weather; crawl inside your sleeping bag to get warm and cook on a back-packing stove. Only a closed structure such as a tepee (page 2020) will keep you warm.

Choose a campsite that provides protection from the prevailing wind and is safe from hazards such as flash floods (look for debris left by previous high water), lightning (avoid solitary trees), falling rocks, falling timber, high tides, poisonous plants or animals, and insects (avoid lush growth). It is a good rule of thumb not to camp on the highest or lowest ground in an area. The best locations are usually in sparse vegetation. Level ground is needed for the sleeping area and the campfire. Try to camp near convenient sources of firewood and water.

Campfire Safety

Whatever type of shelter you build, allow enough room for safe movement around the campfire, and never build a fire where overhead tree branches or the shelter itself could be accidentally ignited. Carbon monoxide is a deadly hazard in enclosed spaces, even in a tent; so make sure of good ventilation before starting a fire. Finally, never line a fire with smooth rocks that may have been in water for long periods—such as those found near stream beds or lakes. Water trapped in them, when heated, can cause the rocks to explode.

Opposite, Roger Coco converts a thunder shower into a cozy coffee break at Claudius Smith's, a rock ledge in New York's Ramapo mountains. Natural shelters like this one (named for a colonial horse thief who hid here for years) were used by man long before any handmade shelters existed.

1: Begin putting up the tarp suspension tent by tying one end of a rope to a corner of the tarp and looping the rope once around the first of three trees that form a roughly equilateral triangle, with one tree at each end of the tent and one in front of it.

Outdoor Activities
Simple shelters

Countless types of simple shelters can be thrown up easily and quickly, using only materials provided by nature or lightweight aids that you can carry with you. The five examples here represent the principles involved in all rudimentary shelter making. More important than mastering any one model is the ability to see what is needed and possible in any situation.

A Suspension Tarp-Tent

I never venture into the wilderness without a waterproof tarpaulin. An inexpensive 9-by-12-foot sheet, or fly, of urethane-coated nylon with eight grommet holes (at the corners and the middle of each edge) can be purchased at sporting goods stores. With this tarp and 150 feet or less of ¼-inch nylon rope, you can make each of the first three shelters pictured. (Also recommended for your pack are a few spring-type clothespins, for a wind-tight pup tent, page 2017.)

For quick cover in a light to moderate rain, suspend a tarpaulin from three trees as shown in the photograph opposite. Select trunks that form a roughly equilateral triangle. Tie a rope end to a corner grommet so the dull side of the tarpaulin will be on top, and run the line around one of the trees about 5 feet above ground level (photograph 1).

Lead the rope back to the tarp, and push a small loop through the grommet in the middle of the longer edge next to the first corner. Pin the loop in the grommet hole with a twig (photograph 2 and Figure A). From there, run the line once around the tree in front of the tarp shelter and then around the third tree in line with the first. Finally, bring the line back to the tarp, pull up the slack, and tie the rope end to the remaining grommet on the top edge (photograph 3). The tarp will hang vertically with its bottom edge draped on the ground.

Pull the bottom edge out from the triangle of trees, and attach ropes 6 feet or longer to the two remaining corner grommets. Stretch first one, then the other lower corner of the tarp diagonally out from the triangle (photograph 4). Drive 12-inch stakes halfway into the ground at a 45-degree angle to the tarp, a few feet in from the rope ends. Loop each rope around its stake (photograph 5). To adjust the tension of the lines, tie slider knots as follows: Run the short end of the rope over the long end and back through the resulting loop (photograph 6). Repeat an inch or so farther from the stake (photograph 7), and again an inch or so closer to the stake (photograph 8). When both ends are tied, slide the knots to balance the tension in the lines; then tighten the knots to secure the tarp.

2: Bring the rope back to the tarp, and pass a small loop of rope through the center grommet hole on the tarp's upper edge, holding the loop in place with a twig.

3: Run the line around the tree that the tarp's open side will face, and around the tree at its other end, then back to the tarp. Tie the rope to the upper tarp corner nearest the third tree.

A suspended tarp provides one of the quickest and easiest means of keeping dry in the woods. This shelter requires three trees, a 9-by-12-foot waterproof tarpaulin, and 100 to 150 feet of rope.

4: Tie individual ropes to the lower tarp corners and stretch the tarp out from each corner, diagonally away from the triangle of trees. The dull side of the tarp should be on top.

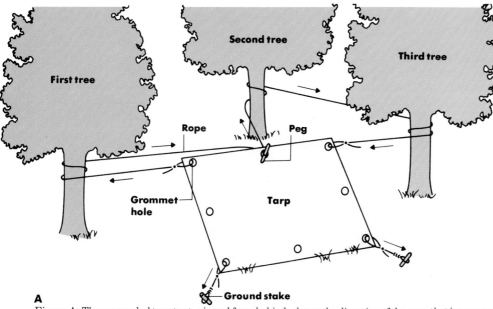

Figure A: The suspended tarp tent, viewed from behind, shows the direction of the rope that is wrapped around three trees, and of the rope and stake connections.

5: Near the rope ends, drive tent stakes halfway into the ground, with their tops pointing away from the tent at a 45-degree angle. Loop each rope around its stake.

6: The slider knot, which allows the tension in the tent-stake lines to be adjusted, is begun by passing the short end of the rope over the long end and back through the resulting loop.

7: The short end is again passed over the long end to form a new loop—this time an inch or so farther from the tent stake—then back through the loop as before.

8: A third pass, identical to the first two, is then made an inch or so closer to the tent stake. When slack, the knot slides freely along the rope; when tightened, it will hold tenaciously.

9: To put up the tarp lean-to, tie the two lower corners to tent stakes. Then wrap each of the two remaining corners of the tarp around a post and secure each one with one end of a 20-foot length of rope as shown.

10: Extend the post ropes diagonally from the tarp. Hold the first one in place temporarily with a rock while you tie the other to a tent stake.

11: With a slider knot fasten the end of the second post rope to a ground stake (page 2015). Then do the same with the first post rope.

A Tarp Lean-to

A similar tent, the tarp lean-to (pictured below), can be pitched in a sparsely wooded area if two more or less straight 4-foot sticks can be found. In a place where you are unlikely to find even this much wood, you can carry hollow aluminum tubing with you. Whatever material you use for poles, it helps if the bottom ends are pointed.

Place the tarp flat on the ground, dull side up. Stake two corners of a long edge with slider knots, the ropes running diagonally out from the corners (photographs 4 through 8, page 2015). Wrap the remaining corners around the tops of the poles, tying each with the end of a 20-foot length of rope (photograph 9). Set one pole in a nearly vertical position, just leaning slightly out from the tarp. Extend the line diagonally out from the upright pole, and weight the end with a rock (photograph 10). Then set up the second post in the same way. Secure both lines with stakes and slider knots (photograph 11).

A tarp lean-to uses two posts for support and requires less rope than a suspension tent. Four taut lines running diagonally out from the corners hold the tarp in place on the posts.

12: To put up a tarp pup tent, first suspend the center of the tarp lengthwise between two trees, tying the rope at both ends. Hold the rope chest high, and keep the line fairly taut.

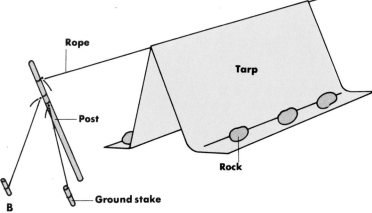

Figure B: When trees are not available, you can suspend a pup tent between two 4-foot posts. Drive the posts into the ground with their tops slanted away from the tent, and hold each one with two ground stakes.

A Tarp Pup Tent

For heavy rain and wind, and for slightly more protection against cold, use a pup tent, as pictured below. Place the tarp flat on the ground, dull side up, and run a line under it, passing it through the two grommets at the midpoints of the longer edges. Select two trees, about 20 feet apart, that line up at a right angle to the prevailing wind. Tie the rope ends to the trees, pulling up the slack (photograph 12). Branches like the ones used in the tarp lean-to (opposite) or aluminum poles may be substituted for trees, but they will need to be driven well into the ground, then made to lean away from the tent with at least two diagonal lines pulling on each pole (Figure B).

Spread the sloping sides of the tent away from the center rope, and weight the edges with rocks (Figure B). In extremely heavy rain, dig a small trench around the tent to divert water running off the tarp and to stop ground water from seeping in. Fill the trench with small stones, and extend a runoff chanel from the low point to still lower ground. Before you move on, cover the trench with twigs and leaves.

In a very heavy rain, sacrifice a little elbow room for extra protection by pulling in the ends of the sloping sides so they lie flat beneath you and holding them with rocks (Figure C). In driving rain, and for protection from wind and cold, seal off the draftier end of the tent by pulling in the tarp corners until one triangular opening is closed. Three or four spring-type clothespins can be used to hold the edges together (Figure D).

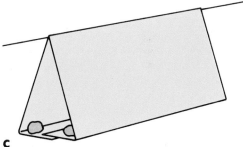

Figure C: To keep dry in a heavy rain, fold the lower edges of the tarp under the shelter until they meet, and anchor them with rocks. They will act as a ground cloth to seal the water out. Digging a shallow drainage trench around the tent also helps.

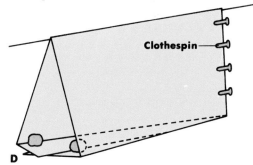

Figure D: If a wind-driven rain penetrates one of the open ends of the lean-to, seal it by drawing the two edges together and fastening them with spring-type clothespins or safety pins.

A pup tent can be as simple as a tarp suspended between two trees, with the outer edges weighted with rocks. The farther you stretch the sides, the lower the peak will fall and the more cover you will get.

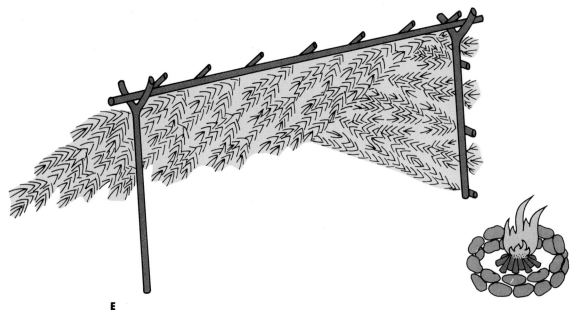

E

Figure E: If you build a lean-to of natural materials, face it away from the prevailing wind. The one illustrated has two forked posts, a ridgepole, and a sloping roof made of evergreen boughs. One or both of the triangular side openings may be sealed for added protection. A small fire located 6 feet to leeward is safe and cheerful, but will not contribute much real warmth.

A Traditional Lean-to

A lightweight tarp and rope take much of the work out of shelter making. But in an emergency, you can pitch an adequate shelter made of natural materials.

The original lean-to is just a simple wood frame on which any available covering may be hung, bound, leaned, woven, or otherwise attached. A practical model is shown in Figure E. To make it, find two straight sticks about 4 feet long ending in a fork. (Two tree trunks can be used instead, provided they can be spanned by a ridgepole.) At right angles to the prevailing wind, drive the sticks into the ground with the forked end up, 6 or 8 feet apart, and lay a pole across the two crotches. Make a sloping roof on the windward side by leaning or propping a tight row of evergreen boughs or other foliage-bearing branches at about a 30-degree angle from the ground to the ridgepole. In wind, lash the boughs to the ridgepole with flexible roots or other binding material. In heavy rain, reinforce the roof with vines or leafy vegetation, bark, moss, or reeds held in place with clumps of sod or loose earth. To keep warmer, close the small triangular side openings by stacking or leaning evergreen boughs against the posts and roof ends. A fire can be built in front of the open side—but never within the shelter or close to flammable roof boughs. A small fire enclosed with rocks piled on three sides to direct the heat toward the lean-to, located about 6 feet from the open side, will give a little warmth. But for more comfort, you can dig a shallow pit inside the lean-to and fill it with heated rocks from the outside fire.

A Sand Trench

In most cases, the idea of quick shelter suggests protection from wet, cold, or windy conditions, but shelters can be equally important in hot, dry climates. In the desert, the period from midmorning to late afternoon can be punishing for the hiker. It is often hard to find natural shade if vegetation is sparse and the sun casts nearly vertical rays into every ravine and gully. If you do not have a tarp and rope, shade can be arranged with little effort in the form of a protected trench (Figure F).

On low ground, dig a narrow east-west trench, about 2 feet wide and 6 feet long. The depth will be determined by the angle of the sun and your desire for the refreshment of the cooler sand a few feet below the surface—but 2 to 3 feet is generally sufficient. Pile the excavated sand as high as possible on the south edge of the trench, and crown the hill with sagebrush or whatever other growth is available, tilted toward the north to cast a shadow over the trench.

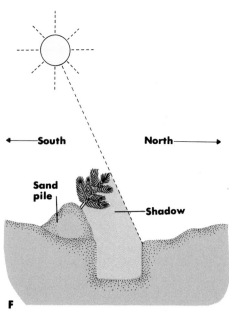

F

Figure F: A sand trench for shade during the heat of the day—perhaps 2 feet deep, 2 feet wide and 6 feet long—should be located at the bottom of an east-west gully. Pile the excavated sand on the south side and top it with any available brush at an angle to cast a shadow on the trench.

CRAFTNOTES: WATER SEAMING AND WINDPROOFING A TENT

If you already own a tent, you may find that it is not quite watertight. Good tents have waterproof floors and sides, but even in a good tent, the top is only water-repellent. If so, you can cover it with a separate piece of waterproof nylon, called a fly, as shown in the before-and-after photographs (above and below). Drape the fly over the peak of the tent and stake out the four corners with slider knots (photographs 4 through 8, page 2015). Water will be less likely to trickle or seep through the double protection of fly and tent than if the two were touching, and most of the wind's force will be spent before it reaches the tent. The poles that support both the tent and the fly should have lengths of shock cord attached to give them stability in high winds.

To prolong the life of your fly, care for it as you would your tent. Dry it carefully after each use to prevent mildew from forming, and do not leave it out in the hot sun, or it may begin to crackle and develop leaks. As much as possible keep it rolled—rather than folded—when it is not in use.

Tenting information

For where to set up your tent in the National Parks, see: **Camping in the National Park System** (I-29.71:972 Series 2405-00473), available for 65 cents from the Superintendent of Documents, United States Government Printing Office, Washington, D. C. 20402.

For information on camping in the National Forests, consult the Supervisor's Office of the forest you intend to visit, usually located in the nearest large town.

In addition, most states, counties, and municipalities have a bureau of parks and recreation which can provide information on camping areas within its jurisdiction.

Tenting supplies by mail

Eddie Bauer
P. O. Box 3700
Seattle, Wash. 98124

L. L. Bean, Inc.
Freeport, Maine 04032

Bishop's Ultimate Outdoor Equipment
6804 Milwood Rd.
Bethesda, Md. 20034

Eastern Mountain Sports
1041 Commonwealth Ave.
Boston, Mass. 02215

Don Gleason's Campers' Supply
9 Pearl St.
Northampton, Mass. 01060

Herter's, Inc.
Waseca, Minn. 56093

Recreational Equipment Co-op
1525 11th Ave.
Seattle, Wash. 98122

Stephenson's
23206 Hatteras St.
Woodland Hills, Calif. 91364

Tent and Trail
21 Park Place
New York, N. Y. 10007

Further reading

The Golden Book of Camping, by William Hillcourt, The Golden Press, New York, N. Y.
Shelters, Shacks, and Shanties, by D. C. Beard, Charles Scribner's Sons, Totowa, N. J.
Camping and Woodcraft, by Horace Kephart, The Macmillan Co., Riverside, N. J.
The Indian Tipi, by Reginald and Gladys Labin, Ballantine Books, Inc., New York, N. Y.
Light Weight Camping Equipment and How to Make It, by Gerry Cunningham and Margaret Hansson, Colorado Outdoor Sports Corporation, Denver, Colo.

An early twentieth-century Blackfoot Indian lodge on the plains of Montana (above, left) and a contemporary tepee near Woodstock, New York (above, right) are two among dozens of types of tepees. These shelters vary in size, shape of flaps and door and many other aspects.

Outdoor Activities
An Indian tepee

The tepee is a great design achievement, offering ease and simplicity of construction, versatility, durability, and beauty—even without decoration. It can be made and pitched by one adult and in the dead of winter can be heated comfortably with a small fire. It takes longer to assemble than the shelters already described, and requires more material and greater precision. So you shouldn't expect to erect a tepee casually. At least two or three days are needed to do the job right.

The Sioux word tepee means "used for dwelling in," and there are still people who use it as a primary residence. The tepee pictured (above, right) is a contemporary dwelling at Woodstock, New York. To its left is a turn-of-the-century Blackfoot Indian tepee in Montana. A tepee is the least expensive shelter I know that you could live in permanently if you liked. It makes an ideal backyard playroom or guest house, and it will serve admirably on a fishing or camping trip if you plan to stay in one place for a while.

To build a tepee 11 feet tall and 11 feet in diameter at the base—adequate for a small family and slightly smaller than those pictured—you will need: 44 feet of 6-foot-wide 8-ounce (or heavier) waterproof canvas duck for the cover; a sewing machine with a heavy-duty needle (hand sewing is possible but laborious); 300 feet of strong, rot-resistant thread; a tape measure; chalk; straightedge; scissors; awl; 14 poles 12 feet long and tapering in diameter from 2 inches to 1 inch; 23 feet of strong cord; 2 yards of rope; 11 pointed ground stakes, 1 foot long and 1 inch thick; a hammer for driving stakes; eight sticks 12 inches long and ⅜ inch thick with points on both ends (to use as lacing pins to fasten the cover on the frame); and a 13-foot length of flexible wood for the door-flap frame.

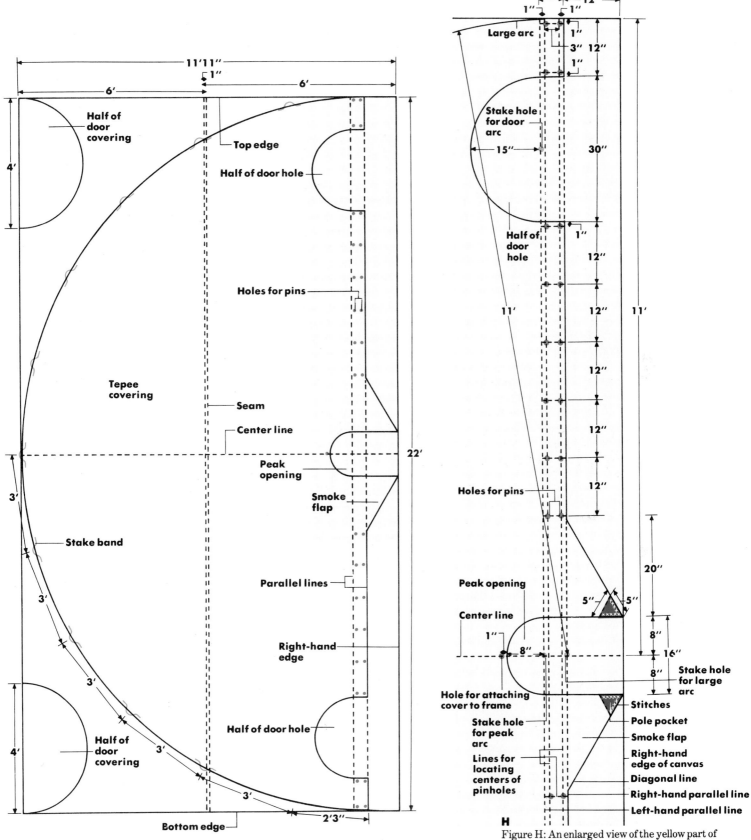

G

Figure G: The covering for an 11-foot-tall tepee begins with a rectangle of canvas, 22 feet by 11 feet, 11 inches, created by sewing two 6-foot-wide pieces together. Follow the instructions in the text (page 2022) for scribing the outline, cutting the pattern (along the solid lines), making holes for lacing pins (shown in red), and attaching stake bands (shown in green). Save the large corner scraps to make a door flap, cut in two semicircular sections, as indicated in the drawing above. The area in yellow is shown in greater detail in Figure H, right.

H

Figure H: An enlarged view of the yellow part of Figure G shows detailed measurements of the tepee cover. The section that lies below the center line will be a mirror-image of the section shown. The stake holes used for scribing arcs are shown in green, those of the lacing pin holes in red, and the pole pockets in purple, with stitching marked in crosses.

2021

The Tepee Cover

To make the tepee covering, join two pieces of canvas 22 by 6 feet (or if this width is not available, four pieces 22 by 3 feet) by placing them right sides together and machine-stitching along their length ½ inch in from the edge. Sew a second seam in the opposite direction for extra strength; then open the canvas and spread it flat on the ground outside, right side up.

To prepare to cut the canvas to shape, measure and mark it carefully, as shown in Figures G and H (page 2021). The large semicircle in Figure G will become an inverted cone when the center of the straight edge is fastened to the top of a conical framework of poles. The canvas is pulled around the poles until the straight edges meet; then these are fastened together with lacing pins. With chalk, draw a center line across the width of the canvas (perpendicular to the seam and 11 feet from either top or bottom edge). Next draw two lines parallel to the seam, 11 and 16 inches respectively from the right-hand edge. Next draw the large semicircle as follows: At the intersection of the center line and the right-hand line, drive a 1-foot pointed stake through the canvas into the ground. (The stake hole is in a waste area of canvas.) Knot the ends of a 23-foot length of strong cord; place the knot so the cord forms a loop exactly 11 feet long. Drop one end of the loop over the stake, and stretch the cord along the right-hand parallel line to either the top or bottom of the canvas. Hold a stick of chalk vertically inside the free end of the loop and pull the cord taut. The tip of the chalk should rest at the edge of the canvas. Mark off the semicircle by moving the chalk in an arc across the canvas.

Now mark the smoke flaps and peak opening. To do this, draw chalk lines 8 inches above and below the center line and parallel to it, extending from the right-hand edge of the canvas to the left-hand parallel line. Then mark a pair of points on the right-hand parallel line 28 inches above and below the center line. Draw diagonal lines from these points to the points where the lines drawn above and below the center meet the right-hand edge of the canvas. Then connect the left-hand ends of the lines above and below the center with an 8-inch semicircle, again using a loop of cord and chalk. Drive the stake for this arc at the intersection of the center line and the left-hand parallel line.

Mark the two halves of the door opening as follows: Draw two pairs of short lines between the long parallel lines, 12 and 42 inches respectively in from the top edge and at the same distance from the bottom edge of the canvas. Midway between each pair of lines, drive stakes through the left-hand parallel line, and chalk off 15-inch arcs.

Cutting the Covering

This completes the outline of the tepee covering. But before cutting, mark the centers of the 32 lacing-pin holes and the additional hole at the peak opening, shown in red in Figures G and H. To do this, draw two additional parallel lines the length of the canvas, 1 inch inside each of the existing parallel lines, as in Figure H. These new lines will be 3 inches apart. Intersect these lines with 16 perpendicular lines, eight on each side of the center line. Working from either the top or the bottom, locate the first line 1 inch in from the edge of the canvas, the second and third 1 inch from both sides of the door opening, and the five remaining lines at 12-inch intervals, moving toward the center (Figure H). These intersections mark the centers for eight pairs of holes on each side of the center line, a total of 32 holes. Plot the center of a final hole on the center line, 1 inch to the left of its intersection with the semicircular peak opening.

With scissors, cut out the shape shown in solid lines in Figure G. Double-stitch around the entire shape, ¼ inch in from the edges.

Next, make holes by pushing the point of an awl through the canvas at the 33 points marked. Open the holes to a diameter of about ¼ inch by forcing a wider object such as a pencil through them. Finish the holes with a buttonhole stitch (Figure I).

Then attach 11 stake bands in the locations shown by curved green lines in Figure G—where the center line meets the large arc and at 3-foot intervals in both directions. These bands may be of ¼-inch rope or ½-inch strips of doubled and stitched canvas. In either case, make the bands 12 inches long. Secure them to the canvas by double-stitching the last 3 inches at both ends of the band to the outer

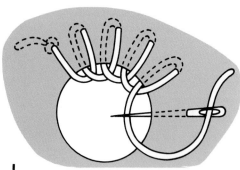

I

Figure I: To make a buttonhole stitch to reinforce holes in the tepee cover, knot the thread and push the needle up through the fabric near the edge of the hole. Then push the needle and thread down through the fabric slightly to the right. Keep the thread loose, and return to the top via the hole, passing the thread through the loop of the preceding stitch. Pull the thread tight and repeat around the hole.

face of the canvas at the curving edge. Allow the unstitched area of the band to bunch slightly so a 1-inch stake can be passed through the resulting gap.

To make pockets for the ends of the poles that operate the smoke flaps (shown in purple in Figure H), cut two 5-inch equilateral triangles from scrap canvas, and stitch them to the flaps along the two legs of the sharp protruding angle.

The Tepee Frame

The tepee frame will consist of twelve 12-foot poles, about 2 inches in diameter at the base, tapering to 1 inch at the peak. Two additional poles are needed to operate the smoke flaps. Young trunks of tamarack, white cedar, red cedar, birch, aspen, yellow pine, or lodgepole pine make good tepee poles. Cut them to size, removing branches and bark. Whittle the last 3 inches at the thicker end to a sharp point. If trees are scarce in your neighborhood, ask a local lumber dealer for 1-inch-round dowels, which, though not tapered, will be an adequate substitute. Aluminum pipe is another alternative.

To erect the tepee, tie three poles together about 2 feet from their tops and set them up in a tripod arrangement on flat, open ground (Figure J). Space the bases 9 feet apart. Then carefully add eight more poles to the circle, resting their tops in the Vs at the roped tripod intersection. Space them evenly (at 3-foot intervals on the ground), and leave a space for one pole on the side of the prevailing wind. Arrange the tops so none protrudes above the others and so they take as little space as possible where they meet.

Returning to the canvas tepee cover, pass a rope through the hole next to its peak opening, and tie the canvas securely to one of the three remaining poles, 2 feet from its top. Set the pole into the place reserved for it in the framework, and spread the canvas, right side out, around the frame. Where the straight edges of the canvas meet (opposite the prevailing wind), overlap them just enough for the paired pin holes to line up. Fasten them at these points by passing sticks—⅜ inch thick, about 12 inches long, and pointed at both ends—through the holes. Begin from the top and work your way down to the bottom, closing the tepee cover as you would button a shirt from the collar to the waist. Then go inside the tepee and reset the poles so they press out against the canvas at all points on the circle. Fasten the bottom edge of the canvas to the ground by passing sharpened 1-foot stakes through the bands and driving them 6 inches into the ground at a 45-degree angle.

Slip the tops of the two remaining poles into the triangular pockets in the smoke flaps. To keep the flaps open, set the bottoms of the poles on the ground to the rear of the tepee; to close the flaps, move the poles forward. If you want to keep a fire going in rainy weather, a piece of canvas may be placed over the tops of the poles. Lift the canvas into place with a pole and fasten it to ground stakes using three or four cords. But in all but the heaviest rains, the amount of water entering the tepee without a top flap is not enough to make the fire splutter.

The Door Flap

For a door flap, cut a circle 48 inches in diameter from scrap canvas, in two semicircular sections, as shown in Figure G. Join the two pieces by placing them right sides together and double-stitching along their diameter ½ inch in from the edge. Open the flap and spread it face down on the ground. For structural support, make a hoop 40 inches in diameter by bending any thin, flexible wood 13 feet long into a circle and tying the overlapping ends together with rope. To fasten the door flap to the hoop, center the hoop on the flap and fold the 4-inch canvas border back over the hoop, pleating where necessary. Enclose the hoop in the circular hem thus formed with hand-stitching.

To hang the door, pierce two holes 5 inches apart and just within the hem on what will be the top part of the door flap. Ring the holes with buttonhole stitches. Run 8-inch loops of rope through the holes so the flap can be hung from the pin located directly above the door hole. In stormy weather, a strand of rope similarly connected to the bottom of the flap will make it possible to secure the flap—from the inside—to the bottom lacing pin. A fire in a closed tepee is safe, because smoke and carbon monoxide leave through the peak opening.

For related projects and crafts, see "Bicycling," "Canoeing," "Hammocks and Slings," "Kayaks," "Weather Forecasting," and "Yard Environments."

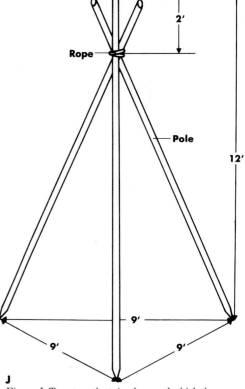

Rope

Pole

2'

12'

9'

9'

9'

J

Figure J: To set up the tripod around which the tepee frame will be placed, tie three 12-foot poles together 2 feet from their tops, and spread their bottoms on the ground 9 feet apart. Nine more poles will complete the tepee cone's framework.

SHIP MODELS
The Art of Small Craft

William Fox majored in naval architecture at Virginia Polytechnic Institute and has been building models of sailing ships for as long as he can remember. A member of the Society of Naval Architects and Marine Engineers, and the Nautical Research Guild, he also takes to the air occasionally, piloting his own plane. He is a native of Newport News, Virginia, where he lives and works. He imports European ship model kits for sale in this country.

Eighteenth-century British Admiralty models, like the 20-gun ship above, are considered the finest examples of the modeler's art. Complete in every detail, these prototypes of actual sailing ships were built by naval architects, master shipwrights, or ship builders, then submitted to the Admiralty Board for approval. The model shown is built of pear wood and is 36 inches long overall. It is built to a scale of ¼ inch to the foot.

If I were asked to choose the most beautiful and adventurous of mankind's creations, I would have to name the sailing ship in all its varied and graceful forms. Ship modelers of every time and place have shared this sentiment, so it is easy to understand why, for centuries, they have been re-creating these beauties in miniature. Of course, models are constructed for more than esthetic reasons. Designers use them to develop prototypes of actual ships—the Admiralty model at left is one made for such a purpose. The process of building a ship model familiarizes you with myriad details of a ship's construction and with a new and colorful nautical vocabulary. You learn how and why the ship was built; you gain intimate knowledge of its structure and operation; and all the while, you develop new skills and abilities to work with your hands, eyes, and wits. In the end, a miniature of a vessel probably long gone from the seas is yours to keep and admire.

Contrary to appearances, ship modeling requires only the most basic of manual skills, and the materials and tools needed are not very expensive. But there are two things you must possess in large measure: time and patience. If you have these, your rewards will be great and your models will be sources of satisfaction for years. The fundamental process in ship modeling is simply looking at a drawing, shaping the material to look like the drawing, and installing the part in its proper place. Whether simple or complicated, all ship-model construction consists in repeating these steps over and over until the model is completed.

I think it is best to start with a model that is detailed enough to be interesting but not so complicated and difficult to build that you will become discouraged or lose interest. Many people have started too ambitious a project only to put it aside and leave it forever unfinished. The model of the Revolutionary War gundalow (rowing galley), *Philadelphia*, pictured opposite, uses simple materials and construction methods to prepare you for building more complex models. The project should not cost more than $10 or $12 for materials and takes about 40 hours to complete. Before beginning work, read this entire entry to familiarize yourself with the sequence of construction. Some of the basics of ship modeling are described below; on pages 2027 and 2035, you will find listings of suppliers, organizations, books, and museums of interest to ship modelers.

Basics of Ship Modeling

Apart from the type of ship you choose as a subject, the principal characteristic which distinguishes one model from another is the method of hull construction. Basically, hulls may be either carved from a solid block of wood or built up from many small pieces of wood, as were the full-sized wooden ships they represent. You can build a ship model from one of the kits available or from scratch, as the *Philadelphia* is made. In building from scratch, you can select from many plans that are commercially available and buy your own materials as they are needed. Kits usually include all materials required and vary in complexity from small, solid hulls costing a few dollars to large, built-up ones costing several hundred. Most kits produced in the U. S. include machine-carved solid hulls. Fittings (anchors, guns, and the like) are generally of cast white metal which is soft—like lead. Larger kits produced abroad often call for built-up hull construction and provide fittings of wood or brass. Carved decorations simulated with cast and gilded metal are sometimes included; these contribute to the high cost of such kits.

For building from scratch, wood is the basic material. Advanced modelers use fine cabinet woods such as holly, apple, cherry, boxwood, and walnut. But inexpensive soft pine is often recommended for solid hulls because it is easy to cut. Balsa wood is not often used for ship models because of its fragility and open grain, but I

The simple lines and rigging of the *Philadelphia*, a Revolutionary War gundalow (rowing galley), make it an ideal first project. This vessel was one of the first to fight under the flag of the United States.

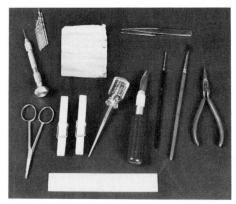

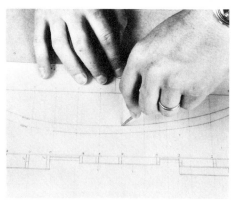

1: Tools used to build the *Philadelphia* are, clockwise from upper left, a pin vise for holding drills and pins, miniature drill bits, sandpaper, tweezers, needle-nose pliers, paintbrushes, craft knife, scratch awl, clothespin clamps, and manicure scissors. A ruler is at the bottom.

2: Punch through the tracing paper with an awl at closely spaced intervals along each line to create an outline on the cardboard pattern underneath.

Associations

There are three for sailing ships, one for steamships:

The Nautical Research Guild, Inc., 6413 Dahlonega Rd., Md., Washington, D.C. 20016. Publication: Nautical Research Journal. Dues $7.50.

Nautical Research and Ship Model Society, 6849 South Keeler, Chicago, Ill. 60629. Publication: Fife Rail. $4 dues, $7.50 in Chicago area.

Northshore Deadeyes, 1900 Central, Evanston, Ill. 60201. Publication: Deadeye. Associated with Ships Unlimited.

Steamship Historical Society of America, Inc., 414 Pelton Ave., Staten Island, N.Y. 10310. Publication: Steamboat Bill. Dues $10.

personally find it acceptable for some models. The model of the *Philadelphia* is built of balsa wood. In the instructions that follow, materials and tools are described in detail, but to get an overall view of projects, materials, and tools, order a catalog from one of the suppliers listed opposite. To learn even more about modeling, visit museums in your area to look at ships and models, and read some of the books listed on page 2035.

Designs and Decorations
The Philadelphia of 1776

The relic of the *Philadelphia* was raised from the bottom of Lake Champlain in 1935. It is now on permanent exhibition at the Smithsonian Institution in Washington, D.C.

The *Philadelphia* was one of the first armed vessels to serve America. As part of an attempt to capture New York state in 1776, and thus cut the rebellious colonies in two, the British assembled a fleet in Quebec and sailed down Lake Champlain. To meet this challenge, the Americans, under the command of Benedict Arnold, hastily built a small fleet largely made up of rowing galleys called gundalows, one of which was the *Philadelphia*. On October 11, 1776, the two fleets met near Valcour Island in Lake Champlain for what was to be the first battle between the American and British fleets. Outnumbered and ill-equipped, the Americans managed to hold out for two days before the enemy caught up with them and sank their entire fleet.

This could have been the end of the *Philadelphia*, but the little vessel was found in 1935 on the bottom of the lake and raised. It was in a surprisingly good state of preservation and was subsequently restored and moved to the Smithsonian Institution in Washington, D. C. where it is on display (see photograph, above). You can learn much about both the vessel and the battle from Howard Chapelle's *The History of the American Sailing Navy*.

The Model
The model of the *Philadelphia* (pictured on page 2025) is constructed with sheet balsa wood, obtainable at hobby shops, making a built-up hull. It is outfitted with both white metal fittings that you order from a catalog and with balsa fittings that you make. You probably can order most items on the following list of materials from a single supplier (opposite page).

Materials Required and Preliminaries

Balsa wood: One sheet 1/16 by 1 by 36 inches; two sheets 1/32 by 4 by 36 inches (3-inch width will do if you can't get wider); one sheet ⅛ by 3 by 36 inches; two pieces ⅛ by ⅛ by 36 inches (cut from ⅛-inch sheet if you can't find it in ⅛-by-⅛-inch size). If you mail-order the wood you will probably receive it in 18-inch lengths.

White metal fittings: One 2-inch cannon and carriage; two 1½-inch cannons and carriages; eight ½-inch swivel guns; two 1½-inch anchors; one dozen ⅜-inch belaying pins (brass); four dozen 1/16-inch cannon balls (or ask a hunter friend for some buckshot); six 5/16-inch cleats; one dozen ⅛-inch deadeyes; two dozen ⅛-inch single metal blocks. (Wooden deadeyes and blocks are available at a slightly higher price and look better than the white metal ones I used.) Each supplier has its own catalog numbering system for these items, so you will have to have the catalog in hand before you can order with precision.

Other items: One box of brass straight pins; two spools of rigging line (one fine and one medium); a small square of beeswax; one 5/32-by-6-inch wood mast; one ¼-by-9-inch wood mast; one 3/32-by-5-inch wood yard; one 5/32-by-7½-inch wood yard; white glue; one dozen eyebolts (or shape them from straight pins with needle-nose pliers); one spool of soft wire; one model-boat paint kit; a small can of rubbing stain (I used medium oak); tracing paper; light cardboard for patterns (14-inch file folders are best); and an assembly board of wood or thick cardboard at least 6 by 18 inches to use as a work surface. You will also need a small can of clear semigloss varnish and one of thinner. Some of the items (paints, rigging line, pins, beeswax, and some wood) will be left over for use on future models.

Tools: Tools required to build this model are shown in photograph 1. A sharpened piece of paper-clip wire held in the pin vise will do as an awl. You could do without the pin vise and drills, but they will make your work easier.

Even before you begin to collect the materials and tools, study the instructions, plans, and patterns carefully. The working drawing (Figure B, page 2032) consists of a profile and a deck plan. Ten construction details (Figures C-L) will clarify some of the more complicated areas. Together, they also will serve to define nautical terms, from keel to topmast, which may be unfamiliar to you. While the patterns in Figure A, pages 2028-2029, are shown full size, the profile and deck plan are drawn to a scale half that of the model; keep this in mind as you work. To find a length on the model, simply take the corresponding length from the profile or deck plan and double it (for example, the flag is ¾ inch long on the drawing; so it should be 1½ inches long on the model). But this applies *only* to the profile and deck plans. Figures E, F, and G are shown actual size. The rest of the details are near actual size but should not be used to check measurements. The profile, in addition to showing the outside detail, also shows some of the internal structure with dashed lines. By noting these dashed lines and comparing them with construction photographs 10 and 11 (page 2031), you will have a good idea of how the model goes together. The deck plan is simply a view of the ship from above, looking down on the deck. Compare the detailed photographs of the model on page 2033 with the profile, deck plan, and detail drawings, and you will be ready to start building.

Balsa Patterns

Accurately trace the balsa patterns (Figure A, pages 2028-2029) onto tracing paper. To align and join the long pattern pieces bridging two pages, first trace one page; then shift your paper and trace the other (you can save time by photocopying each page, then taping them together) along the dotted line. Make cardboard patterns of everything outlined with solid lines. This includes the web (cross-piece) of each former but not its side frames. (The formers are the U-shaped hull braces that together, in effect, form or shape the hull.) To make the patterns, place the tracing over light cardboard and gently punch through with an awl (photograph 2) outlining the pattern with a series of tiny indentations. Remove the tracing, connect the indentations with pencil lines, label each piece as it appears on pages 2028-2029, then cut out the cardboard pattern. Make one pattern at a time to avoid confusion. Formers A, B, and C (hull braces) have been superimposed to save space but you will need to make a separate tracing and pattern for each (patterns for the webs only, remember). The quarter deck, forecastle deck, and main deck have also been superimposed and must be cut as three separate patterns.

Sources of models and gear

America's Hobby Center, 146 West 22nd St., New York, N.Y. 10011. Ships catalog $1. Kits, supplies, tools. Model catalog, also $1, has balsa wood.

James Bliss & Co., Inc., Route 128, Dedham, Mass. 02026. Ship model catalog 75¢. Major kits, fittings, plans, tools.

Bluejacket Shipcrafters, 145 Water St., South Norwalk, Conn. 06854. Catalog 75¢. Kits, fittings, materials, tools, books.

The Channings, 35 Main St., Marion, Mass. 02738. Whaleship plans.

Coker Craft, Box 124, Charleston, S.C. 29402. Catalog $1. Plans, books, waterline models.

A.J. Fisher, Inc., 1002 Etowah St., Royal Oak, Mich. 48067. Catalog 60¢. Plans, fittings, kits, books.

International Marine Publishing Co., 21 Elm St., Camden, Maine 04843. Book list, free.

Marine Model Co., Inc., 95 New York Ave., Box 206, Halesite, N.Y. 11743. Catalog $1. Own line of kits and fittings, tools, tapered spars.

Marittima Models, Box 1156, Newport News, Va. 23601. Brochure 75¢. Ten plank-on-former kits from Italy, also plans.

Model Shipways, 39 West Fort Lee Rd., Bogota, N.J. 07603. Catalog 75¢. Own kits, fittings, books.

Polk's Hobbies, 314 5th Ave., New York, N.Y. 10001. Kits, tools, balsa wood. Catalog $3.95.

Preston's, Main Street Wharf, Greenport, N.Y. 11944. Catalog 25¢. Kits, books, decorative items.

Rockport Marine Center, Box 410, Rockport, Mass. 01966. Catalog $2. Kits, tools, fittings, fine woods, brass, cordage, sailcloth.

Scientific Models, 340 Snyder Ave., Berkley Heights, N.J. 07922. Free catalog, own kits.

Ships Unlimited, 1900 Central, Evanston, Ill. 60201. Many kits, tools, supplies. Write for catalog price.

Silvo Hardware Co., 107-09 Walnut St., Philadelphia, Pa. 19106. Catalog $1. Tools.

Woodcraft Supply Co., 313 Montvale Ave., Woburn, Mass. 01801. Catalog 50¢. Wood and carving tools.

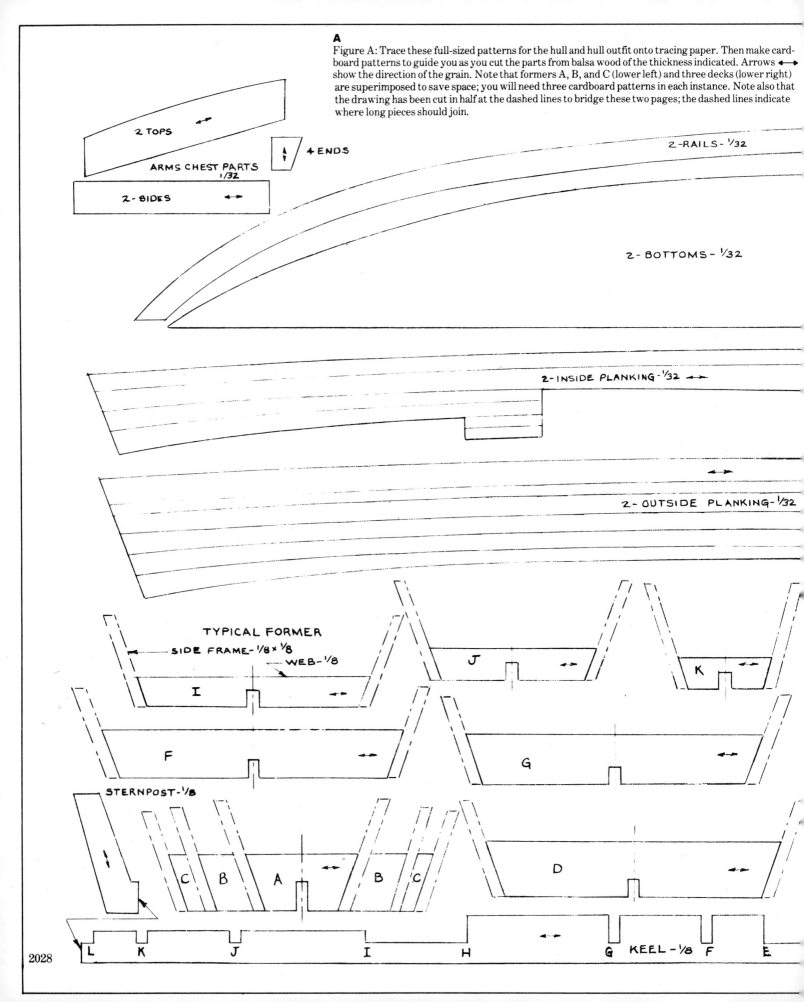

A

Figure A: Trace these full-sized patterns for the hull and hull outfit onto tracing paper. Then make cardboard patterns to guide you as you cut the parts from balsa wood of the thickness indicated. Arrows ◄—► show the direction of the grain. Note that formers A, B, and C (lower left) and three decks (lower right) are superimposed to save space; you will need three cardboard patterns in each instance. Note also that the drawing has been cut in half at the dashed lines to bridge these two pages; the dashed lines indicate where long pieces should join.

2 TOPS

ARMS CHEST PARTS 1/32

4 ENDS

2-SIDES

2-RAILS- 1/32

2- BOTTOMS- 1/32

2-INSIDE PLANKING- 1/32

2- OUTSIDE PLANKING- 1/32

TYPICAL FORMER

SIDE FRAME- 1/8 × 1/8

WEB- 1/8

I

J

K

F

G

STERNPOST- 1/8

C B A B C

D

L K J I H G KEEL- 1/8 F E

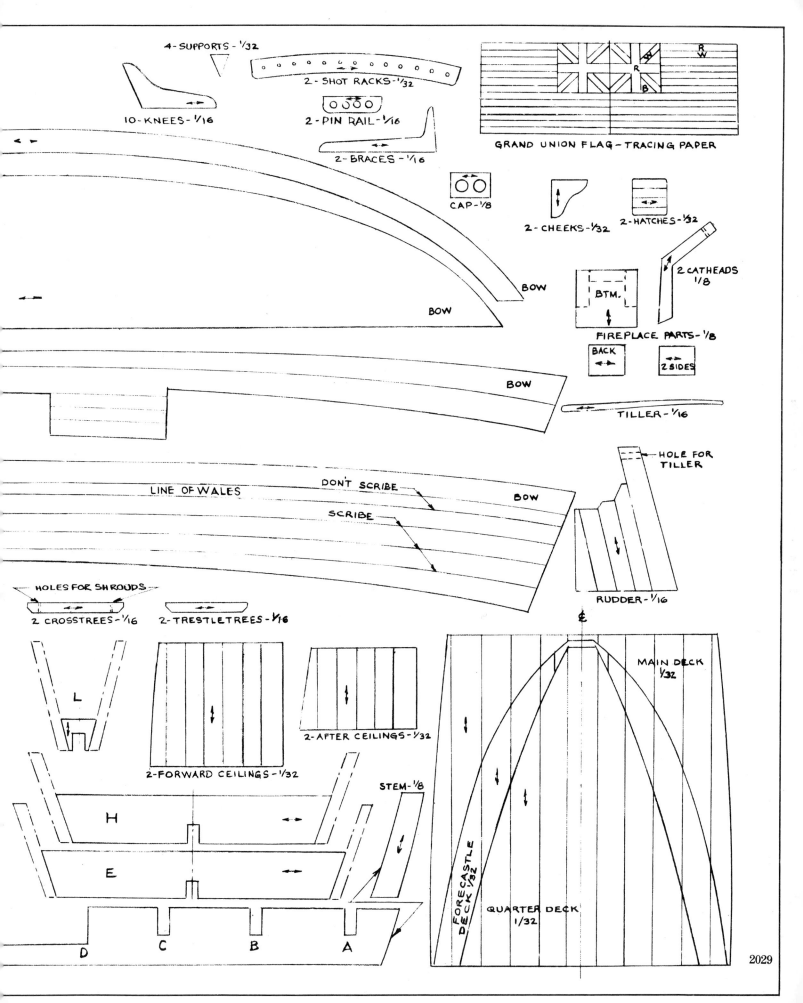

4 - SUPPORTS - 1/32

2 - SHOT RACKS - 1/32

10 - KNEES - 1/16

2 - PIN RAIL - 1/16

2 - BRACES - 1/16

GRAND UNION FLAG - TRACING PAPER

CAP - 1/8

2 - CHEEKS - 1/32

2 - HATCHES - 1/32

2 CATHEADS 1/8

BTM.

FIREPLACE PARTS - 1/8

BACK

2 SIDES

BOW

BOW

BOW

TILLER - 1/16

BOW

HOLE FOR TILLER

LINE OF WALES

DON'T SCRIBE

SCRIBE

BOW

RUDDER - 1/16

HOLES FOR SHROUDS

2 CROSSTREES - 1/16

2 - TRESTLETREES - 1/16

L

2 - FORWARD CEILINGS - 1/32

2 - AFTER CEILINGS - 1/32

STEM - 1/8

MAIN DECK 1/32

H

E

FORECASTLE DECK 1/32

QUARTER DECK 1/32

D   C   B   A

2029

3: Place each of the cardboard patterns over the balsa wood as shown above (the main deck), and cut out the wood with a craft knife.

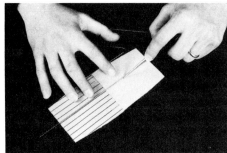

4: To scribe planking lines, lay the cardboard pattern and the cut-out deck end-to-end. Extend and scribe the lines with an awl and a straightedge.

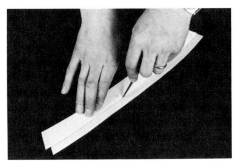

5: To scribe curved lines representing the outside planking of the vessel, use the bottom of the cardboard pattern as a guide.

6: A former (web and side frame) is shown under construction. Pin webs over tracings of actual-size patterns; then glue side frames to the webs and trim ends.

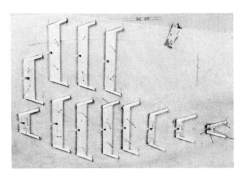

7: All formers are shown completed, with webs and side frames glued and notches cut for the keel. Each former is labeled with a letter corresponding to the keel pattern.

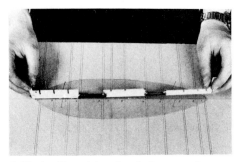

8: The keel is positioned on the bottom so its notches are aligned with the previously drawn parallel lines. Glue it squarely on the center line. Hold it in place with straight pins (photograph 9) until the glue dries.

Preassembly

Place the cardboard patterns over the piece of balsa wood indicated (by its fractional thickness) and cut out the webs of the formers and the keel, stem, sternpost, and bottom. The decks, planking, and other pieces will be cut out later. Note that only half the pattern for the bottom is given. Trace this; then flip the tracing paper, align and trace the other half. Cut one bottom from this doubled pattern. If you were unable to get 4-inch-wide balsa, use 3-inch and make the bottom of two pieces, joining them at the center with tape and a small amount of white glue. Photograph 3 shows a deck being cut out with a craft knife; use the same method to cut out all the parts. Be sure to follow the direction of the wood grain as indicated in the patterns.

To assemble the formers (webs and side frames), place the original full-sized tracing on the model's assembly board and either cover the tracing with transparent wax paper or rub soap on it at the points where webs and side frames join. This will keep glue from sticking to the paper. Pin each web in place; then cut out and glue on the side frames (photographs 6 and 7). Accuracy is important here. Also, glue the stem and sternpost to ends of the keel (photograph 8). Allow glue to dry. Stain those portions of the keel that will show between formers D-E and H-I. To stain, simply brush on the stain and wipe off immediately with a rag.

Hull Assembly

Before beginning the hull assembly, draw a single line lengthwise across the center of your building board. Then, holding the keel on this center line and using the keel notches as a guide, mark their location on the board with a pencil. With a triangle, draw lines at right angles to the center line over each mark. This will give you 12 pairs of parallel lines. Take care to get them precisely ⅛ inch apart, representing the thickness of each former. As shown in photograph 8, pin the bottom to the building board so that its long axis lies directly over the center line. Draw parallel lines across the bottom, connecting those that show on the edge of the building board. Now glue the keel, stem, and sternpost unit onto the bottom, making sure that the guidelines for the formers and the keel notches line up (photograph 9). Glue each former onto the keel and the bottom in its proper place (photographs 9 and 10). If the notches are too tight, enlarge them slightly with sandpaper; if they are too loose, place a sliver of wood in them to get a snug fit. Let the glue dry and remove the model from the board. Using fine sandpaper wrapped around a piece of scrap balsa to hold it firm, smooth the tops of the formers' webs where the decks will set. Try the cardboard deck and ceiling patterns onto the model in their respective places. If the patterns don't fit exactly, trim them as required or enlarge them. This may be necessary to compensate for variations in wood dimensions. Cut out all decks and ceilings. If you were unable to get 4-inch-wide wood, use 3-inch and make the decks in two pieces, as you did for the bottom. Note that both the forward and after ceilings are made in two pieces with one fitting on either side of the keel. The pattern given for the forward ceiling fits the portside of the vessel; turn the pattern over to make the starboard side. Likewise, the pattern for the after ceiling fits the starboard side of the vessel; turn it over to trace and cut out the portside. Lay the pieces down as they appear on the deck plan (Figure B, page 2032). The lines on the decks and ceilings represent planking and are scribed with a point and straightedge (photograph 4). Make the lines deep enough to be evident, but not so deep that you

9: Fit and glue each former to the keel and bottom in its appropriate notch. If the fit is too tight, ease it with light sanding.

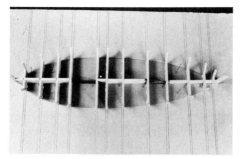

10: With all formers installed on the keel, the bottom and framework of the hull are completed. The decks may now be laid.

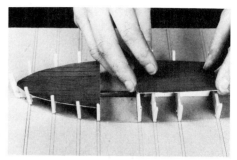

11: Lay the scribed and stained deck pieces over the formers. Adjust the fit if necessary; then glue them in place.

12: Fit the scribed and stained forward and aft ceiling pieces in place over their spacers of scrap balsa; then glue in place.

13: Before installing the inside planking, bevel the inside edges of the side frames with sandpaper so they match the curve of the deck.

14: Install the inside planking. Sand the formers (as shown in photograph 13) to adjust the fit if necessary; then glue the planking in place.

cut through the fragile wood. Practice on some scrap first. The lines representing outside planking, however, are curved, so the bottom of the cardboard pattern is used as a guide instead of a straightedge (photograph 5). Stain the decks and ceilings, brushing the stain on and wiping it off immediately. Now glue down the decks (photograph 11) holding them down temporarily with small weights until the glue sets. As shown in photograph 12, glue scrap pieces of 1/16-inch balsa in the depressions between the forward and after decks to support the ceilings. Glue the ceiling pieces onto them.

Planking

Before laying the inside planking, sandpaper and shape the inside of each side frame so that the inner edges make the same curve as the edge of the deck below (photograph 13). This will insure that the inside planking strip will lie flat when installed. As you sand, brace each side frame with your thumb, as shown, to avoid breakage. Try the inside planking cardboard pattern on the model (the pattern shown is for the portside; turn it over for the starboard side, and trim or adjust it as necessary to fit. Cut out the two wood pieces of inside planking and scribe the inner planking (photograph 5). On one side glue the planking in place to the side frames and to the stem and sternpost (photograph 14) and clamp with clothespins (photographs 15 and 16). To prevent the clothespins from marring the soft balsa, you can glue a small pad of scrap balsa into each side of the jaws. Use clear tape to hold the ends temporarily if necessary. When the glue dries, do the other side. When the inner planking is dry, the outer planking can be fitted and applied. Try the outside pattern (for the starboard side) on the model and adjust as necessary to fit. Sand the side frames outside as you did inside. Then cut and scribe the planking. Wet it with warm water on the ends and bend it slightly over a curved form such as a bottle. This will help shape the wood to the curve of the boat and will facilitate the fit. Glue the planking and clamp (photograph 16). Tape the planking at the ends while the glue dries. When dry, lightly sand the entire model. Cut out and glue on the rails to cover the raw top edges of the inside and outside planking. Then cut out the wales—strips that run the length of the hull on either side (see outside planking pattern, Figure A, pages 2028-2029). Wales are cut in strips ⅛ by 1/32 by about 14 inches long. Trim the ends to fit and glue them in place.

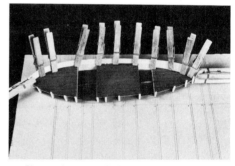

15: Use spring-type clothespins to clamp the inside planking to the formers until the glue dries.

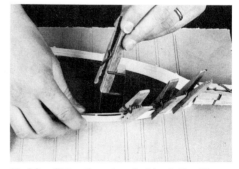

16: After fitting the outer planking to the side frames, glue and clamp it in place with clothespins over the side frames.

B

Figure B: This profile drawing (top) and deck plan (bottom) of the *Philadelphia* are exactly one-half actual size. Refer to these drawings frequently during hull construction and rigging. Yards are shown swung fore and aft here for clarity, but are actually oriented port and starboard on the model. The deck plan shows the placement of all hull outfitting details.

ALL RUNNING RIGGING SHOWN IN RED

LIFT

TOPSAIL HALYARD
TOPSAIL YARD
E

TOPSAIL BRACE

TOPMAST
TOPMAST SHROUDS

CAP
F
C
TOP
LIFT
MAIN YARD

MAIN HALYARD
D

MAIN BRACE

FORE TOPMAST STAY

FORESTAY

BRACE

MAIN SHROUDS

MAINMAST

BACKSTAY (ONE ON EITHER SIDE)

DEADEYE

SPREADER

UPPER BLOCK

TILLER
CLEATS
SWIVEL GUN
BITT
ROWING THOLES
DEADEYE
MAST BEAM & BRACE.
RAIL
ANCHOR
CATHEAD
KNIGHTHEAD
CUT OUT HAWSE HOLE
STEM

RUDDER
WALE

OUTLINE OF REEL & LINE OF DECKS
FORMERS
MAST BRACE

L K J I H G F E D C B A

PORT
DEADEYES

PROFILE
1/8"=1'-0"

FWD. BLOCK W/ EYEBOLT
BITT

STANCHION SOCKET
BLOCK W/ EYEBOLT
CLEATS
SWIVEL GUN

ARMS CHEST

AFTER CEILING

SHOT

FIREPLACE

9 POUND GUN

CATHEAD

A
B
C
D
FORWARD CEILING
E
F
G
H

GUN RAIL
EYEBOLT
12 POUND GUN
KNIGHTHEAD

QUARTER DECK

HATCH

KEEL

MAIN DECK

MAST

PIN RAIL
PINS

LASHING
MAST BEAM

MAST BRACE
TRANSVERSE

FORECASTLE DECK

EYEBOLT
KNIGHTHEAD

STERNPOST

AFT

BRACE

BLOCK W/EYEBOLT

ROWING THOLES

9 POUND GUN

KNEES

SHOT

SHOT RACK

FORWARD

CATHEAD

ANCHOR

BITT
FWD. BLOCK W/ EYEBOLT

RAIL

INNER PLANKING
DEADEYES
STARBOARD

DECK PLAN
1/8"=1'-0"

DRAWINGS BY WILLIAM FOX BASED ON PLANS BY H.I. CHAPELLE AND USED WITH HIS PERMISSION.

Outfitting the Hull

To me, the most enjoyable part of the construction is making and installing all of the wooden hull items: the rudder, tiller, arms chests (Figure C), hatches, knees, mast beam, braces, pin rails, bitts (Figure D), mast brace and transverse, gun rails, shot racks, catheads, and knightheads. Patterns are given in Figure A, pages 2028-2029, for all but the following rectangular pieces which you can cut from balsa by simply measuring their dimensions as given in parentheses: mast beam which runs across the deck from one inside planking to the other just in front of the mast (1/16 by ¼ inch, length to fit); mast brace (⅛ by ⅛ by ⅞ inch); transverse (⅛ by ⅛ by ⅝ inch); two gun rails (⅛ by 3/16, length to fit from bow to transverse); and knightheads (3/32 by 3/32 by ½ inch, trimmed from a piece ⅛ by ⅛ inch). Cut out these parts and the hatch pattern pieces. Sand and stain the hatches, mast brace, transverse, and gun rails. Make the fireplace and paint it dark red or create a more authentic brick red, as I did, by using a red felt-pen color slightly darkened with a black felt pen. Locate and install each of these items, using the color detail photographs below and deck and profile plans opposite as guides. Make and install the arms chests (Figure C) and the six bitts (Figure D). Make 24 rowing tholes (an old form of oarlock) from straight pins as follows: Using wire cutters or pliers, trim off the last ¼ inch of the pointed end of the pin. Install tholes in pairs ⅛ inch deep into the rails as indicated in the deck plan. Install the white metal cleats. (Most of the white metal fittings will require some trimming and finishing.) Drill holes in the rail for each item. Make stanchion sockets (16 small, square holes around the rail; see deck plan) by drilling a 1/16-inch-diameter hole and shaping it square with the point of a knife. Finally, make the cutout through the inner and outer planking for the 12-pound cannon that fits in and projects over the bow (see photograph below, left, and profile diagram). Now paint all of the hull and outfit with hull-red model-boat paint, using the color photographs as a guide. One coat should be sufficient. Paint all of the stained parts with clear semigloss varnish cut with one part thinner to four parts varnish. Remove the wheels from the 12-pound gun with a knife or file; then sand the axle projections smooth. Now paint the cannons black and their carriages hull-red. Paint the swivel guns black; then install them. Glue the fireplace into position. Make piles of cannon balls (buckshot) by assembling a layer, gluing with tiny drops of glue, and then repeating the process, using tweezers to build the pile.

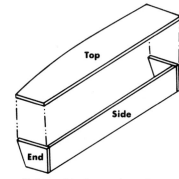

C

Figure C: Assemble the two arms chests, as shown above, using pieces cut from the pattern on page 2028. The deck plan (opposite) shows the placement of the chests in the stern, or after section, of the ship.

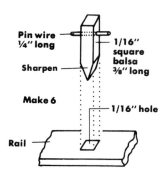

D

Figure D: Bitts are used as lashing points for lines. Make six, as shown above, and install them on the rail, as indicated on the deck plan.

This view of the model looking down at the bow shows the rigging of the anchor and the lower end of the forestay with its spreader and deadeyes just above and behind the cannon.

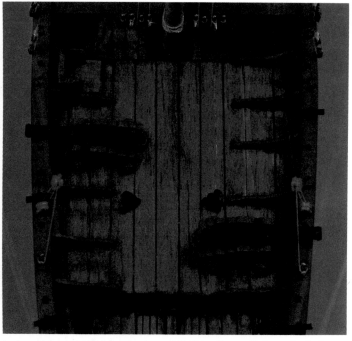

A view of the main deck looking toward the bow (forward) shows, in clockwise order from top left: the fireplace, the pin rail, mast lashing, the cannon, and backstay rigging.

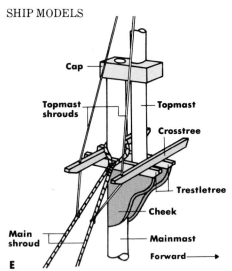

E

Figure E: This is a full-sized detail of the top where topmast and mainmast are joined. Topmast shrouds and main shrouds are shown. Cut the remaining mast-support pieces from patterns (page 2029) and assemble as shown. Compare this view with the profile drawing (page 2032) and the color detail photograph (opposite).

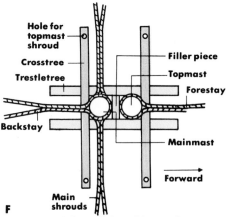

F

Figure F: A full-sized view of the top shows how the filler piece is inserted between the masts. Note that the backstay loop lays over the main shrouds and crosstrees.

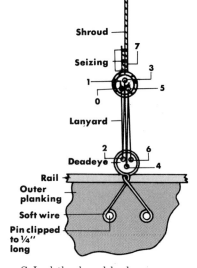

G

Figure G: Lash the shroud deadeyes together, following the numerical sequence given in the full-sized detail above.

2034

Preparing Masts and Rigging Hardware

The *Philadelphia* is rigged but not fitted with sails. Apart from being very difficult to reproduce realistically, sails hide much of the rigging detail that is the pride of every modeler. Most museum models, like the Admiralty model pictured on page 2024, are built without sails; so your model will be in good company.

Before the model can be rigged, you must prepare and install the following items associated with the rigging. First, sand and stain the two precut masts and two yards. Using the patterns on page 2029, cut out and stain the cap, crosstrees, trestletrees, and cheeks. Now, referring to Figures E and F and the color photograph of rigging details, opposite, begin to assemble the masts in the following sequence: Insert one end of the mainmast into the cap and glue. Slip the topmast into the other hole in the cap from above and allow it to project ⅞ inch below the cap. Do not glue it at this time. Make sure that the masts are perfectly parallel when viewed from any direction. The assembly shown in Figure E—called the top—can now be put together. Glue a trestletree on either side of both masts at the bottom of the topmast. Glue one cheek under each trestletree. Drill vertical holes in the crosstrees, as indicated in the pattern, and glue them over the trestletrees. Cut a small filler piece (shown in Figure F) ⅛ inch square and glue between the masts in line with the trestletrees. Coat the mast assembly and yards with thinned varnish.

Deadeyes and Blocks

Four deadeyes—round discs with three holes (see Figure G)—must now be fastened to the hull with soft wire at the places indicated on the deck plan and profile. Following Figure G, bend a piece of soft wire about 2 inches long around a deadeye, and twist it once bringing the free ends out at angles. Be sure the deadeye holes are oriented as shown with two above and one below. Clip straight pins ¼ inch from the heads, wrap the ends of the soft wire several times around the pinheads and clip off the free end of wire. With the pointed end of another pin, make holes in the outer planking of the hull where the pinheads will go. Insert the pins with wire and deadeye attached, and apply a spot of glue to each pinhead to hold it in place. Attach the three remaining deadeyes in the same manner.

Using fine line, tie and knot four eyebolts onto four blocks. Put a tiny drop of glue on these and all knots in the rigging to hold them in place. Two eyebolts must now be installed along the rails on each side of the stern, as indicated on the deck plan. Punch holes in the rail with a pin and insert the eyebolts. Since these eyebolts have no threads, they are not screwed in. Now unroll the rigging line from the spools, and stain it a very light tan, using wood stain or strong coffee. When the line is dry, pull it between your thumb and a chunk of beeswax to give it a smooth finish without fuzziness. Now the actual rigging can begin.

Running and Standing Rigging

There are basically two kinds of rigging on every ship. Standing rigging, shown in black in the profile in Figure B, page 2032, includes the stays and shrouds; it supports the mast and is permanently fixed in place. Running rigging, shown in red, includes lifts, halyards, and braces; it is movable and runs through blocks by which the yards are raised and trimmed. The standing rigging is done first.

Deadeye and Spreader

The forestay and fore topmast stay, shown in the profile, are attached to the hull by means of a pair of deadeyes and a spreader tied to two eyebolts attached to the deck on either side of the forecastle just behind the catheads (Figure B, page 2032). To make them, take a 6-inch length of medium line and wrap it once around a deadeye. Where the threads cross, bind them together with several turns of fine line as close to the deadeye as possible. This is called binding and seizing, and is illustrated in Figure G. Be sure the deadeye holes are oriented as shown in the profile. Tie eyebolts on the free ends of this line, about 2 inches below the deadeye. Glue the knots and trim the loose ends; then attach the eyebolts to the forecastle deck as indicated on the deck plan.

Cut out the spreader (¾-inch-long piece of 1 1/6-by-1/16-inch balsa), stain it, and notch the ends. Insert the spreader between the two lines and glue. This detail is shown in the color photograph (page 2033) of the forecastle deck.

Compare this view of the top and main yard with Figures E and L. Note the crosstrees, trestletrees, and parral. The rigging of the main lifts and halyard, forestay, and shrouds is also visible.

The masts can now be temporarily set up with four pieces of common sewing thread each about 15 inches long. Tie one end of each thread halfway up the topmast. Run the lines down and tie one to each cathead (forward) and one to each of the bitts closest to the stern (aft). Use slip knots for these ties. Adjust the mast unit so that it is positioned between the pin rails and against the mast beam. The masts should be perfectly vertical when seen from the bow but angled slightly aft (toward the stern) when seen from the side. This is called mast rake and is shown in the profile drawing. Now lash the base of the mast to the mast beam with medium line. It is not necessary to glue the mast in place. Even on an actual ship, a mast is never fastened rigidly to the hull.

Shrouds

The shrouds provide lateral support for the masts; the stays provide lengthwise (longitudinal) support. The shrouds are rigged in pairs and flank the mast, attaching to the deadeyes you have already wired on either side of the hull. To make the first pair of shrouds, seize a deadeye to one end of an 18-inch piece of medium line (as was done for the forestay deadeye and spreader). Orient the deadeye holes as shown in Figure G, with two below and one above. Loop the free end of the line above the trestletree (Figure E), around the mainmast, then back down near the deadeye. Seize another deadeye to the free end so that both of these deadeyes hang about ⅜ inch above the deadeyes on the rail. Bind the shrouds together where they loop around the mainmast with several turns of fine line (Figure E). Now rig the deadeyes with lanyards as in Figure G. The lanyard is a 12-inch piece of fine line which is knotted at zero in Figure G, then is threaded through hole 1, then back and forth through holes 2 through 6, then up to 7 where it is tied but not knotted tight for the moment. Now rig the shrouds on the other side of the model exactly as you did the first pair. The loop around the mast for the second pair lays over the loop of the first pair (Figure F). To make the topmast (or upper) shrouds, tie the center of a 15-inch length of medium line to the topmast about 1¼ inches from its top. Run each end down through a hole in the crosstrees and tie to the main shrouds (Figure E). Repeat for the other side of the mast.

Books for reference

Many books are available. Those listed here are generally inexpensive and will help you get started. Many of the suppliers listed on page 2027 have them.

The Neophyte Shipmodeller's Jackstay, by George F. Campbell. Model Shipways.

The History of American Sailing Ships and **The History of the American Sailing Navy,** by Howard I. Chapelle. Bonanza Books reprints.

The Ship Model Builder's Assistant, by Charles G. Davis. Marine Research Society, 1929. Reprint.

American Ship Models and How to Build Them, by V.R. Grimwood. Bonanza Books reprint.

Ships in Bottles, by Donald Hubbard. McGraw-Hill.

Ship Model Building, by Gene Johnson. Cornell Maritime Press.

Lusci's Ship Model Builder's Handbook, by Vincenzo Lusci. Lusci, 1970. Available from Coker.

Modelling Ships in Bottles, by Jack Needham. Collier Books.

The Lore of Ships, by Tre Tryckare. Crescent Books.

Where to see ships and models

There are hundreds of museums featuring ships and ship models, but these are the major ones. Check the Nautical Museum Directory, Quadrant Press, New York, N.Y., for a complete listing.

California: San Francisco Maritime Museum, Maritime Museum Association of San Diego.

Connecticut: Mystic Seaport.

District of Columbia: National Museum of History and Technology (part of the Smithsonian Institution—the Philadelphia relic is here); Truxton Decatur Naval Museum.

Georgia: Ships of the Sea Museum, Savannah.

Maine: Bath Marine Museum; Penobscot Marine Museum, Searsport.

Maryland: Naval Academy Museum, Annapolis; frigate Constellation, Baltimore; Chesapeake Bay Maritime Museum, St. Michaels.

Massachusetts: USS Constitution and Boston Museum of Fine Arts, Boston; Marine Museum, Fall River; Whaling Museums, New Bedford and Nantucket; Peabody Museum, Salem.

New York: South Street Seaport Museum, New York City.

Pennsylvania: Philadelphia Maritime Museum.

Virginia: Mariner's Museum, Newport News; Norfolk Naval Shipyard Museum, Portsmouth.

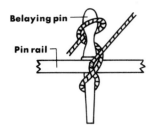

H

Figure H: To belay or tie a line to a pin or cleat, describe the figure-eight loops of the line as demonstrated above. Note that the first turn here is made on the underside of the belaying pin and that the final loop is above.

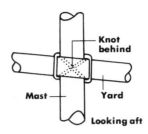

I

Figure I: Attach the yards to the masts with a parral as shown in this view looking aft (toward the stern).

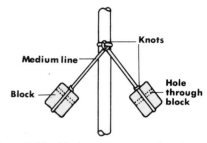

J

Figure J: Tie a block to a mast or yard, as shown, so that the line is perpendicular to the hole in the block indicated by dotted lines.

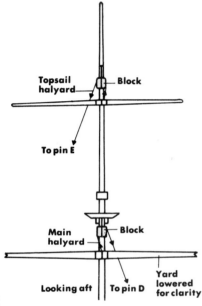

K

Figure K: The halyards (the lines that raise and lower the yards) are tied to the center of the yards, then run up through the blocks tied above them on the masts, then down to pins E and D on the pin rail (deck plan, page 2032).

GUNDALOW
PHILADELPHIA of 1776
MODEL
SCALE: 1/4" = 1'-0"

Trace or photocopy this identifying plate for your model of the *Philadelphia* of 1776 and mount it with the model for display.

The Forward Stays

There are two forward stays: the forestay and the fore topmast stay (profile, page 2032). For these forward stays, take a 24-inch length of medium line and seize a deadeye at its center with holes oriented (Figure G, page 2034). Then run one end around the topmast, tying it where the topmast shrouds are attached. The deadeye on the other end of this fore topmast stay should hang about ⅜ inch above the deadeye and the spreader below (see color detail of bow, page 2033). Run the other free end (the forestay) up over the forward crosstree and loop it around the topmast. Bind the line back on itself (Figure F, page 2034) and trim off excess. Rig a lanyard between the deadeyes as shown in Figure G. Now you can remove the temporary threads that help up the mast while you were installing the standing rigging as it is now held up by shrouds and forward stays.

Backstays

The backstays, shown in the profile drawing, are rigged on each side of the masts and attach to the blocks and eyebolts already installed along the stern rails near the arms chests. Take an 18-inch piece of medium line and tie a block to one end. Run the free end over the crosstrees that face the stern (aft) and loop it around the mainmast between top and cap (Figure F); then lead the free end down and tie a block to the end. Bind the line where it loops the mast as shown in Figure F. The blocks on the lines should hang about 1 inch above the forward blocks on the rail. The line blocks and rail blocks must now be rigged together. Tie a 6-inch piece of fine line around each of the upper blocks; then lead the free ends down through the holes in the lower blocks, up through the holes in the upper blocks, and then down to the bitts just behind (aft of) the lower block and tie, belaying (fastening) the line similar to Figure H. This completes the standing rigging.

Running Rigging

Now we can rig the running rigging. Refer to Figures I, J, K, and L, the profile (page 2032), and the color photograph (page 2035) as you work. The main (lower) yard is rigged first. Take a piece of medium line about 5 inches long, and tie two blocks onto it about 3 inches apart; then trim the loose ends. Tie this line to the main yard about ⅛ inch from one end so that each block is the same distance from the yard (Figures J and L). Make up another identical line with two blocks, and tie it to the other end of the main yard in the same way. Take a piece of medium line about 4 inches long, and tie two blocks 1½ inches apart. Tie this around the topmast just above the cap (Figure L). These are the blocks for the lifts. The block for the main halyard (Figure K) is tied to the mainmast just under the cheeks so that it hangs just below the topmast. Tie the main yard to the mast with a parral of medium line (Figure I). For the main parral on my model, I used a short length of key chain (see rigging detail pictured on page 2035. You may duplicate this if you wish but a rope parral is also correct. When the parral is completed, tie a piece of fine line about 12 inches long to the center of the yard, and run it up through the hole in the block you have just hung below the topmast; then take it down to pin D on the pin-rail (see deck plan) where it should be belayed (Figure H). On a real ship the main halyard raises the yard.

Lifts

The lifts (Figure L), rigged next, raise and support the ends of the yard and keep it horizontal. Cut two 18-inch pieces of fine line. Tie one line around the starboard block at the cap, run it down and through the hole in the blocks at the end of the

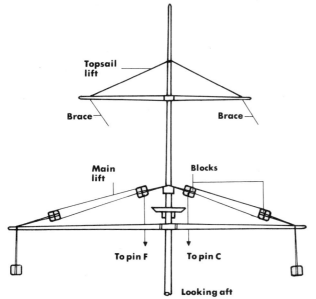

Topsail lift

Brace — Brace —

Main lift — Blocks

To pin F — To pin C

L — Looking aft

Figure L: Like the halyards, the lifts are also used to raise and lower the yards. They are lines tied to the masts and both ends of the yards. As shown above, the main lifts are threaded between the blocks tied to the mast and the yards; the lines then continue down to the pin rail where they are belayed on pins F and C (deck plan, page 2032). The topsail lifts are simply tied between the ends of the topsail yard and the topmast.

yard, then back up through the hole in the block where it started. Then carry it down to pin F on the pinrail. Repeat for the port side, bringing the line down to pin C on the pin rail. Belay the lines.

Braces
The main braces (profile, page 2032) which trim and set the main yard will be rigged next. Tie a 20-inch piece of fine line to each of the aftermost blocks on the rail. Run the free ends up through holes in the blocks hanging below the ends of the main yard (Figure L). Bring them down through the holes in the blocks where they started; then secure them to the cleats just forward of the blocks on either side of the hull. (Note arrows indicating the direction the lines run on the profile drawing.)

Topsail Yard
The running rigging for the topsail yard is fairly simple. Tie a block to the topmast about 1½ inches from its top (Figure K). Parral the topsail yard to the topmast (Figure I). Then tie a 15-inch piece of fine line to the center of the yard, lead the free end up through the block above, then down to pin E on the pin rails (see deck plan). This line is the topsail halyard. To make the lifts on this yard, tie an 8-inch piece of fine line to one end of the yard. Run it up to the mast about 1 inch from the top and tie it there. Lead it down the other end of yard and, after straightening the yard so it is parallel to the deck, tie it there. (All knots in the rigging should be dotted with glue; trim all ends when the glue dries.) For the topsail braces, tie a 15-inch length of fine line to each end of the topsail yard; then run the free ends down to the cleats furthest aft (nearest the stern) on either side of the hull. Go back now and adjust the deadeyes of the shrouds, tightening them if necessary. Then tie and glue the lines.

Finishing Touches
Trace and make the flag from tracing paper, coloring it as indicated on the pattern with felt-tipped pens. Fold the flag and glue both sides together; then punch holes along the staff edge at top and bottom, and tie the flag to the topmast. Drill about a 1/16-inch hawse hole (opening for the anchor chain) through the outer planking on each side of the hull just under the forward swivel guns. These are shown in the profile (page 2032) in front of the catheads. Assemble each anchor and paint the flukes (hooks) and shank black, the crosspiece hull-red, and the crosspiece bands black. Attach a 1½-inch piece of medium line to the hole in each anchor. Tie a loop of fine line through these same holes, and attach to their respective catheads. Sling the anchors along the bow as shown in the color detail of the bow (page 2033) by tying the flukes to the nearest bitts. Place the end of the medium line into the hawse hole you drilled and glue it in place.

The model is finished now and you should go back over it carefully, snipping off any loose ends, cleaning up, and touching up the paint. Cut out or trace the label plate (opposite), and display it with your model. You may wish to build a glass case (Craftnotes, right) to protect it and keep it on display.

CRAFTNOTES: SHIP MODEL DISPLAY CASE

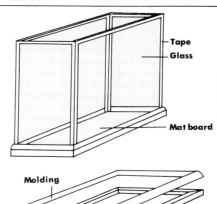

Tape
Glass
Mat board
Molding
Base

A glass display case is desirable for a fragile ship model with its many dust-catching details. It will also enhance its appearance and add to the importance of the model. The single-strength window glass needed to build a case for the **Philadelphia**, about $5 worth at a glass or hardware shop, is as follows: one top 16⅛ by 9⅝ inches; two ends 16½ by 9½ inches; two sides 16½ by 16⅛ inches. You will also need: a piece of heavy cardboard or mat board 12 by 18 inches; about 6 feet of ½- or ⅜-inch quarter round or other pine molding; white glue; clear tape; and ½-inch black electrical tape.

First set up one long side. Carefully apply glue along one vertical edge of each end piece (be very careful not to cut yourself), and put them in position against the side piece. (Note that they are set in.) Hold the pieces together temporarily with clear cellophane tape while the glue dries. Attach the other long side in the same way. Apply glue around the top edge, lay on the top, square it up, and let the glue dry. Then remove the clear tape, and seal all outside seams with electrical tape. Place the case on the mat board and trace its outline. Add the width of the molding all around; then cut out the board along this line. Cut the molding that will frame this baseboard, allowing enough wood so you can miter the corners. Glue the molding to the baseboard, and paint the molding and baseboard flat black with model paint. Center and glue the model onto the mat board. Glue the label plate against the hull. Then carefully place the glass case over it and onto the board inside the molding. The case is attractive and quite inexpensive but it is also fragile (as is the model). Move the case only when it is necessary and then with great care. Should the tape or glue loosen, just rebuild as above.

Ship in a bottle

Born in Port Neches, Texas, on the Gulf of Mexico, Gary Smith has lived near the sea most of his life. After a four-year tour of duty with the Marines in Vietnam, he traveled across the U.S. working at odd jobs. He eventually made his way to New York City, where he now works as a ship's carpenter's apprentice at the South Street Seaport. He has built more than 200 ships-in-bottles, some of which are exhibited at the South Street Seaport Museum.

17: Modeler's tools useful for making a ship to put in a bottle are, left to right: file, small drill bits, razor saw, copper wire, forceps, wood-carving tools, scissors, gouging tool, pin vise, craft knife, and beeswax.

18: The bottle is prepared with a blue plastic-clay sea, inserted in strips, then waved with a length of wire from a coat hanger. The bamboo skewers will be used as masts. The tiny boxwood hull is shown in preliminary stages of carving.

If you love the sea and sailing ships, and if, like me, you are fascinated by things that seem impossible to do, you might like to build a ship in a bottle. Sailors the world over have been practicing this unique nautical craft for more than a hundred years, and the methods they have devised all use the same basic principle. Regardless of the complexity of the model, it is constructed, complete with rigging (and sails, if desired) outside the bottle. The width and depth of the tiny hull usually measures half the diameter of the bottle neck it must pass through. Masts are hinged to the deck so they are collapsible. The yards—wooden crosspieces on the masts—are tied to the masts in a manner that allows them to swivel vertically. Thus, the entire model can be folded up and inserted into the bottle in one piece, as photograph 21 on page 2041 shows. Once inside, the hull is settled down on a blue plastic clay sea, and the superstructure is unfolded by pulling on lines that run out of the bottle. Although almost any ship design can be scaled down to bottle size, I advise beginners to use full-sized plans like those shown here or the ones given in the model-building books by Donald Hubbard and Jack Needham, listed in the bibliography on page 2035.

Some of the tools needed to build a ship in a bottle are shown in photograph 17. In addition, I improvise long-handled tools for working inside the bottle from lengths of wire coat hangers. The forceps enable me to set the ship inside, but the coat-hanger tools are better for trimming the sails (photograph 23, page 2041), applying glue (photograph 24, page 2041), and cutting the lines of the bowsprit, the final steps in construction. You will also need fine- and medium-grade sandpaper, small amounts of mahogany stain, glossy black paint, and white paint.

The Sea

Although old-timers used caulking putty or ordinary clay to simulate a sea in a bottle, I prefer plastic clay, because it does not require drying and does not mildew. In addition, plastic clay is sticky enough to hold the model in place. For a bottle the size shown in photograph 18, cut three strips of blue plastic clay the length of the bottle from bottom to neck. It can be purchased from art shops and toy shops or J. L. Hammett Co., Braintree, Mass. Insert these one at a time; then smooth the

An American merchant brig, built around 1870, ploughs through choppy seas, all sails set and the lee rail awash. Though a model ship in a bottle may seem a small miracle, how it was launched on its miniature ocean is described here.

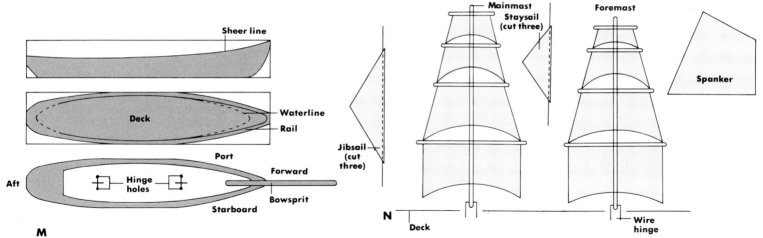

M

Figure M: Actual-size patterns for the boxwood hull are at left, above. Cut a rectangle of wood (top) and draw the pattern lines on it with a pencil. Carve it to the shape shown (center and bottom). Gouge out the deck to a depth of 1/16 inch to make the rail. Drill holes for the mast hinges where indicated. Cut a bowsprit from a bamboo skewer; cut a notch for it in the bow, and glue it in place.

Figure N: Masts, yards, sails, and mast hinges are shown here full size. When installed in the vessel, sails on the masts will curve toward the bow.

seams and make waves with a wire-hanger tool. Smooth an area in the center approximately the size of the hull. With the bottle prepared (needless to say, it must be clean inside) the modeling can begin.

The Model

Building the model is the most time-consuming and difficult part of the process because you work on a very small scale. The hull is carved from a single piece of boxwood (Figure M), a very close-grained wood that is less likely to crack or split than most other woods. After it has been shaped, screw the hull to a wooden base (Figure O and photograph 19, page 2041) for painting and rigging. I make the masts of ⅛-inch-diameter bamboo skewers which are less apt to split than the beech doweling usually used by modelers. These can be purchased at hardware stores or variety stores. For rigging, I use black silk thread. Unlike ordinary modeler's rigging line, black silk need not be coated with beeswax.

Begin the model by cutting a piece of boxwood with a razor saw to the dimension shown in Figure M (top). Outline the top and side of the hull in pencil on the wood. First, cut the sheer—the sharp curve of the deck from bow to stern. Then shape the sides of the hull. Using the pattern lines in Figure M (top and middle drawings) as guides, shape the bow and stern with carving tools, tapering back the underside of the hull to the dotted lines which represent the waterline on which the vessel will eventually rest. With a craft knife, scribe the inside rail line as shown in the drawing. With wood chisels, gouge out the deck between the rails to a depth of 1/16-inch. Sand the hull with fine sandpaper. Simulate ship's planking by scribing bow to stern lines 1/32 inch apart on the deck. Cut the bowsprit from a bamboo skewer to the length shown in Figure M (bottom) and sand; cut an opening in the bow rail, and glue the bowsprit in place. Make a rigging base (Figure O) and secure the hull to it with the bow pointing to the push pin (see photograph 19, page 2041). Drill tiny holes ¼ inch deep for the wires that will hinge the masts to the deck (Figure M, bottom). (The hinges are U-shaped pieces of wire; the wire legs are glued in the deck holes, and the masts fold on the cross wire.) Stain the bowsprit and deck dark mahogany; paint the hull glossy black. Line the rail, the wale (around the hull), and the hatch covers on the deck in white as shown in the color photograph opposite.

Figure N shows masts, yards, and sails full size. Use this drawing as a pattern for measurements and for making the sails later on. Cut two masts and eight yards. Next, make a drilling block (Figure Q) to facilitate drilling holes in the masts. Rest the masts in the block's groove, and using a No. 78 bit, drill four holes through each mast, one for each yard, at the points shown in Figure N where the yards cross. Also drill a hole near the bottom of each mast, approximately 1/16 inch from the base, for the wire mast hinges; these holes run in a port-to-starboard direction. Now drill two more holes in the mainmast for the gaff (just below the hole for the lowest yard) and the boom (just above the hole for the wire hinge).

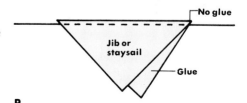

O

Figure O: Make a rigging base from two notched pieces of scrap wood. A single screw inserted through the base from below is enough to impale the bottom of the hull and hold it in place (see photograph 19, page 2041). A pushpin on one end serves as a securing point for rigging lines.

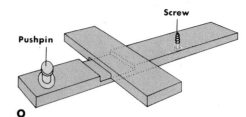

P

Figure P: To attach jibs and staysails to the line, apply glue to the inside surface of the paper, avoiding the fold line. Fold the sail over the line and press glued surfaces together.

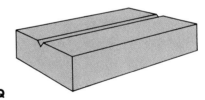

Q

Figure Q: Make a drilling block for the masts by cutting a 1/16-inch V in a piece of scrap wood. Lay the masts in the V to keep them from rolling as they are drilled.

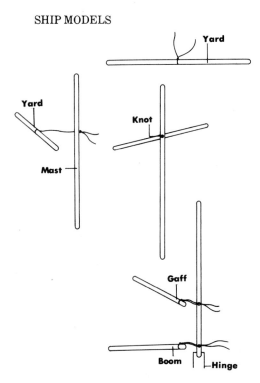

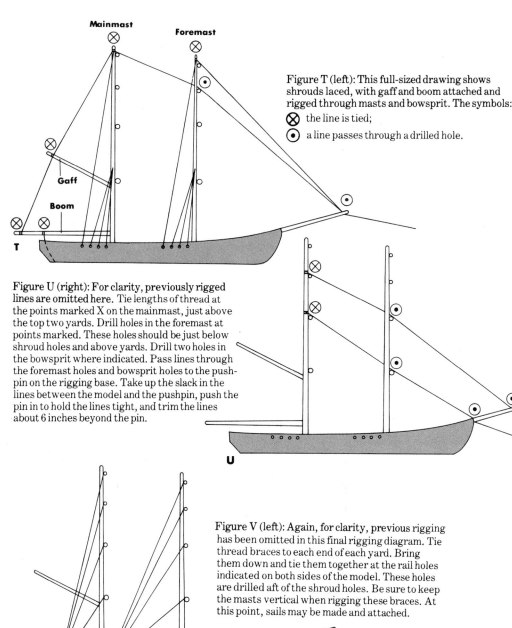

Figure T (left): This full-sized drawing shows shrouds laced, with gaff and boom attached and rigged through masts and bowsprit. The symbols:

⊗ the line is tied;

⊙ a line passes through a drilled hole.

Figure U (right): For clarity, previously rigged lines are omitted here. Tie lengths of thread at the points marked X on the mainmast, just above the top two yards. Drill holes in the foremast at points marked. These holes should be just below shroud holes and above yards. Drill two holes in the bowsprit where indicated. Pass lines through the foremast holes and bowsprit holes to the push-pin on the rigging base. Take up the slack in the lines between the model and the pushpin, push the pin in to hold the lines tight, and trim the lines about 6 inches beyond the pin.

R

Figure R: Find the center of each yard (top), and securely tie the center of a 3-inch length of thread at that point. Pull the free ends of the thread (left) through a hole drilled in the mast. Draw the yard tight against the mast, and knot the thread until the knot is larger than the drilled hole (center). Cut off excess thread and dot with glue. Make sure each of the yards pivots smoothly. Tie the ends of gaff and boom (bottom, right) tightly at the center of a 3-inch length of thread. Pass the ends through the mast holes and knot as for the yards. The U-shaped wire hinge on which the mast swings (bottom, right) fits into holes drilled in the deck.

Figure V (left): Again, for clarity, previous rigging has been omitted in this final rigging diagram. Tie thread braces to each end of each yard. Bring them down and tie them together at the rail holes indicated on both sides of the model. These holes are drilled aft of the shroud holes. Be sure to keep the masts vertical when rigging these braces. At this point, sails may be made and attached.

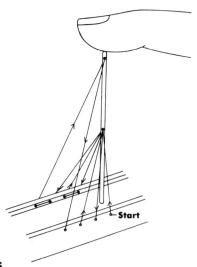

S

Figure S: To lace the shrouds, knot a 12-inch length of thread at the rail hole marked *start* in the drawing. Follow the pattern given for taking the thread back and forth through the lower mast hole. The final line threads through a shroud hole drilled at the top of the mast. Hold the mast vertical with one finger as you tie off the final line.

The method used for attaching yards, gaff, and boom with knotted thread is shown in Figure R. When these are attached, cut two ½-inch pieces of copper wire; insert a piece in the lowest holes in each mast and bend into a U shape as shown in Figure R (lower right). Insert the wire ends at least ⅛ inch into the holes drilled in the deck. Bring the masts as close to the deck as possible while still permitting them to fold on the wire hinges.

With the masts in place, you can drill holes in the bulwarks (rails) and masts for the shroud lines. As shown in Figure S, drill four rail holes just behind (aft) and on either side of each mast, spaced about 1/16 inch apart. The position of the holes allows slack in the line when the masts are folded back. Hold your model against the full-sized drawing in Figure T to determine the placement of the rail holes. Complete one mast at a time. Drill the first shroud hole just above the top yard. Both shroud holes must be drilled in a port-to-starboard direction. Cut a 12-inch length of thread, and tie and knot it through the hole marked *start* in Figure S. Dot the tip of the other end with clear nail polish to stiffen it. Follow the lacing pattern in Figure S, taking the line through the lower shroud hole in the mast back and forth from starboard to portside rail holes. When three holes are laced, hold the mast in a vertical position with your finger, and bring the final line up through the top shroud

19: The completed model is shown on its rigging base. A screw through the underside of the base holds the model steady, while the pushpin (right) serves as an anchor for the rigging lines.

20: To fold the masts, release the lines from the rigging base and carefully lower the mainmast. Be sure the spanker clears the hull. Then lower the foremast. Unscrew the ship from the base.

21: Insert the model into the bottle stern first. As it enters the mouth of the bottle, swivel the yards to one side to let the dropped masts enter.

hole and down to the final rail hole; then tie it securely (Figure S). Lace the shrouds for the other mast in the same way.

When all the shrouds are laced on both masts, drill a hole through the hull at the stern, indicated by a dotted line in Figure T. Knot a 12-inch length of thread and pull the other end through from the bottom, as shown, and tie snugly at the point indicated on the main boom. Bring the thread almost to the end of the boom and tie again. Bring the line up to the end of the gaff, tie, and bring up to the mainmast cap and tie. Next drill a hole in the foremast in a bow-to-stern direction where indicated in Figure T, just above the second yard from the top, and pass the thread through. Drill a hole through the end of the bowsprit; slip the thread through and out to the pushpin on the rigging base and secure. Tie a line to the foremast cap, above the top yard; pass it through the same hole in the bowsprit, and tie it to the pushpin in the base. Complete the rigging as shown and described in Figures U and V, drawn with previous rigging omitted for clarity.

22: After the ship passes the bottleneck, anchor the bottle with plastic clay. Position the hull on the smoothed area inside, using forceps; then press it down with coat-hanger wire.

Sails

Trace the square sails and spanker shown in Figure N (page 2039), and cut them out of bond paper. Paint each sail with coffee for an antique look and let dry. Before applying glue, bend each sail slightly around a pencil to simulate a lengthwise billow. Put glue on the top edge of each of the sails, and glue one to each yard, following the drawing. Attach the spanker—the sail at the stern of the boat—by gluing it to the main gaff only. Be careful not to get glue into holes of the rigging.

For the three jibsails at the bow of the ship, trace the pattern shown in Figure N three times and cut these out along the folded edge of a piece of bond paper to create a double sail (Figure P, page 2039). Put glue on the inner surface of these bowsprit jibsails, but not along the fold line. Fold one jib over each bowsprit line. Since the crease is not glued, the jib should slide on the line. Finally, trace, cut out, and attach the staysails between the masts in the same way. When the glue is dry, the ship is ready to be inserted into the bottle. Photographs 19 through 24 detail the technique to use for inserting the ship into the bottle.

23: Gently pull on the lines that run outside the bottle to raise the masts. Do not force. If the masts do not rise easily, check for tangled rigging and straighten them with coat-hanger wire as shown, then proceed.

Shipshape Bottles

People often ask me which I select first, the ship or the bottle. Usually, I have a specific ship in mind—often someone's favorite yacht or schooner—and I find that the vessel tells me what kind of bottle will suit it best. The rigging and square sails of the brig pictured on page 2038 for example, suggested a rectangular bottle with the same proportions as the rigging. But I also collect unusual bottles wherever I find them, and each one also suggests a specific type of ship to me. In any case, you must know the exact inside dimensions of the bottle, carefully estimating the thickness of the glass overall, before you can design a model to fit inside. If your estimate is wrong, you may complete a beautiful model only to find that the masts are too tall and the yards too wide when you try to raise them. Or you may find the collapsed model will not fit through the bottleneck. Though I have built more than 200 ships in bottles, I always breathe a sigh of relief as the newest one passes through that crucial point, thinking, one more coat of paint and it wouldn't have made it!

For related entries see "Models and Mock-Ups," and "Wood Carving."

24: When all the masts are up and the rigging is taut, anchor the strings at the neck of the bottle with a rubber band. Dab glue on the bowsprit holes, as shown, and let it dry overnight. Finally, cut the threads at the bowsprit with a narrow razor blade taped to the end of coat-hanger wire.

SILHOUETTES
Instant Communication

A silhouette is usually thought of as a profile cut from black paper. But it can be any shadowlike representation obtained by filling the outline of an object with black or another solid color. The silhouette is probably the oldest graphic-art form. In limestone caves at Lascaux, France, and Altamira, Spain, are found silhouettes of animals and humans that were drawn 20,000 to 30,000 years ago. The Egyptians and Greeks of antiquity embellished their own surroundings with flat but decorative silhouettes. The Greeks outlined shadows of figures cast by the sunlight; according to one legend, painting was invented when Corinthia drew the shadow of her departing lover on the wall so that she could retain his image.

Portrait Silhouettes

Profile portraits were common in seventeenth-century Europe. At that time, the usual manner of obtaining a silhouette was to use a candle or a lamp to cast a shadow on a wall or screen (see drawing, left). Often the subject sat immobile in a chair between the light source and a piece of paper that had been oiled to make it translucent. The portraitist traced around the outline of the shadow, then filled it in to form a solid silhouette. Then, as now, this technique could be used by anyone, even a novice, to create an accurate silhouette of any subject. The only knack required was that of getting living subjects to remain absolutely still, since the slightest movement distorted the silhouette.

Another more challenging way to do a portrait silhouette developed with the sudden availability of inexpensive paper and the manufacture of cheap scissors during the Industrial Revolution. Using the new method, a silhouettist needed artistic ability and keen perception, since the profile was cut directly from a sheet of black paper without any guidelines. The best-known American silhouette artist, William Henry Brown, was reputedly able to cut remarkably realistic silhouettes, often from memory, in ten minutes.

In the mid-1700s Étienne de Silhouette, France's frugal finance minister, initiated unpopular financial reforms. His hobby was cutting out silhouettes, a form of portraiture that was quicker and less expensive than the painstakingly executed oil paintings customary at the time. It was around that time that shadowgraphs or shades, as they had been called, came to be known as silhouettes. The expression "à la Silhouette" became synonymous with things that were cheap and paltry, including portraits cut from paper.

The Unique Silhouette

The silhouette is still with us because it has the ability to communicate instantly on a basic level. Today, silhouettes are used by artists for book and poster illustrations because of this immediate impact. International traveler's and traffic signs are done in silhouette style for the same reason. Even though many more sophisticated and complex techniques are available (such as using pencil, pen, or brush to add detail, shading, or color), the bold, simple silhouette with its uncompromising shapes and its crisp, definite edges has no equal as a powerful graphic representation.

In addition, the few tools and materials needed to make a silhouette are easily obtained and are inexpensive. The projects in this article describe the basic techniques you will need to design and cut a silhouette and show three designs you can reproduce. These three designs are each shown in two forms. Instead of cutting silhouettes from black paper, I always use plain white bond paper because it is inexpensive, it is easy to cut, and a design can be sketched on it with a pencil. Then I mount the design on black paper. But often when these designs are reproduced in a newspaper or magazine, they are made to look as if they were cut from black paper by printing them in negative form (that is, with black and white areas reversed). Here, they are shown in both positive and negative form, so you can choose the style you prefer and cut your design from either white or black paper.

There's a touch of the Renaissance in Diana Bryan, a sculptor, illustrator, and teacher who, as director of the Full Moon Puppet Theater, first makes puppets, then brings them to life as she and her fellow puppeteers perform throughout New York. Since graduating from the Tyler School of Art in Philadelphia, and from Pratt Institute in Brooklyn, her paper cutouts have appeared in many publications, including The New York Times, National Lampoon, Harper's Weekly, New York *magazine, and* Print *magazine. Ms. Bryan shares her skills with others by conducting workshops devoted to paper cutouts and puppetry (both building and performing); the participants have ranged in age from four to 80.*

Portraiture is usually easier in profile, and the contraption shown here was a popular device with seventeenth- and eighteenth-century portraitists. The subject's shadow was cast on paper, and the shade, as silhouettes were then called, was painted or otherwise filled in.

The delicacy of some silhouettes from the past, such as this one made in Germany during the eighteenth century, could only be achieved by painting rather than cutting them. At one time such portraits, painted on glass, ivory, plaster, vellum, wax, or paper, or cut from black paper and elaborately mounted, were popular through most of Europe.

These silhouettes were cut from ordinary bond paper. They are the first attempts by (left to right) Anita Karl, age twelve, Toni Adams, age ten, and Alice Bush, age thirteen. Designing a silhouette is easy, and the technique is one that anyone can perfect with practice.

Paper Cutting and Folding
For children of all ages

Children everywhere enjoy paper cutting. But the technique is usually associated entirely with holidays. Endless streams of cookie-cutter decorations clutter homes and classrooms—heart-shaped cutouts for Valentine's Day, black cats and pumpkins for Halloween, trees and snowflakes at Christmastime, turkeys at Thanksgiving.

So it is no wonder some people think that cutting paper is child's play. But when approached creatively, silhouette making is a craft that can be as simple or as elaborate as you please. Everyone can produce worthy results, regardless of age or level of experience. Since both children and adults will experience similar pleasures and difficulties when trying the technique for the first time, the directions that follow are not specifically for children but for anyone who has never cut a silhouette before. You will find suggestions on how to create your own designs, as well as the best and safest ways to use the cutting tools. Directions for repairing mistakes and for mounting finished silhouettes are in the Craftnotes, page 2047.

Materials
For your first silhouette, use an ordinary pencil and plain white bond paper. Bond paper is inexpensive and widely available; patterns can be easily penciled in on it and then erased. I began using bond paper years ago, and it is still the only paper I ever use. You will also need single-edged razor blades or a small, replaceable-blade craft knife and blades (sold in art supply stores), and clear cellophane tape to mend any inadvertent cuts or tears in the silhouette. As a cutting surface, use a piece of cardboard—the back of a notebook or sketch pad, a cut-up carton, or a shirt cardboard will do, as long as the surface is smooth rather than corrugated.

If you are helping children learn the principles of silhouette making, show them examples of successful silhouettes.

1: To make a symmetrical silhouette, fold the paper in half. With experience, you will be making more elaborate, asymmetrical designs later.

2: Draw the border on one half of the paper; then draw the center design on the same half, making sure all elements remain connected.

Creating the Design

The first step is to imagine a design and draw it on paper. Until you gain experience, fold the paper in half (photograph 1). Then draw the design on one half of the paper (later you will cut through both layers simultaneously). This will result in a symmetrical (and therefore balanced) design; it will also give you faster results than if you had to draw a design to fill the entire sheet of paper. Then cut out all the elements individually. Make sure your design includes a border. This border can be made with simple lines that parallel the edges of the paper, forming a rectangle, or any other geometric shape such as a circle, square, triangle, or diamond. The border is very important, not only because it serves to organize the design, but because it gives you a framework to which you can attach the center shapes of the design. When you draw the internal part of the design (photograph 2), keep it simple and bold; a geometric design, a flower, a person, or an animal would be suitable. To adapt your design to the silhouette-cutting technique, make sure that each design element is connected either to the border or to another element that touches the border. To make this easier, remember that when you have cut it out, the silhouette should be in one piece, with each part linked with another. This takes planning and some ingenuity, but this is part of the fascination of the craft. For your first designs, you may simply enlarge the center elements until they touch the border. Or you may bridge gaps by drawing short, straight, or curved lines connecting shape to shape and shape to border. (Note the short connecting lines between the butterfly and the border in the silhouette opposite.) As you gain experience, you will be better able to plan designs with the limitations of this technique in mind, and you will discover connecting devices that are much less obvious (see the silhouettes on pages 2046 and 2048).

It will be necessary to adapt your design to the silhouette technique in one more way. Each pencil line in your finished design will be a cutting line; but unlike a single line made with a pencil, a single cut will not appear as a line in the finished silhouette. Rather, you must make two parallel cuts in order to leave a strip of paper between them that will appear as a line. To avoid confusion when you cut, draw a double line for every line you wish to appear as a paper line. If you draw these lines no less than ⅛ inch apart, they won't be too fragile and prone to tear after they have been cut.

The next step will also help avoid confusion when you cut. With the pencil, shade in all the areas of the design that will be cut away and discarded. This will give you a clear picture of how the finished silhouette will look (photograph 3).

Cutting the Silhouette

To cut the silhouette, place it on the cardboard, and keep it flat on that surface until the cutting is finished. Make sure you start out with a sharp, new, single-edged razor blade or craft-knife blade. Cut with enough pressure so the point of the blade penetrates both layers on the paper, but not so much that you lose control of the tool. For safety's sake, *always* position the hand that is holding the paper behind the cutting blade, and pull the blade toward you to make the cut (photographs 4 and 5). Do not place your hand or finger in the path of the blade (photograph 6); nor should you try to cut away from you (photograph 7). Both mistakes are invitations

3: The silhouette is ready for cutting. All the necessary lines have been doubled, and all the areas to be cut out and removed have been shaded.

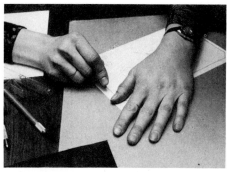

4: The safest way to cut with a single-edged razor blade or a craft knife is toward you, with the hand that holds the paper behind the blade.

5: When you begin to cut, use the entire hand, as in photograph 4, to keep the paper from shifting as you cut, but when most of the areas have been cut away, a more delicate touch is required.

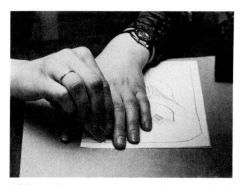

6: Wrong: One wrong way to cut with a razor blade is toward your hand or finger, as pictured. If the blade slips, this index finger lies right in its path.

7: Wrong: If you try to cut with the razor blade gliding away from you, the pencil guideline is hard to see, and you lose control of the tool.

8: To separate large pieces from the silhouette, pull them apart gently and carefully. Smaller pieces can be speared with the blade.

to injury. Do not attempt to cut curves in a single stroke; make a series of little cuts along the curved pencil line, shifting the paper with each cut so your free hand is always behind the blade, and you are always cutting toward you.

Where cuts meet at angles, make the cuts cross each other a bit to make sure the corners will be sharp. If such corner cuts do not intersect, you will have a fuzzy, ragged corner rather than a clean, sharp one. If you find your blade is beginning to drag along the paper, rather than gliding smoothly, and the cuts are becoming ragged and more difficult to make, it is time to change to another blade (or to the unused point, if you are using a razor blade). If you hold the blade up to the light, you can actually see the rounded tip of a dull blade. Depending on the complexity of your design and the number of cuts to be made, you will need three or four razor blades per silhouette. But razor blades are inexpensive, and a sharp point can make a great difference in the ease of cutting and in the final product.

A silhouette of two men toasting each other, a symmetrical design cut from folded paper, is shown full size as it appears when cut from black paper (above) and reduced as it would appear if cut from white paper (opposite). To reproduce the design in either version, make a pattern by tracing half of the full-sized design.

Depending on the design, you may remove the pieces as soon as you finish cutting them. An easy way to remove small pieces is to pierce them with the point of the cutting blade so you can use the blade to pick them up and lift them out. Large, continuous pieces may be separated from the silhouette with your fingers (photograph 8, page 2045).

Paper Cutting and Folding
Three silhouettes

The design shown opposite and the two on page 2048 demonstrate three types of silhouettes and the variations on the basic techniques (pages 2044 through 2046) used to cut them. Each silhouette is shown full size (for tracing the pattern) in negative form, and in a reduced size in positive form (to show how it looks if it is cut from white paper, as these were).

If you wish to cut the design in positive form from white paper, simply make a pattern by placing a piece of tracing paper over the full-sized design; then trace the outlines of the design, using a soft lead pencil that will give you a dark line. Place the pattern, face down, on plain white bond paper and tape it in place. Rub the back with the bowl of a spoon or other dull tool so the pattern is transferred to the paper. Then cut out the silhouette with a razor blade or a craft knife.

If you wish to cut the silhouette in negative form from black paper because you prefer the way that looks, you will need to stick the tracing-paper pattern onto the black paper. The best adhesive to use for this is rubber cement, because it allows the pattern to be peeled off when you are through. Coat the back of the pattern with rubber cement; then quickly (before the cement dries) smooth the pattern over the black paper. Let the cement dry, and cut out the silhouette, following the pattern lines. When the silhouette has been completely cut out, carefully peel away the remaining pieces of the pattern, and gently rub off any rubber cement that remains on the black silhouette. Mount the finished silhouette as described at right.

To simplify any of the designs, you can omit some of the elements, such as the windows in the first design or some of the animals in the second design.

Two Men Toasting Each Other
This is a symmetrical design, as are the children's silhouettes shown on page 2044. Since one half is the mirror image of the other, make your pattern by tracing only half of the design. Fold the white or black paper in half; then transfer or rubber-cement the half-pattern onto the folded paper. Cut out the silhouette (pages 2044 through 2046), cutting through the two layers of paper simultaneously.

Noah's Ark
Cutting an asymmetrical design, such as the one shown at the top of page 2048, is more time consuming than cutting a symmetrical one from folded paper, but the result can be more interesting. Trace the entire design; then transfer or rubber-cement it to the white or black paper from which it will be cut. Cut the silhouette carefully, cutting through the single layer of paper.

Adam and Eve
The Adam and Eve silhouette pictured on page 2048 illustrates a third silhouette-cutting technique that opens additional possibilities. Some of the design elements, such as the border and the tree, are symmetrical; others, such as the Adam and Eve figures, are asymmetrical. The way this is accomplished is simple and logical. First, using a half-pattern in which the design elements common to both halves are drawn, the silhouette is cut with the paper folded so these elements appear in both halves. Then the paper is unfolded and the unwanted elements in each half are cut off and removed.

To cut the Adam and Eve silhouette using this technique, trace over Eve's half of the design. Then flip the tracing paper over to Adam's half. With the wrong side of the paper up, line up the traced elements on Eve's half so they match the corresponding elements on Adam's half (the pencil tracing will be visible on the wrong side). On the wrong side, add Adam's hat to Eve's body. Turn the tracing over and transfer the hat to the right side of the pattern by tracing over it.

Transfer or rubber-cement the pattern to the folded white or black paper, and cut out the design, including all the elements in both halves. Then open up the paper and cut the hat off Eve's head. Then make the narrow cuts for her breasts. To finish Adam, cut off the hair and the apple.

For related entries, see "Block Printing," "Greeting Cards," and "Valentines."

The full-sized silhouette opposite is shown above in reduced form as it would look if you were to cut the design from white, rather than black, paper.

An animal menagerie on its way to Noah's ark, an asymmetrical design cut from unfolded paper, is shown full size in black-on-white (above), and reduced in white-on-black (left) so you can choose the look you prefer. Trace the full-sized version to get a pattern that you can use to cut the design.

Symmetrical and asymmetrical design elements are combined in this silhouette of Adam and Eve and friends. To get a pattern of the design, trace half of the full-sized black-on-white version (above). When the design is cut, modify the figures as explained in the text (page 2047). The white-on-black version is shown reduced (left); the black-on-white version, full size, is above.